ULYSSES AND US

Declan Kiberd is Professor of Anglo-Irish Literature at University College Dublin. Among his books are *Synge and the Irish Language* (1979), *Men and Feminism in Modern Literature* (1985), *Inventing Ireland: The Literature of the Modern Nation* (1995), *Irish Classics* (2000) and *The Irish Writer and the World* (2005). He introduced and edited *The Annotated Students' Ulysses* (1992) in the Penguin Twentieth-Century Classics series.

Professor Kiberd is a director of the Abbey Theatre. He has been Parnell Fellow at Magdalene College Cambridge, and a visiting professor at Duke University and the Sorbonne.

by the same author

SYNGE AND THE IRISH LANGUAGE
MEN AND FEMINISM IN MODERN LITERATURE
IDIR DHÁ CHULTÚR
INVENTING IRELAND: LITERATURE OF THE MODERN NATION
IRISH CLASSICS
THE IRISH WRITER AND THE WORLD

Ulysses and Us

The Art of Everyday Living

DECLAN KIBERD

faber and faber

First published in 2009
by Faber and Faber Ltd
Bloomsbury House
74–77 Great Russell Street
London WC1B 3DA

Typeset by Faber and Faber Ltd
Printed and bound in the UK by CPI Mackays, Chatham ME5 8TD

A CIP record for this book
is available from the British Library

ISBN 978-0-571-24254-2

2 4 6 8 10 9 7 5 3

In memory of John McGahern

'Níl ann ach lá dár saol'

Contents

Acknowledgements

For almost thirty years the students of University College Dublin have been teaching me about their famous forerunner. I am particularly indebted to those who shared their work on doctoral dissertations with me: Deborah Reid, Dermot Kelly, Urs Bucher, Michael Howlett, Minako Okamuro, Peter Quinn, Tony Tighe, James Pribek SJ, Seokmoo Choi, Enrico Terrinoni, Diana Pérez García, Graham Price, Patricia Gorman, Katherine O'Callaghan, Malcolm Sen, Vivien Igoe and Jill Hastings.

Some of the themes in this book were rehearsed in guest lectures given at other places: Cambridge, Athens, Rome, Seville, the Sorbonne (Paris 3), Emory, Duke University and the University of Notre Dame.

John Hobbs of Oberlin College suggested the project, and was also kind enough to offer many forms of support through its gestation. His close attention to an earlier version was most helpful. I am grateful to Tom Van Nortwick, Jessica Pinto, Bob Pierce and Grover Zinn for responding to particular chapters, and to my dear friend Noreen Doody for her generous reading of the typescript. Derek Hand and P. J. Mathews offered vivid conversation on many themes: their support and friendship were a constant inspiration. Thanks also to Seán Freyne for lending me many books on the textual issues raised in the

ACKNOWLEDGEMENTS

Old and New Testament, and to John Dillon for his thoughts on Homer. Janet Clare, Anne Fogarty and Maud Ellmann made helpful observations on particular chapters; and Terence Killeen saved me from many errors of detail, as did Joseph O'Connor – my debts to both of these kind helpers are great indeed. Pat Donlon and her wonderful colleagues at the Tyrone Guthrie Centre in Annaghmakerrig provided just about perfect conditions in which to write the final draft. I am thankful also to Jana Fischerova; to Wendy Toole; to Alison Worthington; to Paula Turner at Palindrome; to Dave Watkins at Faber; and to my editor Neil Belton for much assistance in preparing the work for publication.

My understanding of Joyce and his world has been enriched over many decades by conversations with my father and mother, brother and sister; with wonderful teachers, including Brendan Keneally and Richard Ellmann; with my children, Lucy, Amy and Rory; and, most of all, with my beloved wife, Beth.

Note on the Text

The edition of *Ulysses* quoted throughout is that published by the Bodley Head in 1960, reissued by Penguin Books as part of their Twentieth-Century Classics series in 1992.

Joyce and his critics used Homeric names (such as 'Proteus', 'Wandering Rocks', 'Cyclops', 'Nausikaa', 'Ithaca' or 'Penelope') for specific episodes. He did not include these titles in his final text but they are used occasionally in this commentary. A full exploration of their meaning may be found in *James Joyce's Ulysses* (1930) by Stuart Gilbert.

ULYSSES AND US

How *Ulysses* Didn't Change Our Lives

When a painter visited James Joyce in his Parisian apartment, the famous author pointed out of the window to the son of the concierge playing on the steps. 'One day,' he said, 'that boy will be a reader of *Ulysses*.' Already the book had a reputation for obscurity as well as obscenity, but Joyce remained confident that it would reach and move many ordinary readers. On its publication in 1922, he gave a copy as a present to François Quinton, his favourite waiter at Fouquet's. In those years, he preferred not to discuss literature with experts or writers, but 'loved to carry on a dialogue about Dickens with some unknown attendant at the post-office window or to discuss the meaning and structure of Verdi's *La Forza del Destino* with the person at the box office'. Sylvia Beach, whose bookshop published Joyce's masterpiece when nobody else would, noted how he treated everyone as an equal, whether they were writers, children, waiters, princesses or charladies. He confided in her that *everybody* interested him and that he had never met a bore.

Ulysses is one of the masterpieces of modernism, accorded the same exalted status as Marcel Proust's *In Search of Lost Time* or Robert Musil's *The Man Without Qualities*, yet it has become a defining element in the life of the city where it is set. Like the prelates of the Catholic

Church, Joyce was perhaps cunning in setting aside a single day of the year on which to celebrate a feast. When Leopold Bloom and Stephen Dedalus sit down together at the book's climax over coffee and a bun, neither man says 'do this in memory of me', yet every year the cult grows. Like all such cults, it has its routes of pilgrimage, special foods, ritual observances and priestly decoders of the sacred text. Many of the surrealists who lived near Joyce in Paris had also grown up as Catholics – but their displaced religion was filled with edicts, dogmas and ex-communications, while he, by contrast, appropriated the more celebratory rituals of Catholicism. As is the case with all emergent religions, the cult of James Joyce – known jocularly as the Feast of Saint Jam Juice in Dublin – has spawned its own loyal opposition. On 16 June 2004, when 10,000 Bloomsday breakfasts were served on Dublin streets to mark the great centenary, a spray-painter went to work and wrote 'Bloom is a cod' on a building-site wall. There were no inverted (or even perverted) commas around the quotation.

Every year, hundreds of Dubliners dress as characters from the book – Stephen with his cane, Leopold with his bowler hat, Molly in her petticoats, Blazes Boylan under a straw boater – as if to assert their willingness to become one with the text. They re-enact scenes in Eccles Street, Ormond Quay and Sandycove's Martello tower. It is quite impossible to imagine any other masterpiece of modern-ism having quite such an effect on the life of a city.

And yet, one has to ask the obvious question – how many of those celebrants have actually read the book through? Ernest Hemingway worshipped Joyce as the leader of intellectual Paris in the 1920s, yet his copy of

4

Ulysses lies in the John F. Kennedy library with all but the early and final pages uncut. Many of the early editions put on sale by art auctioneers seem not to have known the first reader's knife. It is as if Joyce's work has been co-opted by that very art market which he despised. *Ulysses* set out to change the world and to liberate its readers, but now often seems more famous for the prices at which first editions change hands. In his Parisian years, Joyce often complained about the commodification of modernist painting: 'Picasso gets 20,000 to 30,000 francs for a few hours' work', he moaned, while he who laboured 10,000 hours writing each section of *Ulysses* was 'not worth a penny a line'. The man who once told a college classmate on the steps of the National Library of Ireland that his stomach muscles were tight from hunger might have been even more amazed to discover that the same library would one day acquire the papers that he left to Paul Leon for millions of euro. While he would doubtless have enjoyed the drinks and japes of Bloomsday, he might also have sadly noted in them an attempt by Dubliners to reassert a lost sense of community, a poignant assertion of ownership of streets through which on other days of the year they hurry from one private experience to another. The celebration of Bloomsday may in fact be a lament for a lost city, for an earlier time when Dublin was still felt to be civic, knowable, viable.

My father loved *Ulysses* as the fullest account ever given of the city in which he lived. There were parts that baffled or bored him, and these he skipped, much as today we fast-forward over the duller tracks on beloved music albums. But there were entire passages which he knew almost by heart. In 1982, the centenary of Joyce's birth, I enticed him to attend a Joyce symposium at Trinity College, but as we walked through the hallway, a passer-by said, 'I think I'll go into "The Consciousness of Stephen",' at which the old man baulked and bolted for the nearest door.

It was the peculiar curse and blessing of *Ulysses* to have appeared just as the curricular study of English literature in universities really took off. The book which set out to restore the dignity of the middle range of human experience against the false heroics of World War I was soon lost to the common reader. Yet *Ulysses* was arguably one of the major artworks to register the effects of that conflict on ordinary people. Bloom's uncertain sexual potency, though an element of a book set in 1904, seemed to prefigure the impotent or damaged protagonists of Hemingway, Eliot and Lawrence, while his emphasis on the need for a tolerant and peaceful response to the experience of betrayal held many lessons for a world coming out of war.

Many of those who enlisted for military service in 1914–18 diced with death in order to heighten their sense of being alive. Joyce understood from the start that this cult of death arose out of a disillusion with everyday life. He intuited a link between a more democratic politics and a belief in the significance of people's quotidian practices. In making the central character of *Ulysses* an ordinary Jewish citizen, he may have foreseen that the Jews could easily become victims of the general disenchantment with the complications of modernity. If you make the rejection of everyday life, of work, of happiness a mass phenomenon rather than just a response of baffled individuals, writes Henri Lefebvre, 'you end up with the Hitler Mystique'.

6

A book which set out to celebrate the common man and woman endured the sad fate of never being read by most of them. Was this a case of bad faith or bohemian hypocrisy in a work which idealised just the sort of simple souls who could never hope to read it? It was first lost to those readers even as it triumphed in bohemia and then in the academy; but today it is lost also to most students, lecturers and intellectuals. Many of the people who read Joyce now are called 'Joyceans' and appointed as specialists in university departments, most of whose other members would never dream of attempting *Ulysses*. There are, of course, plenty of amateur readers and determined autodidacts out there in society, who study it as a sort of furtive activity to which they would never own up for fear of seeming pretentious. Then, also, there are dozens of Dublin taxi drivers who 'know the main characters but haven't got too far into it yet'. Most people who study it closely tend, like reforming alcoholics, to join groups in which to share and discuss the challenges. It is almost as if *Ulysses* anticipated not only the growth of the university seminar but also the rise of the suburban book club, both of which offer an antidote to the loneliness of the long-distance reader.

The development of modular systems of education, offering wide choices of subjects to students across many disciplines, could have been the saving of *Ulysses*. A class containing individuals who had already studied, say, Homer, romantic music or Irish history could have really hummed, but this has not often happened. What has been lost in these systems is a sense of chronology, an understanding of the evolution of English literature on which so much of the meaning of the text depends. Even before that defeat, however, *Ulysses* was wrenched out of the hands of the common reader. Why? Because of the rise of specialists prepared to devote years to the study of its secret codes – *parallax, indeterminacy, consciousness-time* being among the buzz words. Such specialists often tend to work in teams. Many of them reject the notion of a national culture, assuming that to be cultured nowadays is to be international, even global, in consciousness. In doing this, they have often removed Joyce from the Irish context which gave his work so much of its meaning and value.

The middle decades of the twentieth century were the years in which the idea of a common culture was abandoned – yet *Ulysses* depends on that very notion. Joyce himself was *not* forbiddingly learned. He cut more classes at University College Dublin than he attended, averaging less than 50 per cent in many of his exams. His classmate Con Curran noted that he made the little he learned there go a very long way. When he left secondary school at eighteen, Joyce knew most of the basic things you need for reading (or writing) *Ulysses* – the Mass in Latin, the life and themes of Shakespeare, how electricity works, how water gets from a reservoir to the domestic tap, Charles Lamb's version of the adventures of Ulysses. In his youth he described himself as a socialist artist and a believer in participatory democracy – that everyone, whether wealthy enough to have a higher education or not, should have equal access to this common culture. He would have agreed with R. H. Tawney's contention that 'opportunities to rise are no substitute for a general diffusion of the means of civilisation', something that was needful for all, both rich and poor. To his brother Stanislaus he wrote from Austria in May 1905:

It is a mistake for you to imagine that my political opinions are those of a universal lover: but they are those of a socialistic artist. I cannot tell you how strange I sometimes feel in my attempt to live a more civilised life than my contemporaries.

Ulysses took shape in a world which had known for the first time the possibilities of mass literacy and the emergence of working men's reading libraries. Virginia Woolf, perhaps unintentionally, captured that element when she sneered at it as the book 'of a self-taught Dublin working man'. Its succession of disparate and discordant styles seemed to her an embarrassing example of an autodidact conducting his own education in public. (The same complaint would be made about the very different styles in which Picasso painted each of the figures in *Les Demoiselles d'Avignon*.) These were the years in which H. G. Wells's *Outline of History* sold over two million copies; and books by Ruskin, William Morris and Macaulay sold in tens of thousands. As Richard Hoggart observed, 'The reading of working men was likely to be wide, solid and inspiring.' The later years of World War I and the years just after witnessed a decline in deference to church and state authority and an assertion that the working man, landless labourer and voteless woman were persons of dignity in their own right. This was the era when democracy meant that *anyone* could enjoy Shakespeare. When a group of travelling players asked a porter in Limerick railway station whether they had reached their destination, the man raised his cap in mock-salute and said, 'Why, sirs, this is Illyria.'

Nobody then spoke of *Hamlet* as an example of elite art

being imposed on the helpless children of labourers, for in those years a radical populism meant training readers in the art of self-reliance. These were the conditions in which Joyce made free play with texts like the *Odyssey* or *Hamlet*, not as specialist knowledge but as the property of all who shared in a common culture. One of his favourite party pieces in his student years was to dress up as Queen Gertrude and keen the death of Ophelia in the accents of inner Dublin, while his friend Willie Fallon, dressed as the tragic heroine, strewed cauliflowers across the drawing-room floor.

After the mid-twentieth century, that common culture was replaced by the creation of specialist elites. Democracy was no longer seen as the sharing in a common fund of textual knowledge, but as providing access to this or that super-educated grouping. No longer was the prevailing idea that anyone bright enough could read and understand *Hamlet* or *Ulysses*, but that anyone sufficiently clever could aspire to become one of the paid specialists who did such things. Today's social movements aim at the inclusion of gifted souls in the dominant structure rather than at the revolutionary transformation of social relations. Hence the pseudo-radical interpretations of Joyce produced over the past two decades of 'critical theory' have challenged neither the growing corporate stranglehold over universities nor the specialist stranglehold over Joyce. They have in fact strengthened both forces. And that is because 'theory' is rarely concerned with linking analysis to real action in the world.

Ulysses was written to celebrate the reality of ordinary people's daily rounds. From Baudelaire to Flaubert, much of the most powerful writing of the previous century contained corrosive critiques of everyday life, motivated by their authors' rebellion against the repetitive character of city routines reduced to mere banality. Most persons who are bored to numbness cannot even perceive this malady, but Baudelaire and Flaubert set out to bring them to a consciousness of it. 'Boredom is the everyday become manifest,' observes Maurice Blanchot, 'and consequently, the everyday after it has lost its essential, constitutive trait of being unperceived.' But Joyce took a very different line. He believed that by recording the minutiae of a single day, he could release those elements of the marvellous latent in ordinary living, so that the familiar might astonish. The 'everyday' need not be average, but a process recorded as it is lived – with spontaneity and openness to chance. For all their radical newness, Joyce's methods were a return to the aims of the romantic poets in the aftermath of the French revolution: as Coleridge said of Wordsworth, the hope was to awaken the mind from the lethargy of custom to deal with persons from common walks of life and 'to give the charm of novelty to the things of every day'.

It is time to reconnect *Ulysses* to the everyday lives of real people. The more snobbish modernists resorted to difficult techniques in order to protect their ideas against appropriation by the newly literate masses; but Joyce foresaw that the real need would be to defend his book and those masses against the newly illiterate specialists and technocratic elites. Whereas other modernists feared the hydra-headed mob, Joyce used interior monologue to show how lovable, complex and affirmative was the mind of the ordinary citizen. *Ulysses* gives such persons the sort of ceremonial treatment once reserved for aristocrats. While other writers followed Nietzsche in attacking mass culture ('the rabble spit forth their bile once a day and call the results a newspaper'), Joyce offered *Ulysses* as a counter-newspaper, which would capture even more acutely the events of a single day. As others voiced their fear of the passivity and tractability of the mob, he tried to democratise intelligence and to produce a more active, creative kind of reader. The more frightening the world became, the more abstract the arts seemed to become, but Joyce tried to keep everything concrete.

Although *Ulysses* is a book of privacies and sub-jectivities, an astounding number of its scenes are set in public space – libraries, museums, bars, cemeteries, and most of all the streets. Its characters enjoy the possibilities afforded by those streets for random, unexpected meetings. And it is this very openness to serendipity which allows Joyce to renew his styles and themes with each succeeding episode. Far from seeing 'street people' as a problem, he treats them as the very basis of a civilisation – the civic bourgeoisie.

Ulysses is an epic of the bourgeoisie. Modern epics, however, far from being confident statements from the heart of a successful civilisation, are more often laments for its fragile greatness and imminent decline – Milton on the English Revolution, Walt Whitman on the promise of American democracy. Joyce in 1922 published a cele-bration of the bourgeois Bloom, but he sensed that the man's versatility and openness of mind were already in jeopardy.

The bourgeois saw that even a modest income carried social obligations – to one's neighbours, fellow citizens, even to one's nation. Accordingly, Bloom doesn't just help a blind stripling to cross the street or give beyond his means to the fund for the bereaved Dignam family. He also frets about how to improve transport systems in Dublin and how to combat cruelty to animals. It's even suggested that he may have given the idea for Sinn Féin to Arthur Griffith. Insofar as he identifies with the Jewish people, it is less with their suffering sense of victimhood and more with their achievements, those of Mendelssohn in music and Marx in social thought.

One of the most attractive features of Bloom is his blend of imagination and practicality, of theory and practice. He sees no contradiction whatever between bohemian and bourgeois. That is the meaning of his climactic meeting with Stephen Dedalus near the close of the book, a book which may be unique in the history of modernism because it suggests concord rather than eternal enmity between poet and citizen.

Joyce remained always steadfast in his belief. In his youth he had tried to establish a daily newspaper in Dublin called *The Goblin*, to be published like certain continental papers each afternoon. 'Its establishment', commented a friend, 'would cost a sum that in the Dublin of that day was fabulous.' Later, he would open the city's first movie house, the Volta, as a going concern in 1909, with financial backers from overseas. Unlike their European counterparts who had learned to detach them-selves from the hated bourgeoisie, Irish intellectuals were still bedazzled by the idea of business success. Wilde and Shaw wrote their plays avowedly for money; Yeats ran the Abbey Theatre without government subsidy as a business; Joyce even tried to sell Irish tweed in Trieste. He had little truck with bohemians, preferring to stress the practical value of art for a full life. As his college classmate Mary

Colum said, he lacked 'any of what are called Bohemian qualities'. The Irish painter Arthur Power recalled how 'he hated Bohemian cafes and anything to do with them. His life was very regulated and it was bourgeois in all its aspects. He was a great family man.'

He recreated these qualities in Bloom who, for instance, had a belief that the works of Shakespeare were important for the practical wisdom they conveyed. In the 'Ithaca' episode Bloom is described as using Shakespeare to help solve 'difficult problems in imaginary or real life' (791) but with imperfect results. That view of Shakespeare is not much in fashion today, when expert commentators treat his plays more as technical performances than as guides to a fulfilled life. Yet even the intellectual Stephen had in the world of 1904 tried to put *Hamlet* to such a use, hoping it might help him to sort out his troubled relationship with his father. Through Stephen, Joyce voiced his objection to the cult of the Shakespeare specialist when he mocked Edward Dowden's dominance of that field. Perhaps sensing that a Joyce industry might one day curtail his expressive possibilities as Dowden had those of Shakespeare and Company, he had Stephen deride the Trinity College Dublin professor's patent on the Shakespeare industry: 'Apply E. Dowden, Highfield House' (262).

Joyce knew that national epics give people their ideas of what sort of persons they should be. The *Odyssey* even gave the Greeks their notions of what gods they could make their own. Joyce set his book alongside Homer, the Bible, Dante and Shakespeare precisely because he believed that it could project ideas of virtue. Only when it is read and taught as if it *says* something will it gain the influence over youth of which he dreamed. Any teacher knows that many students today sprinkle their essays with quotations from the lyrics of rock music and from popular films. This suggests that they still yearn for instruction from artists on how to live. It may well be that rock artists provide the only common culture which most of those students know. The need now is for readers who will challenge the bloodless, technocratic explication of texts: amateur readers who will come up with what may appear to be naïve, even innocent, interpretations. Today's students have been prevented by a knowing, sophisticated criticism from seeking such wisdom in modern literature. In it they seek mainly tricks of style, rhetorical devices, formal experiment, historical insight, but seldom if ever lived wisdom. The contemporary gulf between technique and feeling cries out to be bridged in the classroom, through the work of teaching and learning.

How It Might Still Do So

Ulysses itself offers many models of how a more honest kind of teaching might work. In the second episode, 'Nestor', Joyce mocks rote learning by boys who have little idea of the inner meaning of the words they parrot. They seem to prefigure a world, our world, in which the steely precision of Latin has declined, only to be replaced by a new priestly discourse of critical jargon. In the classroom Stephen rejects all ideas of mastery and asks to be coached in his teaching role by the students. Rather than make a fool of a boy who says 'Pyrrhus . . . a pier', he turns the error into a portal of discovery, calling a pier 'a disappointed bridge' (29). Afterwards, he tells the headmaster, Mr Deasy, that he prefers to see himself as a learner rather than a teacher.

Mr Deasy believes in 'progress'. In an age of disillusion, he holds on to the one great illusion that still governs our technocratic world, the illusion of mastery. The scholar who seeks a repressive mastery of *Ulysses* may not be greatly different from the man who fears that he cannot control the actual world. Stephen's educational theory is rather akin to Joyce's: teachers should ask questions, open children to ancient legends, ask them to contemplate the faraway and the remote – as children naturally want to do. Democracy should educate and education should

16

democratise. But even in Joyce's time, education was being flattened out, with the result, lamented by Oscar Wilde, that everyone 'who has forgotten how to learn has taken to teaching'. A hundred years later, long, challenging books like *Middlemarch*, *Moby-Dick* and *Ulysses* no longer find places on many undergraduate courses, but are the stuff of scholarly conferences, while 'students graduate from college in a condition of profound ignorance about the world' – and about great literature. Too often the papers of academic experts are addressed only to their peers in a jargon that seeks to mimic the rigorous discourse of the sciences: such criticism is published only in expensive volumes destined for purchase by libraries and not by the common reader.

Reading *Ulysses* is undeniably challenging, yet many of the jobs which are done by ordinary people are as complex and exacting as any analysis of that book. Walter Benjamin observed that it would become increasingly difficult for children in a mass culture to find their way back to the exacting silence of a text. The challenge posed for many by *Ulysses* in 1922 proved prophetic of that issued by many other books now. Yet *Ulysses* was designed to produce readers capable of reading *Ulysses* – a sentence which is not the tautology it seems – with the very difficulty intended by Joyce as an intrinsic part of the experience. It offers not only a text but a training in how to decode it.

He acted on the brazen assumption that his book would not defer to the current taste of the public but serve to invent a new sort of reader, someone who after that experience might choose to live in a different way. He wanted to free people from all kinds of constriction, among them the curse of passive readership. This was not as immodest a programme as it might have seemed. Most writers believe that by changing language and style you may in time alter thought; and that by altering thought you may transform the world itself. The painters who worked alongside Joyce in Paris believed that they might yet challenge other media as exponents of the dominant visual form. Eventually, they lost that battle to film, television and the music video. With *Ulysses* Joyce issued a similar sort of challenge to newspapers and it did not entirely fail, though it is hard now to find persons who claim to base the conduct of their lives upon its wisdom. Yet that was Joyce's hope, and it wasn't preposterous. Many who have truly engaged with *Ulysses* will tell you that Dublin looks very different afterwards – and that their own thoughts have taken on a sort of Bloomian contour. As with Freud and Jung, it is difficult for us to gauge just how much of our minds James Joyce has invented. But even that would hardly have been enough for him. He believed that the common culture, already under threat in his day, could be remade along more multicultural lines, with infusions from many national and spiritual traditions, because the future would be what artists like him already were. In that context, *Ulysses* exists like a blasted road sign in a war zone, pointing to a future that is exhilarating to precisely the extent that it is uncertain and open.

The uselessness of much schooling is a subject often returned to in *Ulysses*. Stephen's theory of Shakespeare uses both Socratic and Scholastic methods, but produces only an analysis that not even its sponsor believes. He is a dire example of the intellectual who stands in need of practical wisdom from an older man who would prove both humble and authoritative. Joyce's youthful friend, J. F. Byrne, said in *Silent Years*, 'I do not recall one older person in whose company he was at ease'; yet he also noted the physically weak boy's love of heroic deeds and language. Could it be that Joyce in his book juxtaposed the rude heroes of the *Odyssey* against the oversensitive Hamlet in order to foreground the question of the relation between practice and theory, activity and learning?

In the National Library, after Stephen disowns his theory and the useless education which gave rise to such barren cleverness, the figure of Bloom appears before him, as if offering the beginnings of an answer: 'cease to strive' (280). So he turns his back on literary Dublin and follows Bloom out, finding the practice of everyday life suddenly more interesting. The wisdom which Bloom has to impart to Stephen later that night in the cabman's shelter is nothing so banal as a dogma. Rather, it concerns practical matters, such as why café chairs are piled on tables overnight, or how the intellectual and manual labourer can make common cause. Bloom chides Stephen for fighting while drunk; and the fact that Stephen is inebriated for most of the later episodes suggests just how hard he finds it as an intellectual to fit into his society.

Joyce rejected the idea of a separate bohemia, and in so doing he repudiated the notion of art as a sublimated sphere in which ideas denied in everyday life can alone be enjoyed. He saw the violent actions of the Celtic warrior Cúchulainn staged regularly in the Abbey Theatre as a version of such evasiveness; and he staged in 'Circe' his own counter-truth as a mockery both of Yeats's idealised Cúchulainnoid visions and of downmarket bohemias (such as Dublin's red-light district called

Monto). Joyce understood that bohemia was really a 'stage', used by ordinary citizens who feared that they had lost their expressive abilities and who asked its denizens to perform on their behalf an identity which they had suppressed in themselves. Such an artificial and contrived zone was unnecessary in a Dublin whose citizens had retained their expressive potentials intact.

Joyce insisted on the use-value of art. He praised Ibsen for giving us men and women as we meet them in the real world. He lambasted the replacement of a useful art by the exchange-value of the markets. The irony that his 'usylessly unreadable blue book of eccles' has now become a commercial fetish, vied for at auctions by pluto-crats, should not blind us to its meaning. The difficulty of *Ulysses* is not based on snobbery but on the desire of a radical artist to escape the nets of the market. His 'usylessly' unreadable book becomes an attack on a society based on narrow ideas of utility. It respects the masses by showing not only how admirable they are but also how much more vibrant they might yet become. While newspapers by their sensationalism annulled debate and the very possibility of experience, *Ulysses* offered a diurnal report that would, unlike other news-papers, survive the day of its enunciation.

The underlying intention was that *anyone* reading *Ulysses* could be an expert, at least in the sense that anyone present at a sporting event feels entitled to have a valid opinion on what transpires. The model of education favoured by Joyce is one which does not master the young but rather mediates the relation between the generations as Bloom does. Bloom is more like a guru than an old-fashioned instructor. His object is less to convey a content than to draw Stephen into the process of transmission itself, so that the teacher-turned-learner can himself become a teacher in turn. Like many students, Stephen is quizzical at first, but he does learn a lot.

This is, in intention, the book of wisdom of a new dispensation and, as such, it should be accessible to ordinary readers as once were the *Odyssey*, the *New Testament*, the *Divine Comedy* and *Hamlet*. That doesn't preclude learned exegesis or belittle the contribution of those who perform it, but it does suggest that a great text always appeals on several levels. The popular reading can not only be enriched over time by the learned one, but it can also enrich the learned interpretation. Scholarly notes and commentaries on *Ulysses*, ostensibly designed to help readers, too often scare them off with displays of arid pedantry or institutional power. But this is a book with much to teach us about the world – advice on how to cope with grief; how to be frank about death in the age of its denial; how women have their own sexual desires and so also do men; how to walk and think at the same time; how the language of the body is often more eloquent than any words; how to tell a joke and how not to tell a joke; how to purge sexual relations of all notions of ownership; or how the way a person approaches food can explain who they really are. Before Joyce, nobody had so fully represented the process of thought, that stream of con-sciousness which everyone experiences every day. In previous artworks, such detail was offered only about a noble character like Hamlet as he considered suicide; but Joyce shows the inner soliloquy as a normal prelude to nothing more portentous than drinking a cup of tea. In a sense Joyce was bringing some of the procedures of psychoanalysis into the daylight, as opposed to the old idea of a confession made in a darkened room.

Bloom is, of course, no ultimate paragon. Although a civic-minded bourgeois, he defends capital punishment and flirts with the idea of becoming 'middle class' by the simple expedient of moving to a home called Flowerville or Bloom Cottage or St Leopold's in Dundrum, on the outskirts of Dublin. But he also resists the temptation of suburbia, knowing that it would be a zone of emptiness in which urban and rural qualities cancelled one another out. His inner city retains a village feel of *rus in urbe*, with *Ulysses* itself functioning as a sort of transplanted pastoral, a version of Goldsmith's country village in a city centre. For all its emphasis on deracination – or perhaps as a re-action against it – modernism itself was a kind of village phenomenon (think of the famous windmill in Mont-martre), seeking its virtues of intimate neighbourliness and avoiding its liability of narrow-mindedness. *Ulysses* seems to resolve the conflict between rural and urban which has disheartened so many modern people by pre-senting a world that is at once archaic and avant-garde. Its bohemia is not a voluntary gathering of dissidents in flight from the high rents of gentrification. It is the laboratory that Ireland was at the turning of the nineteenth into the twentieth century. It celebrated the ways in which a life could be simultaneously cosmopolitan and supremely local. After all, the local Irish features are an intrinsic part of the book's meaning and appeal.

Joyce's own first stories appeared in the *Irish Homestead*, and their diagnosis of social paralysis was intended as a basis for remedial action. For him the nation as an ideal created a sense of responsibility for the fate of others in the community. The later decline of nations in an era of global economic forces is linked intimately to the collapse of the civic bourgeoisie and its replacement by a merely consumerist middle class. The civic bourgeoisie saw 'freedom' as the right to produce rather than consume, and, rejecting the idea that *everything* should be privatised, it invested some of its profits in public libraries, museums and parks. The vernacular modernisms of Barcelona, Bombay, New York and Dublin are among the ultimate achievements of that bourgeoisie: so also is Joyce's book an illustration of the ways in which the energies of a bourgeois protagonist might be marshalled.

British pedagogy in the lead-up to World War I reduced many Greek and Roman classics to a cult of mere power as in empire-building, boy-scouting or mountain-climbing. That is the immediate context for Joyce's revision of Homer and for his redefinition of heroics. He sees heroics as a neurotic attempt by men who, fearing emptiness and anomie after the long peace, seek to create a cult of strenuous energy – yet this search led only to the carnage of World War I. Joyce's use of the classics is more humble and wise. The *Odyssey*, a book of cannibals, is itself cannibalised, on the ecological understanding that it's better to recycle what exists before sacrificing present resources to an uncertain future.

That critique of the abuse of classics is part of a wider attack on ideas of mastery. The medieval world also used teams of artisans to achieve a different form of mastery in its great cathedrals. These used up the creativity of generations to inspire awe and obedience in the common person. Joyce's own cathedral, however, was individually erected, with the object of celebrating that same ordinary person. The tragedy of the twentieth century was the replacement of a public-spirited bourgeoisie, not with a fully enfranchised people, but with a workforce now split between overpaid experts and underpaid service providers. The world so lost turns out to have been far better than that which replaced it. The world of pub, café, civic museum and national library produced social democracy, modernist painting and *Ulysses*. The world which supplanted it can generate only the identikit shopping mall, the ubiquitous security camera and the celebrity biography. The middle class has no real public culture or artworks which critique its triumph, because it has assimilated all the oppositional forces of modernism, by reducing them to mass entertainment. Now the streets are places not of amenity but of danger, through which nervous people drive in locked cars from one private moment to another.

This was borne in on me when I taught *Ulysses* to a class of young Californians in 1988. After four sessions, a woman raised her hand. 'Is Mr Bloom ill?' she asked. 'No,' I said, 'not that I'm aware of.' 'Well, he's sure doing a lot of walking,' she explained helpfully, 'and I think he's trying to walk something *off*.' Maybe he was. Maybe he was aware that a class-based society which so absolutely marks off the roles of women and men will create the sort of boredom endured by his wife in their home. I tried to explain, however, that my father and his siblings thought nothing of walking for over an hour to play a game of cards in a friend's house, and of walking for another hour home. The streets were then places which people felt that they owned, whereas seldom did they own their own houses, which Leopold Bloom likens to coffins. For him and for them, it was the public zone which was warm, nurturing and affirmative. It was there that the random encounters which propel *Ulysses* kept on happening, before the rise of the shopping mall put a brake on such unexpected meetings and an end to the idea of a neighbourhood.

How was the bourgeoisie trumped by the middle class? Joyce hated being called a middle-class writer. For him this was the greatest of all insults, to which he responded jocosely by saying that 'nobody in my books has any money'. But he maintained at all times a strictly bourgeois distinction between his art and his life: for instance, he might write four-letter words, but he would on no account utter them. This distinction was lost by many in the years after his death in 1941, so that what had once been permitted only in the imagination might now be enacted by individuals intent on proving how free they were. By substituting the search for sensations for the making of art, these people confused art and life – but Joyce knew that real art required hard work. Among the bohemians he had noticed a culture-worship that rejected the idea of an art devoted to everyday life. Hence his famous put-down of the young man who wished to kiss the hand that wrote *Ulysses*: 'No, that hand has done a lot of other things as well.'

Work in a technocratic society after World War II was often repetitive and boring, but in 'lifestyle' all could aspire to be artists. Labour and intellect became increasingly detached from one another, with a concomitant shift away from the discipline of 'character' to the impulse-ridden cultivation of 'personality'. The episode called 'Circe' foretells in a satiric mode that bleak cultural contradiction of capitalism, whereby (in the words of Daniel Bell) 'straights by day can become swingers by night'. Joyce sought freedom, true enough, but he never made the mistake of equating it with the freedom to consume, for in a book published as early as 1922 he still had hopeful, emancipatory ideas about the possible relation between men and machines.

In a civic society, the artist and entrepreneur, for all their antagonism, had one thing in common. Both were risk-takers, who might feel the need to follow up an initial idea with years of hard work testing its creative potential, much as Joyce did with the Volta cinema and then with *Ulysses*. But in the new order, the artist's role was mimicked by the sensation-seeker and the business person's by the bureaucrat. These groups often voice deep fears of one another, but are in fact opposite sides of the same coin. Life after 1945 became the very antithesis of Joyce's Dublin. Rather than the villagification of the city, European society saw an urbanisation of all zones including the rural.

The intellectuals and radicals of the 1890s who attacked the bourgeoisie never suspected that that class might turn out to have been the high point of modern civilisation. But Joyce gave their targets much credit, for he had grown up in an impoverished land still waiting for a bourgeoisie to appear. His initial pose in *Dubliners* was to mock the paralysis of a provincial town, and then in *A Portrait of the Artist as a Young Man* to cry '*non serviam*'. These were classic strategies of bohemian youth. In those books he depicted a world to which he felt himself fully superior, yet his hauteur was only a pose, easily penetrated by classmates. One fellow student, Con Curran, marvelled at the 'frieze of stooges' which represented

26

Joyce's university companions in *A Portrait*, and quoted the objective witness John Eglinton on how UCD students were 'interested in everything new in literature and philosophy and in this respect far surpassed the students of Trinity College'. Realising the emptiness of that bohemian posture, Joyce moved resolutely on, away from youthful rebellion to a more affirmative stance.

Ulysses suggests – by its closing 'Yes' – that a brake be put on such negation. Joyce's project was an attempt to return to the spirit of 1789, making the bourgeois once again exemplary. Robespierre and others had tried to conceal the fact that they were revolutionary businessmen by commissioning portraits of themselves wearing Roman togas. Karl Marx sneered at the fear of the future behind such a move, which reduced history to costume drama. He believed that when a real revolution came, the people would wear their own clothes. This is why the manifest content of Joyce's Homeric structure must fall away to reveal the latent content beneath. And this is why Bloom really does wear his own clothes, unlike Stephen who feels second-hand in other men's cast-offs. All through the nineteenth century, intellectuals had dismissed bourgeois style as effete. Even Freud derided the businessman as 'not an adventurer' and lamented that the fall of the gentleman was really the collapse of Eros. Not Joyce, who portrayed Blazes Boylan – at one point he carries a melodramatic flower between his teeth – as the fake gentleman of a false Eros, unlike the true Bloom, a real gentleman whom the other man can only play at being.

Like modernism as a movement, *Ulysses* begins in a sort of experimental community at Sandycove Tower. Then it moves rapidly through the world of Hamlet and the self-inflicted wounds of bohemian soliloquists to a counter-tradition in Bloom, whose monologues challenge all tendencies to suicide by asserting that there is still plenty to see and feel. Stephen Dedalus is a carrier of the bohemian virus which so troubled Joyce, and when he tells Bloom at their meeting that he left his father's house to seek misfortune, he is echoing Alfred de Musset on the 'search for heartaches of the modern artist'. Pretending that his marginality is transcendence, he attempts to hide his unimportance in the world by a show of pride. Yet Joyce knew that in labouring so mightily over the production of *Ulysses* he could never be a convincing bohemian. Gustave Flaubert had already observed that an idle dandy could only be idle, while a successful writer must combine hard labour with deep imagination, 'live like a bourgeois but think like a demigod'.

Joyce's own career enacts, therefore, the journey of modernism, as does his greatest book – the move from aesthetic withdrawal in the tower, through the central chapters of major intoxication in 'Cyclops', 'Nausikaa', 'Oxen of the Sun' and 'Circe', when the long hangover kicks in, with the discovery that freedom is just the freedom to be like everybody else and that the sub-conscious is not individualised, but the greatest plagiarist of all. There is a sense of limitation amidst the liberation of the closing episodes, as if the city which had seemed to promise so many possibilities ends up blocking off many of them. Stephen's tragedy of drunken bohemianism is to have felt stimulation followed by emptiness. Joyce uses Bloom to teach him a way of remaining sober in a world that can nonetheless be sacramental. The meeting between the men is the mysterious climax of the book.

What Joyce liked most about his native city was its urbanity. 'What a town Dublin is!' he exclaimed to his friend Frank Budgen. 'I wonder if there is another like it. Everybody has time to hail a friend and start a conversation about a third party.' It was so different from London, where people had a horror of common hallways in which a person might have to talk with a total stranger. *Ulysses*, in recreating the effects of such chance meetings, connects the reader with his or her inner strangeness, helping us to make friends with our buried selves, epitomised perhaps by the Wandering Jew.

Like all epics, *Ulysses* also offers wisdom. In *Finnegans Wake* Joyce wrote that Walt Whitman had 'foredreamed' his own epic. Whitman had said 'no one will get at my verses who insist on viewing them as a literary performance', because whoever touches his book 'touches a man'. In *Democratic Vistas* he complained that European art had never celebrated 'the people, their power and capacity, their reliability in emergencies'. Whitman also contended that the greatest writers were only at ease among the unlearned, and that Homer, the Bible and Shakespeare were great precisely because they tapped the energies of the common people. It is hard for us today to recreate that potential link between a person's expressive capacity and the nature of the state in which democracy means not just elections but a transformation in the relations between people, even between writer and reader.

Joyce knew that European art too often treated ordinary people as clowns or buffoons, and he sought a new style which would show the dignity of everyday living. The exaltation of the humble was the inner meaning of the story of Jesus. And the lesson of that story was that whoever loses his life shall save it, an intuition that has always been at the centre of the epic. The energies of a people converge solely at the moment of their dissolution, so that the exemplary protagonist comes into imaginative possession of his country only as he loses it. Joyce, like Whitman, Milton and Shakespeare, derived inspiration from the idea of the nation. All four men were in a real sense inventors of their nations, because of their willingness to open their art to despised or discarded oral traditions among their people. But in recovering those traditions, they also discovered their doom – that their spoken energies were being replaced by a more bookish and technical culture.

How can a book like *Ulysses* have been so misread and misunderstood? How was it taken as a product of a specialist bohemia against which it was in fact in open revolt? Why has it been called unreadable by the ordinary people for whom it was intended? The legend of its forbidding difficulty has scared readers off, but so has the silly notion of its monumental perfection: as one critic writes, 'each chapter, where not one false note, not one error, not one thing to regret is discernible'. How Joyce would have laughed at that! The Irish novelist Roddy Doyle was nearer the mark when he said that many passages stood in dire need of an editor. A young art lover like Sylvia Beach, intimidated by Joyce's reputation, was in no position to warn him that some episodes go on too long.

When after World War II bohemia broke out of the ghetto and became the new middle-class lifestyle, the assumption behind *Ulysses* that there was never any deep-rooted conflict between bohemian and bourgeois helped to secure its speedy assimilation to the literary canon. But it was the corporate university – and not the liberated individual reader – which took over the work of interpretation. That university praised Joyce as the supreme technician and ignored *Ulysses* as a modern example of wisdom literature. However, modernism, like any other great movement of art, is full of lessons.

Paralysis, Self-Help and Revival

Joyce wrote much of *Ulysses* while reclining on his bed. He often wore a white suit, so that the light would be stronger and his eyes less tired. It must have been an awkward position, but settling into a cramped apartment, surrounded by boisterous children and noisy neighbours, he felt himself in the midst of life. As a compositional tradition, bed-writing can be traced back to the bards of Gaelic Ireland, who created their poetic works while lying on pallets.

Stephen Dedalus is repeatedly called a 'bard' by his acquaintance, Malachi Mulligan, who mocks his 'toothless' condition (27). Once upon a time in ancient Ireland the bard was a powerful figure, standing second only to the chieftain. But those days are long gone, and Stephen is utterly marginal in the colonial society which has since emerged. Yet he carries an ashplant walking cane to evoke memories of those *fili* who carried a rod as a symbol of their vatic power. Those *fili* were often blind or short-sighted, so the rod helped them to feel their way forward, as the stick assists Stephen. The cane was also, of course, an essential part of the dress of Parisian *flâneurs*, as they measured out their walking progress along boulevards, taking their pose from aristocrats and their pace from turtles held on string leads. Joyce bore his own cane through the streets of Paris, while insisting on its Irish origin, 'made from a wood that grows only there'. 'It was a symbol of his country', said Jacques Mercanton, 'that he always carried with him on the roads of the world.'

Working late into the night, Joyce often woke his partner Nora Barnacle with guffaws at his own prose. Like his Gaelic forerunners, he felt himself working in a mainly oral tradition. If anyone couldn't understand a passage, they should just try reading it aloud; and if that didn't work, they should change their drink. *Ulysses*, although its author never overtly said so, is part of the literature of the Gaelic revival, which Joyce saw as a return to a vibrant medieval world in which sacred and obscene stood side by side. The medieval was the true spirit of Europe, he maintained. Even Chaucer's *Canterbury Tales* was a rewrite of Boccaccio's *Decameron*, as Milton's *Paradise Lost* was a 'Puritan transcript' of Dante's *Divine Comedy*, and Shakespeare's plays the work of 'an Italianate Englishman'. What came afterwards for the English was an empire and a literature devoted to the 'manly independence' and 'conscious cruelty' exemplified by *Robinson Crusoe*. At the same time, a richly European literature deriving mainly from Catholic sources shrank to mere Englishness.

Joyce loved to speculate about what Irish culture might have been like if it had remained part of European Catholic tradition: 'Had we been allowed to develop our own civilisation instead of this mock English one imposed on us, and which has never suited us, think of what an original, interesting civilisation we might have produced.' *Ulysses* reconnects with those codes lost during the long sleep of colonial occupation. It is not a novel in any meaningful 'English' sense of that term. Novels deal with already made societies, and Ireland in 1904 was still a society in the making. The short story or anecdote was designed to describe a submerged, colonised people, whereas the novel was more suited to the calibrated world of social classes. *Ulysses* is something more than a collection of stories, yet it is not quite unified enough to be a novel. It belongs to a long-evolving Irish genre, halfway between the two, which took centuries to emerge.

The old Gaelic aristocracy fell after 1600, but it wasn't fully replaced by a confident, native middle class until the central decades of the twentieth century. In between these dates, the key works of Irish prose were collections of micro-narratives, cast in the semblance of a novel but without its smoothly connected and singular plotline. *Gulliver's Travels* by Swift is really four short *contes*, in each of which the protagonist starts a new voyage as if he had learned nothing from the previous one. *Castle Rackrent* by Maria Edgeworth describes many generations in just sixty pages, as if the author were a kind of Gibbon on speed; and the prose trilogy of Samuel Beckett, like *At Swim-Two-Birds* by Flann O'Brien, is structured around anecdotes which never quite shape themselves into a novel. Even Joyce's first prose work, *Dubliners*, was a collection of stories with enough connections to suggest to W. B. Yeats the promise of a novelist of a new kind. However, *Ulysses*, when it finally emerged, was caught in the interstices between these forms. If the epic is the genre of the ancient world, and the novel that of the bourgeoisie, then it is in the troubled transition period between these orders that the forms of art go into meltdown and a radical newness becomes possible. In lands like England or

France that transition was managed in a few decades, but in Ireland it took more than three hundred years.

The Spaniard Miguel de Cervantes wrote a narrative mockery of romantic tales in the early 1600s and the result, although he did not yet call it that, was the novel. Within the Irish language, tellers of old stories also tried to update them to modern conditions. The anti-hero made a first appearance in *Stair Éamuinn Uí Chléire*, a parodic reworking of medieval texts by Seán Ó Neachtain in the Dublin of 1710. Other parodies, such as Brian Dubh Ó Raghallaigh's *Siabhra Mhic na Míchomhairle*, followed later in the 1700s. Frustrated by the two-dimensional characters of the saga world, these writers were caught between the desire to mock them in hilarious send-ups and the wish to supply more realistic psychological motivations. Their protagonists display the virtues and weaknesses of modern characters, breaking into cold sweat at the prospect of battle or seeking to bed each lady they meet without any extended courtesies. Conservative Gaelic scholars find in such anti-heroes 'a noteworthy phenomenon which suggests a decline in cultural standards', but they are really attempts by artists to marry their oral narratives to the forms of Cervantes and Henry Fielding.

That attempt failed because there were so few Gaelic printing presses in eighteenth-century Ireland, and those few were devoted to the production of religious material. Native speakers of Irish still told the old romantic tales, which were filled with supernatural wonders and recited in public to credulous audiences. The novel, on the other hand, was a realistic account of everyday life, to be read silently in private by the sceptical, solitary reader. It dealt in those personal emotions and psychological analyses which were lacking in the world of most storytellers. Ó Neachtain and his contemporaries did their best to conflate both modes, but without a way to publish they could go no further. Almost two centuries later, Joyce simply took up where they left off, generating a form of mythic realism in a narrative which combined everyday events with supernatural interventions (such as Bloom's assumption into the sky on a fiery chariot). In doing so, Joyce was restoring narrative possibilities that had been ousted by the English novel. He sought to awaken Irish narrative from the nightmare of its colonial history.

Calling *Ulysses* a central text of the Gaelic revival sounds preposterous, but only because current definitions of that revival are so narrow. Joyce's early stories had appeared in the *Irish Homestead,* and their exposure of 'paralysis' to its victims was intended as a contribution to that journal's programme for revitalising Irish agriculture and industry. His work, placed in that context, presented itself as part of the self-help movements which renovated Ireland after the failure of Westminster to ratify Home Rule in 1893 – Gaelic League, Agricultural Co-Operation, National Theatre (the Abbey) and, ultimately, Sinn Féin (which means 'ourselves'). As a colonial subject depicted in *Ulysses*, Stephen is painfully aware of how Britannia still rules the waves and waives the rules. For him there are three things to fear – 'horn of a bull, hoof of a horse, smile of a Saxon' (27). Confused, lost and bitter, he sees no hope of rescue, either from older Irish people or from English pseudo-liberals. In the three early episodes, Joyce describes the negative forces which entrap him – empire, church and narrow patriotism – before he can go on to say what the book is *for.*

As an adolescent, Stephen is given a bewildering variety of names in the opening episode (Jesuit, Kinch, mummer, knife-blade, Dedalus, Japhet), showing that his identity is as yet unresolved. 'Nations have their ego, just like individuals,' wrote Joyce in Trieste in 1907, and he saw Ireland at the time as passing through an adolescent phase of growth. Mulligan, who shares the tower with Stephen, wishes to Hellenise the island, while the other occupant, the Englishman Haines, says to Stephen that as an Irishman he should be able to free himself. However, freedom is not so easily seized, for like the Jews, the Irish have been deprived of their true inheritance. The old woman who brings them breakfast milk is called 'silk of the kine' and 'poor old woman' (15), names given her by bards in earlier times, yet she has lost contact with that Gaelic inheritance. The poets of earlier centuries, denied a role by English usurpers, saw in the fate of the children of Israel a version of their own, and hoped to win victory in the end as a chosen people:

> *Urscéal air sin tuigtear libh*
> *Clann Iosraeil a bhain le Dia*
> *faoin Éigipt a bhí i mbroid*
> *furtacht go grod a fuair siad.*

> A story on that theme will explain your plight:
> the children of Israel who stood by God,
> although they were in captivity in Egypt,
> were quickly given help.

In Hellenising Ireland, Joyce would also Hebraicise it, but only because he saw *Ulysses* as part of the Gaelic revival.

Many books other than *Ulysses*, if read in a more liberal spirit, might also qualify as masterpieces of Gaelic

37

revivalism. For instance, *Labour in Irish History*, the socialist tract by James Connolly, contends that socialism would simply be a return to ancient systems whereby the chieftain held the land in the name of all the people, the only difference being that now the state would take control. In a similar spirit, Patrick Pearse argued that a child-centred method of liberal education would be a revival of old fosterage traditions. As leaders of the 1916 Rising, both of these men invoked the ancient epic hero Cúchulainn to underwrite their dream of a welfare state, 'cherishing all the children of the nation equally'.

Although Joyce found the violence of Cúchulainn repulsive, his tactic in *Ulysses* is identical – to gift-wrap a subversive modern idea in some of Europe's most august narratives from the *Divine Comedy* to *Hamlet*. In a world addicted to tradition, the very new is always best presented as a reassuring revival of the very old. This is done to soothe the fears not only of onlookers but of the pro-tagonists themselves, for anybody who is about to innovate will inevitably feel nervous. For such reasons the French revolutionaries of 1789 stilled all fear of the unknown with the suggestion that they were really resurrected Romans rather than businessmen interested in careers that fitted their talents. Looking back on this self-deception (as he saw it), Karl Marx was quite scathing: as Caesar had worn the mask of Alexander, so Alexander adopted the clothes of Miltiades. The whole of history had been a story of mistaken identity in which the participants could never be themselves. History was a nightmare in which the dead past weighed upon the brains of the living.

Whenever peoples had tried to awaken and create themselves out of nothing but their own desires, Marx contended, they had relapsed into the farce of mere revivalism:

> An entire people, which had imagined that by means of a revolution it had imparted to itself an accelerated power of motion, suddenly finds itself set back into a defunct epoch and, in order that no doubt as to the relapse may be possible, the old dates rise again, the old chronology, the old names, the old edicts, which had long become the subject of antiquarian erudition, and the old minions of the law, who had seemed long decayed.

History becomes weary with repetition, as the old plot overwhelms the new one. But when a true revolution began, the people would not mistake themselves for historical actors.

Joyce was well aware of these dangers. His text would not merely repeat his predecessors, but carry their lost potentials into a wholly new form. Old stories, conjured into his mind by a sort of involuntary memory, might yet redeem with their sense of untapped potentials. The 'mask' of Homer, of the Bible, of Dante or Shakespeare, or indeed of Gaelic bardic tradition, need not be a prison but could fall away to reveal the face beneath. Yet the tale of *Hamlet* was a painful illustration of the problem, for in that play a young man tried to seize his life as his own, only to run into a ghost and discover that the old revenger's plot took over his hours and days. By the end of the play, Hamlet has been simplified beyond belief. His rich, multiple identities as courtier, scholar, playwright and artist are all but forgotten by the time he is given the burial of a soldier. In much the same fashion, creative thinkers and artists such as Pearse and Connolly passed into Irish iconography as militarists rather than visionaries. That was not the way forward for Joyce, or for his youthful surrogate, Stephen Dedalus.

1. Waking

The Martello tower in which Stephen awakens with his companion Malachi Mulligan and the English visitor Haines poses the question of inappropriate form. Built by the British to forestall invasion by Napoleonic forces, it is now the edifice in which a homeless, disenchanted youth will improvise what freedom he can. An asylum for the young man who has fled the nets of language, nationality and religion, it is a sort of bohemian outpost, offering a form of organisation for the disorganised. Yet the sins of bohemia are only too evident: the young men, like Ireland itself, talk too much and do too little. Dandies all, they affect the hauteur of middle-class aristocrats, courtiers without a court, and so they feel themselves quite superior to the world around them.

No wonder they are haunted by *Hamlet*, by Elsinore and by the idea of a rotten state. Hamlet insisted that his dark clothes denoted a true mourning, but Stephen feels himself a fraud in a pair of cast-off trousers, borrowed from Mulligan. Stephen seeks liberation but within the constraints of a second-hand home built also for other men's purposes. He has fled his father's house and its hopelessness. Joyce's own father was such a poor provider that he was forced to chop down the banisters of their Cabra dwelling to provide fuel for the winter fire. A family without an adequate father is an analogy for an occupied Ireland without effective leaders. Mr Dedalus, once a gentleman, has declined into a bankrupt and a praiser of his own past. Stephen will have to find a true father in another. 'The Son striving to be atoned with the Father' (22) may be the meaning behind both the *Odyssey* and the Christian Trinity, but Stephen must find his image of authority elsewhere.

Nietzsche once said that if you haven't had a good father, you'd better invent one by becoming a father to yourself. So Stephen becomes an anti-Hamlet, the ghost of his own father, who will establish a radical son's priority over a parent. Rather than follow the dictates of a dead man, he will turn his father into a botched version of himself. Besides, his more pressing problem is that he is haunted by the ghost of a dead *mother*, for whom he is still in deep mourning. Rebuked by Mulligan for his refusal to pray at her deathbed, he feels guilt at that necessary betrayal but also pride at his rejection of a religion in which he does not believe.

The sea around the tower is described as a 'mother' (3). It evokes the unconscious forces at work in the scene, not least the dead Mrs Dedalus. Stephen likens the snot-green sea of Dublin Bay to the bowl into which she spat green bile in her last illness. His response to her request had been art rather than a prayer – he sang a lyric by Yeats:

> And no more turn aside and brood
> Upon love's bitter mystery . . .

He sang it from an adjoining room, because Stephen can never directly confront his own emotion. Ever the gruff

Irish male, he excels in strategies of avoidance, using the Middle English phrase 'agenbite of inwit' as a way of distancing his underlying feeling of remorse of conscience. A little learning can indeed be a dangerous thing, if it comes between a youth and his emotions. Much of the conversation in this episode is conducted between the disembodied voices of three young men who can hear but not always see one another, as if an invincible shyness governs all. That shyness is especially notable in Stephen, who all day will either say too little (as in this scene) or too much (as in his later monologues).

What is repressed by day, however, must always be confronted by night: and so Mrs Dedalus in her grave clothes haunts her son's dreams – but his response is the opposite of Hamlet's:

> Ghoul! Chewer of corpses!
> No mother. Let me be and let me live (11).

Stephen refuses to be 'taken' to another world, according to folk belief, by a recently dead beloved one.

The other female in the episode is the old milkwoman who comes with the morning supply. She is perhaps a messenger, like Athena visiting Telemachus, but her 'old shrunken paps' (15) suggest a different, more local mythology. She is Mother Ireland, 'silk of the kine' (15), '*síoda na mbó*' in the phrase used by Gaelic poets. They believed that the cow would return to her proper field, when the old woman brought the French across the sea to liberate the people. The milkwoman is a figure from Gaelic sovereignty tales in which a young man met a withered old harridan who might be transformed into a ravishing young queen if only he would love, serve and, if

43

necessary, die for her. The myth had been dramatised by Yeats and Lady Gregory just two years earlier in *Cathleen Ni Houlihan*: but Joyce is writing an anti-*aisling*, an anti-vision-poem, in which no such transformation can occur. As an Irish bard, Stephen has a duty of either celebration or satire: 'to serve or upbraid, whether he could not tell: but scorned to beg her favour' (15).

At the close of *A Portrait of the Artist as a Young Man*, Stephen had dreamed of casting his imaginative creations before the daughters of Ireland, so that they might breed a race less ignoble than their own; but now he cannot even keep the attention of an old woman, who is more impressed by her conqueror (the English Haines) and by her betrayer (Mulligan). Stephen well knows the feelings of powerlessness and marginality of the recent arts graduate in the company of the medical man: 'She bows her old head to a voice that speaks to her loudly, her bonesetter, her medicineman; me she slights' (16). Worse still, when they speak Irish to her, she mistakes it for French. Far from offering an image of an Ireland being restored to its rightful self-possession, this woman cannot even recognise her ancestral tongue. Her ignorance of native tradition may provide yet another cue to Stephen to recover it.

The penetration of Ireland by the colonial power proves almost absolute. Mulligan speaks in a prattle copied from Oxford English: 'Thanks, old chap' (2). Everything about him is in inverted commas, from his abject external deference to the English visitor to his secret suggestion to Stephen that they assault Haines. He claims that Ireland has grown out of Wildean paradoxes but presents himself as the very reincarnation of Oscar.

Stephen rejects that old jester's role. He will express rather than exploit his nation.

Far from being the clown-by-appointment to some foreign prince, Stephen will be the bard who rewrites the epic for the community at home. But there are many temptations and traps along the way, one of which is that sentimental and romanticised view of Ireland which simply reinforces English hegemony. Wilde had called the nineteenth-century dislike of realism 'the rage of Caliban at seeing his face in a mirror', but Mulligan mockingly quotes for Stephen the other Wildean wisecrack about the dislike of romanticism: 'the rage of Caliban at not seeing his face in a mirror'. Hamlet had asserted that acting should hold a mirror up to nature, but in Stephen's view the mummers of Yeats's theatre were simply confirming imperial power by producing 'the cracked looking-glass of a servant' as 'a symbol of Irish art' (6).

The problem seems clear enough: the narrow-gauge nostalgia of the Irish revival, whose adherents fail to realise that a cracked mirror, like a cubist painting, projects a multiple, not a singular, self. Fragmented, maybe, but also authentic. Instead of sincere devotion to a single self-image, it calls for a recognition that every person has several selves, which it is the labour of a lifetime to be true to. In being true to a single image, the romanticist is inevitably being false to several others. Modernist art, at the prompting of Wilde, recognised that the only way to intensify personality was to multiply it.

But just when Ireland had been about to innovate and throw off the shackles of the past, 'liberal' Englishmen like Haines had arrived to assure its people that their ancient language and traditions should be retained. Not updated, simply retained. For Joyce such a revival could be nothing more than a celebration of the backwardness of Ireland, 'the most belated race in Europe'. He wished, as did Stephen, to create new forms, not just to repeat old ones. He could sense the English substratum in the Irish revival – the desire of some frustrated Saxons, cheated of their culture at home, to come to Ireland in search of a lost language of Elizabethanisms, folk energy and old tradition. Haines represents all those forces which, having repressed Ireland for centuries, denying it economic development, now come over to cream off the colourful phrases and rich story-making which are the results of such material deprivation. The English had always had a fatal gift for sentimentalising peoples *after* they had conquered them – and Haines is more sentimentalist than emperor. He even has a notebook in which to record Stephen's vivid phrases, as a prelude, doubtless, to making them available in dilute versions for fellow Oxonians back in England. Stephen, however, is reluctant to be pressed into the role of minstrel-show performer. Far more obliging in this regard is Mulligan, who tells a hoary joke about Old Mother Grogan. 'When I makes tea, I makes tea,' she says, 'and when I makes water, I makes water,' only to be told by a neighbour, 'God send you don't make them in the one pot' (14).

There is, nonetheless, a slight touch of mockery in Mulligan's description of the quip to Haines:

> That's folk, he said very earnestly, for your book, Haines. Five lines of text and ten pages of notes about the folk and fishgods of Dundrum. Printed by the weird sisters in the year of the big wind (14).

Joyce is satirising the eccentric sisters of Yeats, who ran the Dun Emer Press from Dundrum, but he is also laughing at annotations to ancient myth supplied by the scholar-pedants who failed to notice their sources in more local demotic.

Behind all these scenes is a simple truth, later expressed by Patrick Kavanagh: that much of the writing of the Irish revival was 'a thorough-going English-bred lie' got up by public schoolboys in order to prevent the Irish people from modernising their culture and country. The Wildean tradition of performing funny one-liners was being reimported into the colony from London by the Haineses of the world, who became for Stephen just one more reason to get out. 'I will not sleep here tonight,' he says of the tower: 'Home also I cannot go' (28).

The last line of the episode is the single word 'Usurper' (28). This captures not just the usurpation of the tower (for which Stephen paid rent) by Mulligan and Haines, but also the denial of Mother Ireland by their macho-imperial use of militarist images to describe the life of the 'messmates' in the tower. Nothing new will come from such bland echoes. Stephen may have only a cracked mirror offering a fragmented, abject image. The trick which he must master is how to do without the distorting mirror of other people's opinions. He must reject all codes imposed by others in order to construct himself out of nothing but his own desire. The homo-erotic tone of Mulligan's language concerning him is just the sort of degraded caricature of the feminine to be heard in officers' mess-talk: 'my love' (2), 'loveliest mummer' (4), 'you look damn well when you're dressed' (5).

Haines's glib attempt to palm off all blame for the past

sufferings of the Irish on to an impersonal force called 'history' is odious to Stephen. It is odious because he knows the true score: 'I am the servant of two masters, an English and an Italian. And a third there is who wants me for odd jobs' (24). Very odd jobs. Yet, in blaming history, Haines provides a major theme of *Ulysses* – the dead, denying power of the past from which the main characters try to liberate themselves. Although Stephen feels the fierce pull of his dead mother, he withstands it. Confronted by Stephen, Haines is reminded of Hamlet and sees that story as a version of the Christian Trinity: 'The Father and the Son idea. The Son striving to be atoned with the Father' (22). Mulligan, aware of Stephen's domestic problems, jokes that his theory of *Hamlet* is pure wish-fulfilment, so that he himself may become 'the ghost of his own father' (21).

The Irish colony has become, like the court at Elsinore, an echo chamber of flatterers. Everything Mulligan says is meant to be instantly decipherable to his lords and masters: but Stephen rejects such easy legibility, just as Joyce scorned to use quotation marks for their conversations. Stephen prefers to remain uninterpretable, as Mulligan rather pointedly observes on behalf of the baffled Haines: 'He can't make you out' (3). Stephen is a rebel, but unlike previous rebels against imperial power, he doesn't press his case in any terms recognisable to the enemy. If there had been one figure whom the British could handle with as much confidence as they did a lackey, that was a rude, rug-headed terrorist – but Stephen is none of those things. He adopts silence, exile and cunning as part of his programme of remaining untranslatable, just as his creator uses the English language and literary traditions, but only to subvert them utterly. Joyce understood that all imitation is slavery, for as Richard Sennett has written:

> Rebellions in *moeurs*, in manners broadly conceived, fail because they are insufficiently radical in terms of culture. It is still the creation of a believable personality which is the object of a cultural revolt, and, as such, the revolt is still enchained to the bourgeois it seeks to overturn.

This may explain why Stephen is at different times glacially polite, boisterously obscene, often silent, sometimes verbose . . . but never entirely predictable. He refuses to be easily decoded. So in truth does Joyce's book. In taking the day as the unit to be seized, it embraces the epic wisdom of that Gaelic life which taught '*níl ann ach lá dár saol*' (it's only a day in our lives). By his focus on a single day from his young manhood, the mature Joyce shows the reader how the hours may be wasted and also how they may be redeemed. A single day may prove the very antithesis of dullness. By recording the hour-by-hour variations in individuals, Joyce can show their selves in transformation. The very fact that no great events transpire on 16 June 1904 leaves the characters free to attend to their own thoughts as a discipline of self-exploration, rather than have those thoughts wholly dictated by others.

The Irish writing of his day positioned itself in a Celtic Twilight (an in-between state of receptivity as the human figure hovered between day and night), but he was scornful of such *fin de siècle* effects, dubbing them 'the Cultic Twalette'. He preferred to emphasise the need for

49

the sleeper, after bad dreams and a life lived below the level of full consciousness, to arise to a new dawn and shake himself awake. 'By night the sleeper abandons himself to death,' joked Freud, 'but in hopes of a morning reprieve.' The night can be heavy going, Stephen discovers. As if haunted by some colonial guilt, the sahib Haines raves about black panthers and tries to shoot them. Stephen is terrified by images of his mother. 'We're always tired in the morning,' he explains to the visitor (21), a further indication of the depth of his depression. But at least the morning promises deliverance from such terrors. If sleep brings forth monsters, then the only way to live well is to wake up.

The bachelors in the tower eat their morning meal with energy, but also with a certain resentment, as if the food cannot fully satisfy. They 'fumble' at the fried eggs, 'slapped out' on three plates; and they jibe 'where's the sugar?' or 'what sort of a kip is this?' (13). Mulligan, who seems to relish male bodies as well as female ones, has his bread 'buttered on both sides' (17). The way in which the men eat is a fair indication of their attitude. There is a kind of bachelor improvisation about their feeding, as if they don't like having to look after themselves and feel the need of a good, caring woman, mother, or lover, but not the withered old milkwoman, who simply reminds them of their poverty.

The narrative, centred in Stephen's head, shares in his refusal to be simplified. The episode is filmic, with jump-cuts and skips, as Joyce already shows how chronological time need not be strictly followed, but can be compressed and edited. Whole phrases of the conversation are lost, as Stephen's thoughts distract him from these exchanges, which they in fact override. Already, a strong hint is given that there may be a pathological element to interior monologue, which has huge appeal for a man who finds it hard to talk to others and often prefers to speak only to himself.

Sometimes, single words ('Chrysostomos', the Greek for golden-mouthed) describe a passing thought of Stephen – on this occasion about the expensive fillings in Mulligan's mouth, which provide a contrast with his own toothless state. Interior monologue is introduced, but sparingly, popping out now and then as an intrusion into the more social scenes. But intrude it does, as an image of those repressed, ousted possibilities of an ancient culture which might yet return. This is figured in the drowned body due to be washed up out of the sea water that afternoon, an irruption from the buried unconscious but also, perhaps, a sign that Homer's epic hero, drowned on this occasion after shipwreck, can only re-emerge in a wholly new form hereafter.

The English visitor seems to sense that something heroic is afoot. 'After all,' says the facile Haines to Stephen, 'I should think that you are able to free yourself' (24). Maybe so. Stephen rejects Mulligan's suggestion that he take the revenger's role and debag Haines. Haines is only a problem at night, when bad dreams, brought on by the guilty past which he is so busy suppressing by day, seem to derange his mind and cause him to reach for his gun. (In 1904, George Bernard Shaw, in *John Bull's Other Island*, had a liberal English Unionist, Tom Broadbent, also pack a gun before coming over to Ireland to mix with, i.e. exploit, the natives.) Shakespeare's Hamlet was another who refused the avenger's part and then found it hard to discover any other. Like him, Stephen looks for a vantage point from which the problems of the present moment might begin to make a kind of sense. He tries to restore some of the cultural possibilities ousted by empire, which closed off many of the potentials for an Irish art that might have been part of Catholic Europe.

His thoughts are filled with speculations about Arius who denied that the Son of God was one with the Father and of Sabellius (who claimed that he was). The son can be atoned with the father in the Christian Trinity, but Stephen wishes to self-invent, to derive ultimately and only from himself. The Irish past, filled with inadequate or absent fathers, is the troubled sleep from which he wants to awaken. 'Who chose this face for me?' (5), he ponders. Cyril Connolly would later joke that, after the age of forty, every man gets the face that he deserves; but Stephen is only twenty-two, far too young for such bleak thoughts. He is a revolutionary, who knows that for centuries the Irish have been doomed to wear masks, like Mulligan playing the Stage Irishman. But now the time has come to reveal to the people their true faces.

2. Learning

Of all the days of the year, why did Joyce choose 16 June 1904 on which to set *Ulysses*? The romantic answer is that it was on that date that he first walked out with Nora Barnacle and she 'made a man' of him. The book might be seen as a sort of anniversary gift, offered by the mature man in gratitude to the lady who brought an end to his emotional and sexual depression, calling him back to life. He learned something new on that day.

But what if there is another explanation? The main event of *Ulysses*, after all, is not a male–female encounter but the moment when a tired and drunken Stephen is rescued by a kindly Jewish man of middle years, one who gives good advice and offers him a bed for the night. An incident of this kind befell the young Joyce in June 1904. We do not know what exactly happened between the two men, but perhaps this secret history is being commemorated. It is as if Joyce were seeking to recapture that passing moment, and asking how it might have developed, before the other major event of June 1904 took over his life. *Ulysses* is a book obsessed with missed or insufficiently developed encounters. It is indeed a revisionist text, in the sense of trying to restore to lost moments in history a sense of the multiple possibilities which might have flowed from them, before a single subsequent event took on the look of inevitability.

As Stephen teaches Roman history in the second episode 'Nestor', he raises just such 'what ifs?':

> Had Pyrrhus not fallen by a beldam's hand in Argos or Julius Caesar not been knifed to death? They are not to be thought away. Time has branded them and fettered they are lodged in the room of the infinite possibilities they have ousted. But can those have been possible seeing that they never were? Or was that only possible which came to pass? (30)

The meeting with Leopold Bloom will provide a 'corrected' version of Stephen's unfruitful conversation with Mr Deasy, headmaster of the Dalkey school at which he teaches this lesson. That encounter with Deasy is but the latest in a long series of unsatisfactory interviews with failed authority figures in Joyce's oeuvre, stretching right back to the opening stories of *Dubliners*. In the first, 'The Sisters', an impressionable boy feels let down by a dead priest who somehow betrayed his sacred vocation; and in the second, 'An Encounter', a sensitive youth goes on a quest for adventure only to be frightened by threats of chastisement by an old pervert in a field. Repeatedly, in *A Portrait of the Artist as a Young Man*, Stephen Dedalus trusts in the authority of fathers, teachers and priests, only to find them all conspiring to rob him of his freedom and self-respect. Joyce's entire work is a sustained meditation on true and false pedagogy, and on how best the young may learn from their elders. The Wilde affair had brought some discredit on to relationships between older and younger men, but the Greek ideal remained intact. Thus, Joyce sets out to Hellenise the island in ways undreamed of by Mulligan.

54

At the start of 'Nestor', Stephen hasn't got very far himself. In fact, he has become one of those bad teachers whom he warned against. The boys in his charge sneak-read the answers to the questions from their textbook, and Stephen himself has to be coached in his teacherly role. A lad named Cyril Sargent copies the answers to sums without understanding the underlying process. This type of external rule-keeping without inner conviction is all too symptomatic of a colonial system of schooling which produces mimic-men but not people prepared for life. So Stephen encourages the boys in their evasive strategies ('I don't see anything', 31), even as they advise him ('Ask me, sir', 31) on how to impersonate the sort of teacher that Deasy wants him to be.

A true education would master not the young but the relationship between generations, a wisdom which Stephen cannot teach until first he acquires it in the presence of Bloom. But, already, he has some inkling of how that process might work: 'You were not born to be a teacher,' Mr Deasy suggests, to which Stephen responds, 'A learner rather,' while silently asking himself, 'And here what will you learn more?' (43). In a true pedagogy, tradition is the medium in which the learner changes constantly into the teacher, and vice versa. Bloom will be exactly such a guru, one who dreams of being an agony uncle in a newspaper, because you can learn a lot teaching others.

Deasy, on the other hand, is all external form. He collects shells for display in mounted cases, 'dead treasure, hollow shells' (36), giving his obedience as unionist and empire man to a set of outmoded systems. He also amasses Stuart coins and apostle spoons, symbols of those twin empires of state and church whose service Stephen has already railed against. In so doing, Deasy has turned his school into a museum rather than a place of spiritual transformation. A happy imperialist, he believes that history is already at an end, finding its consummation in the British Empire, which the boys of his school will be happy to serve. He believes that knowledge is not dynamic, but has been stabilised once and for all. In sum, he is a dismal illustration of Oscar Wilde's complaint that those who have forgotten how to learn have all taken to teaching.

The lesson of Shakespeare, opines Deasy, is that 'he made money' (37). He quotes from *Othello*, 'Put but money in thy purse', while Stephen murmurs 'Iago', recalling inwardly the villain of that play. The Englishman's proudest boast, says Deasy, is 'I paid my way' (37), a comment which causes Stephen to list his various debts even as he prepares to be paid. For all of Deasy's external bluster, he is deeply insecure, surrounding himself with valuable coins and objects in order to compensate for an inner emptiness. As he pays Stephen, 'a sovereign fell' (37), and that line seems to portend the end of the very imperial system which he supports, one which can offer only a schooling obsessed with the adult codes to which the child must be made to conform rather than an education that addresses a child's inmost nature.

Throughout the episode, Stephen feels the sort of pity for the boys which can only be based on identification with their plight. They recite 'Lycidas' badly. Its author, John Milton, was the creator of one of the previous epics in English, and, like Joyce, a devotee of Italian culture who feared that his early promise remained unfulfilled:

How soon hath Time, the subtle thief of youth,
Stol'n on his wing my three and twentieth year!
My hasting days fly on with full career,
But my late spring no bud or blossom shew'th.

Sargent, one of the boys in Stephen's class, had a face only
a mother could love, 'Yet someone had loved him, borne
him in her arms and in her heart' (33). Watching Sargent
stooped over the sums he can copy but never quite
fathom, Stephen feels his childhood bending beside him
and is haunted by *amor matris*, the love of the mother (as
both source and object of such love).

But his own mother, Mrs Dedalus, had died 'scarcely
having been' (33); she was traumatised by a fear of life
that leaves little or no trace. Was she also a mere rule-
keeper? Perhaps. But Stephen knows that there is no
gainsaying a mother's love: 'Was that then real? The only
true thing in life?' (33). Joyce liked to joke that the love of
a woman for her child was equalled only by the love of a
man for lies, but the old, nagging doubt about paternity
lies behind the question. It was dramatised well by Angela
Carter in a feminist fable which tells of a young man who
falls in love with the girl next door, but is told by an
embarrassed father not to marry her, as 'she might be
your sister'. The youth, some months later, brings a
slightly older woman home from another part of the city
and meets the same interdiction. Years later, he returns
from a distant town with a third prospective bride, only to
hear his red-faced father say, 'Son, there is no excuse for
my wantonness, but . . .', at which point the mother looks
up at last from her knitting and proclaims, 'Son, you can
marry whoever you want – he's not your father.'

57

How is one to be an authentic, free person in a world of filiation, derived gestures, rote-learning and conformity? Mulligan's mockery is hardly the answer, though Stephen briefly re-enacts it with his pun for the uncomprehending boys about a pier being a disappointed bridge. He flirts with the idea of re-telling the joke that night to Haines in the pub, but knows that this would reduce him to the role of an Oscar Wilde: 'A jester at the court of his master, indulged and disesteemed, winning a clement master's praise. Why had they all chosen that part?' (29). This is Stephen's dismissal of the subservient role played by Anglo-Irish comedians, from Congreve to Sheridan, Goldsmith to Shaw, in the culture of Britain. The boys from such a colonial school could hope for nothing more – either military/naval service, or becoming apprentice Yoricks, fellows of infinite jest, at the London court. Fearing the capacity of England, like that of Haines, to convert all Irish artists into wit-and-wordplay performers, Joyce wisely turned to Paris, a place in which no such stereotyped expectations preceded the Irish intellectual.

Even in Paris, however, that old problem of authenticity presented itself to Stephen, in the spectacle of the Jewish traders on the Bourse under their maladroit silk hats: 'Not theirs: these clothes, this speech, these gestures' (42). Their clothes were as derived and uncouth as the second-hand breeches worn by Dedalus in the tower. Their melancholy made them hoarders and collectors, like Deasy, but only a real revolution would leave them free to be themselves for the first time.

That new order would derive not from the past but from the present and the future. That is at the root of Stephen's disagreement with Deasy. The boys, dismissed from class, engage in the sport of hockey on the playing field, a zone of contest on which was rehearsed the world war being waged as Joyce wrote the episode:

> History, Stephen said, is a nightmare from which I am trying to awake.
>
> From the playfield the boys raised a shout. A whirring whistle: goal. What if that nightmare gave you a back kick? (42)

The teaching of Roman history, along with the practice of field sports, had fed a cult of manly prowess designed to counteract the enfeebling effects of the prolonged peace before 1914. But Joyce, writing this episode in Locarno in 1917, knew what the 'back kick' of aerial bombardment could wreak. He has Stephen link the apocalypse of William Blake to the devastation of Europe in 1917: 'I hear the ruin of all space, shattered glass and toppling masonry, and time one livid final flame. What's left us then?' (28). So deep did the disquiet about the emasculation of youth become in the years after 1900 that, even in the United States, a preacher named Billy Sunday was dispatched to Ivy League colleges with one purpose only: to replace the old image of 'gentle Jesus, meek and mild' with an altogether more masculine saviour who 'was no dough-faced lick-spittle' . . . but 'the greatest scrapper that ever lived'.

For all his morning depression, Stephen really does want to awaken from the nightmare that weighs like the pressure of the past upon the brains of the living. There is, in fact, no point in having dreams unless you can rouse yourself from them in order to discover what hidden wish lay coiled in their plot-lines, a wish that might only be fully understood when it began to be achieved. The new order, like a new poem, is a process of shaping which may begin in a stray rhythm, a movement, 'an actuality of the possible as possible' (30). Where Mulligan saw the world as dying matter (white corpuscles), Stephen believes that the soul has yet to be born, if only it can find the appropriate form. But Deasy takes a more Protestant view of history, seeing it as a straight line running towards a single destination, the manifestation of God.

It was difficult for Irish people of Joyce's generation to accept such a theory, based as it was on a view of life as a train moving smoothly on tracks towards a definite point – whether the classless society, evolutionary perfection or, indeed, the Second Coming of Jesus. After all, their parents had lived in a country where millions died of starvation in field and street, while in London railways were constructed and the great Crystal Palace erected to proclaim the triumph of Victorian science and industry. For writers like Joyce and Yeats, history would appear more as a circle of recurring traumas than as a straight, progressive, purposeful line. So Stephen, as shy as Telemachus was with Nestor through most of his interview, is nonetheless bold enough to object to Deasy's model. Jerking his thumb towards the window, he insists that God is present here and now as 'A shout in the street' (42). The divine plan must, like the form of a poem or epic, take its shape from everyday experience, or else not at all. This was the surrealist credo espoused by Joyce, ever since the Manifesto of Berlin had castigated 'people who prefer their armchair to the noise of the street'.

Stephen understands the dynamics of creation far better than Deasy. He recognises the good teacher's need

60

to see each child as that child's mother first did – and so he recalls his own mother's love. The fact that he doesn't fully understand what he's teaching seems to be part of the point: that the forms of knowledge emerge only gradually, often in unexpected moments, and are not always completely mastered, even by their bearers. A person of limited intellect and imagination may none-theless teach wisdom to students more intelligent than himself – as will Bloom at the close of the day. Even Socrates relied upon errors – his own, as well as those of his students – for the uncovering of new truths. Deasy commits many howlers in his blame-the-women version of history. He wrongly claims that the wife of Dermot McMurrough brought the English to Ireland in 1169. He falsely alleges that Kitty O'Shea brought her lover Parnell down, when it was in fact the intolerance of the Irish bishops and of the English Nonconformists that sealed his fate. The circular notion of history as eternal recurrence includes the eternal recurrence of errors. However, Stephen can silently correct many of Deasy's mistakes. Moreover, he will observe later that a man of genius sees every error as the portal of a new discovery, an aid to the understanding of the world. We go wrong, but only in order to go right.

Deasy's last mistake is, arguably, his greatest of all. He denounces the Jews, claiming that their merchants are destroying England. A Bible-quoting paranoiac, he insists that 'they sinned against the light' (41). But Stephen, whose natural element is darkness owing to his bad eyesight, asks who has not, as if unconsciously defending the Jewish man who later that day will come to defend him. Minutes later, Deasy will come running after

Stephen to offer his own riddle. Why has Ireland the honour of being the only country which never persecuted the Jews? Answer: because she never let them in. Deasy rushes after Stephen to tell this crude witticism at the end of the episode, from his subconscious need to appeal to a person whose mind is superior to his own, even if that person is dependent on him for employment and income. Once again, however, Deasy is wrong: the Irish authorities had let Jews in, among them one whose son, Leopold Bloom, far better than this old headmaster, will provide wise counsel for the young man.

'Is this old wisdom?' (42), Stephen sardonically asks himself, before telling Deasy that history is nightmare: 'He waits to hear from me' (42). But it is old wisdom, and new wisdom too. The world war raging as Joyce wrote had been made possible by a narrow-mindedness among nations, whose leaders often failed to see the larger context of their actions. The openness of form and the multiplicity of viewpoints in a book like *Ulysses* implicitly challenge the sort of zealotry which had led to the carnage.

After the war, many soldiers were so traumatised by their suffering in the trenches that they could no longer tell stories which carried the pressure of felt experiences. Many also simply fell silent, lapsing into neurasthenia. Even among those who remained eloquent on the topic, there was a sense of the 'unreality' of civilian life, of everyday living. *Ulysses*, though begun around the same time as the war itself, tried to restore the possibility that 'good counsel' might come from a story. Young men who had gone to war in search of stimuli were now in search of a consciousness which would teach them how to protect themselves from over-stimulation.

Ulysses offered that wisdom too. Unlike the shock-horror stories beloved of modern newspapers, these tales would partake of their quotidian quality, but with a wisdom designed to last for more than a day. Joyce's stories of everyday life would be lodged, like the lore of Gaelic tradition, within the room of infinite possibilities ousted by militarism and empire. While Joyce wrote *Ulysses*, sovereigns fell, empires toppled, a world system collapsed: but he knew that he was writing a book for the future community which might take their place. In that book he would explore modes of teaching and learning which answer the emotional and intellectual needs of ordinary people in search of a wiser way of life.

3. Thinking

Those who think often think differently.

Deasy valued shells and money for themselves, and not for the life which they contained or for the uses to which they could be put. But Stephen seeks their inner meaning, the soul which animates the exterior form. To find it, he must abandon his attachment to clothes, ideas and things. If his soul is to reveal itself, he must give up all notions of ownership and control. So at 11 a.m. he walks into eternity along Sandymount Strand, crushing the dead shells of the past under his feet in the attempt to open a different future. Rejecting Deasy's idea of a knowledge that has been stabilised once and for all, he immerses himself in a world of change and flux.

That trick is not easily done. Like the pupils back in Dalkey, he also is the product of a schooling which privileges results over processes, a schooling ill-suited to real human needs. This entire episode is a mocking study of the lethal after-effects of a recent university degree, which immobilises Stephen's thought even as it prevents any significant developments of plot. By the edge of the sea, Stephen ponders images and thoughts from his subconscious, hoping to create something out of nothing. His meditation is filled with evocations of creativity, from midwives to navels, from the Book of Genesis to modern philosophy.

He isn't really in full control of his own thoughts, or for that matter of where his own legs are carrying him. If anything, his walking seems involuntary, beyond his control. The sand underfoot is soft and wet, as if already giving way to subterranean forces of the unconscious. Suffering too much information, carrying too great a learning, Stephen is weighed down rather than illuminated by his knowledge. He is the adolescent as narcissist, but at least his learned quotations are all internalised, impressing nobody but himself. He feels powerless, loveless, inadequate ('If I had land under my feet', 57). Worse still, he is guilty of wanting to feel guilty about all this: 'our souls are shame-wounded by our sins' (61). Many readers drop *Ulysses* at this point, finding themselves unable to keep up with Stephen's remorseless and obscure pedantry: but the truth is that Joyce is laughing at the pitiful pretentiousness of the youth he once was. *Nobody* could understand all that Stephen says or thinks. *Nobody* could take all of his ideas with utter seriousness.

There is a sense of excess about the young man's self-interrogations, which are out of all proportion to his actual problems. His robust insensitivity to others is exceeded only by his exquisite sensitivity to himself. Clearly, he needs to move out into the world, to find a way in which his learning might at last be put to work for him. Yet the many points of overlap between his thoughts in the opening three episodes and the ideas propounded by Leopold Bloom in later chapters suggest that the same basic experiences can be reprocessed by a more balanced mind – ideas such as phone links to the buried dead, or distrust of the big words that make people unhappy, or even the proposition that death by drowning may not be the worst way to go. For the moment, however, this monologue is a cautionary tale about how a college degree in arts may unfit you for the world. Stephen, shy and yet arrogant, always says either too little or too much. Messy food, bad teaching, and now over-interpreting events – all this has been a lesson in how *not* to live.

Stephen's pressing problem is where to sleep that night. Immobilised by theory, he is troubled also by guilt about his dead mother, whose voice had called to him from the sea at the end of the opening episode. His fear of sinking, even of drowning, is somehow linked in his mind to his mother's death: 'I could not save her. Waters: bitter death: lost' (57). But that fear seems to go well beyond feelings about Mrs Dedalus. Stephen feels that he is himself 'wombed in sin' (46). This may all relate to doubts about his father, Simon, who liked to complain about 'the things I married into' (47).

A man's doubts as to whether he is father to his designated children may cause him also to doubt whether he is his own designated father's son. Simon Dedalus is evoked in this episode as the man with Stephen's voice and eyes in a classic reversal of the tradition which sees an anxious world politely seeking traces of the father in the features of his child. Whatever the truth – and it's hard to think of Stephen as other than the eldest son of Simon and May Dedalus – he himself feels lacking in identity, as futile as the landless, loveless, wifeless Fenian who rolls gunpowder cigarettes in a pointless Parisian exile. Although Stephen's self-revelation is neither fully willed nor fully controlled here, it is a confession, albeit a subconscious one.

The danger of thinking, of uninterrupted interior monologue, is the risk run by pure theory unchastened by any sense of fact: that one can wade too far out into the waters of private reverie, either sinking in the shoals or being overwhelmed by the incoming tide. Stephen fears that if there is no God, then he may drown in the spray of phenomena: one damned thing after another. As early as 1899, the Dutch critic Ernst de Peerdt had said that the visual field was not a timeless unity but a sequence of different perceptions: 'It is precisely those moments that we put together as a simultaneity, a *Nebeinander*, which constitute a sequence, a *Nacheinander*, in the seeing of an object.' The figure of a lost soul gazing out to sea is a sign of the melancholic intellectual in late Romantic art. 'My whole life has been spent walking by the side of a bottomless chasm,' said the painter Edvard Munch, 'jumping from stone to stone.'

The drowned man's body is to be fished out of the sea at one o'clock. But Stephen, for a few moments at least, wants to imagine himself subsiding with the drowned one: 'His human eyes scream to me out of horror of his death . . . With him together down' (57). All through *A Portrait of the Artist as a Young Man* he had been haunted by terrifying eyes. Is the fear in this case of drowning in a sea of alcohol and debt, a fate shared with the father who has his eyes? The drowned body may represent the end of the line for Homer's sea voyager, whose story Joyce is already trumping. But Stephen is himself submerged by all his learning. One of the reasons for his immobilisation in this episode is that he can never act without first indulging in a history of the narrative underlying any possible action. (In this, at least, he has something in common with his author, who cannot write *Ulysses* without first reprocessing the classical texts of the past.)

67

Yet Stephen's ultimate fantasy is of self-invention. He would prefer to have no debts to precursors but to be a changeling, 'made not begotten' (46), unlike Jesus who, according to scripture, was 'begotten, not made'. Self-invention was a recurrent myth in the Irish writing that preceded Joyce. Wilde underwent a makeover by which he became all that his father was not; and Shaw suppressed the names 'George' and 'Shaw', those degrading links to an alcoholic father, reinventing himself as GBS, the child of his own writings. Such manoeuvres seemed to presage Sigmund Freud's own version of the family romance, whereby a child seeks to free himself of a crippling sense of obligation to parents by the performance of some sacrificial act which leaves the generations quits and the protagonist free at last to conceive of himself.

Stephen would like to free himself of those eyes which expect so much yet offer so little. Hence his fascination with the idea of creation from nothing, not just as a divine achievement but as one he hopes to make his own. That might also explain why Joyce chose to dispense with all Homeric titles in each episode of the published book: for the 'mask' of ancient Greece would not be central to the actual event, and so it could be dropped off to reveal the core meanings of the new form.

The art of self-invention may recommend itself not just to individuals but to nations. If a country hasn't had a happy history, it may be tempted to invent one – that is, to rewrite the national story along lines more helpful to current self-esteem. This was the process already under way in the Irish Revival. But at the level of the individual, such self-invention was also a major feature of European modernism. Wilde had advised Yeats to form a conception of himself, as a result of which the poet affected a black cape which made him look 'like an umbrella left behind after a picnic'. Scott Fitzgerald's Jay Gatsby had inherited the less imposing name of Jimmy Gatz but decided to spring 'from some extraordinary Platonic conception of himself'. And Jean-Paul Sartre in his autobiography *Words* summed up Stephen's dilemma in speaking of himself: 'Being nobody's son, I was my own cause and was filled with both pride and wretchedness . . . I always preferred to accuse myself rather than the universe, not only out of simple good-heartedness, but in order to derive only from myself.' Such ideals were an inevitable result of the speed of social change, for the world had altered more in a few modern decades, it was generally agreed, than it had since the birth of Christ. This left the older and younger generations with little common ground on which to meet; and it meant that parents, whether they wished to or not, were more and more compelled to leave children to their own devices.

But creation from nothing, though a pleasing fantasy, is in the end impossible. The navel cords lead right back to our first parents. Stephen has fantasies of a phone line which would link him back to them ('Put me on to Edenville', 46), but he knows in his heart that intellectuals need the wisdom of past experience. Seeing two midwives walking down the beach, he thinks that one such person dragged him into the world. Nobody really gives birth to themselves. Except, possibly, the artist in the artwork.

Joyce once told Pádraic Colum that lyric art began in 'the simple liberation of a rhythm'. This is Stephen's intuition too. As he walks, he tries to compose a poem which might capture his very movements: 'Rhythm begins, you see. I hear. A catalectic tetrameter of iambs marching' (46). Joyce believed that, if anything, form was anterior to content: and that new forms and rhythms would, if perfected, be filled in time by their destined contents. Such newness was more likely to be found outside the traditional genres of literature. 'A major work will establish a genre or abolish it,' said Walter Benjamin, 'and the perfect work will do both.' As Joyce composed this episode he was under no pressure to conform to any given rules. He had grown up in a Dublin whose citizens, lacking any great responsibility for their society, felt quite free to mouth off about everything. Yet, because he came from a society that was undercapitalised and technically underdeveloped, he felt all the more investment in pioneering new and modern forms.

His object, in rendering a single day, was to capture a sense of life in full flow. This might necessitate a severely reduced role for plot-lines and external events. He was, however, greatly influenced by some of the advances made by impressionist painters. Claude Monet had said that *time* was a far more important element than *plot* in any convincing painting. As a modern artist, he was less interested in narrative of the Victorian kind than in returning to the feel of a moment. 'One does not paint a landscape, a seascape, a figure,' said Monet. 'One paints an impression of an hour of the day.' *Ulysses*, with its successive episodes keyed to the various hours through a summer's day, seems the literary implementation of this programme.

The flux of life, at the centre of this episode, which Joyce called 'Proteus', and of all the interior monologues that follow, is a central element of *Ulysses*. If Joyce had an obsession with systems of classification – and he surely did – that was the understandable reaction of a man who felt some need for a point of stability in the midst of all that uncertainty. Proteus was the god of change, and the episode is concerned with the ways in which matter is constantly transformed. This is true especially of human bodies. Stephen's teeth are so rotten that they are turning into shells, much like those hollow shells which he is trampling underfoot. The drowned body to be taken from the sea is already decomposing. All created things feed off one another: 'God becomes man becomes fish becomes barnacle goose becomes featherbed mountain' (63) – a truth informed by Hamlet's famous observation that death levels all. 'A king may fish with a worm that hath eat of a king, and eat of the fish that hath fed of that worm,' observes Hamlet, so that a king 'may go a progress through the guts of a beggar', or find his noble dust 'stopping a bung-hole'.

The very quotations from past authorities that fill Stephen's thoughts prompt him to consider that even the air he inhales on the beach has been exhaled by many deceased people: 'Dead breaths I living breathe, tread dead dust, devour a urinous offal from all dead' (63). Matter is transformed in all kinds of ways, sometimes by the simple expedient of changing verbs from one language to another in order to describe the progress of a midwife: 'She trudges, schlepps, trains, drags, trascines her load' (60). Stephen sees a cloud and recalls how the deferential courtier Polonius was forced by Hamlet to admit that it was 'very like a whale'. The carcass of a dead dog rots on the sand and a live dog urinates. Stephen, poor dogsbody (ever since Mulligan called him so), is frightened of both. But he himself effects some of the most notable transformations of all.

He makes himself resemble the dog by urinating in the sand. Once again the text confronts a challenge to the limits of language, as the sound of pissing mingles with the speech of the nearby waves: 'seesoo, hrss, rsseiss, ooos' (62). Stephen composes a poem, or more accurately recomposes a lyric of Douglas Hyde's. Appropriately, the poem is about a vampiric act:

> He comes, pale vampire, through storm his eyes, his
> bat sails bloodying the sea, mouth to her mouth's
> kiss (60).

And finally, he removes a piece of snot from his nose, depositing it upon a rock, for want of the handkerchief he had loaned earlier to Mulligan.

The pissing, the poem and the picking of the nose are all ways of reprocessing matter. The equation of the creative act with the two decreative ones may be Joyce's little joke against those who would deify art. Although Stephen dons a Latin Quarter hat in order to dress in the character of a poet, it may well be that his poem is the least impressive of his acts. As if to suggest as much, he imagines the loss of his rod of bardic authority at this moment with the possibility that his ashplant cane will float away.

In the later stages of his monologue Stephen hopes that there might be 'someone' with whom to share all this intensity. The call is scarcely to a definite person, but perhaps it contains the secret language used by Joyce to Nora Barnacle on their fateful date:

I am lonely here. O, touch me soon, now. What is that word known to all men? (61)

Earlier, he had closed his eyes to conduct Bishop Berkeley's experiment: does a world which exists only in his perception of it remain nonetheless present and substantial, while his own perceptive powers are suspended? Of course the world does remain. The 'ineluctable modality of the visible' (45) is simply the solidity in space of the world which we see.

For all his interiority, Stephen will soon have to learn about that world. The daredevil artist, depositing snot on a rock, affects indifference but he glances behind himself in some embarrassment to ensure that nobody has spotted his dirty little deed: 'Behind. Perhaps there is someone' (64). That last sentence is the beginning of wisdom, the moment when Stephen starts to open a relationship to the world. Almost at once, he is ratified in this by the sight of a sailing ship homeward bound into Dublin port, a ship whose crew have trusted themselves to the water and to a collective enterprise.

The lesson is clear. In order to find the self, one must first agree to lose it. If individuals, like nations, have their egos, then these must at some point be surrendered, so that a transformation may occur. Milton had written 'Lycidas' in celebration of 'the dear might of Him that walked the waves'. Mulligan had saved drowning men. But Dedalus remained scared of water, refusing to swim, unwilling to wash ('Only dirty people has to wash' is a noted Dublin proverb). Now, however, he must allow his old ego to die in the hope that a truer self might be born. The shells thrown out of the sea by crashing waves epitomise the fact that all of life is a search for an appropriate form. Water *is* the flow of life, the living stream. It cannot be owned (despite the Englishman's claim to rule the waves), nor can its flow be stopped.

In order to open himself to a new adventure, Stephen must recall his own dawning wisdom. If there is, perhaps, someone, that someone may be a shouter in the street. In order to expose himself to that other being, he may have to take a risk, the risk of abandoning his pose of self-sufficiency and of opening himself to another. So Stephen's deliverance is at hand. The nightmare from which Haines awoke him was actually a dream of his future liberation by a man of Eastern appearance, who teaches him to conquer selfish fears in the act of being reborn:

> Street of harlots. Remember. Haroun al Raschid . . . That man led me, spoke. I was not afraid. The melon he had he held against my face. Smiled: creamfruit smell (58–9).

Already Stephen is tiring of his bohemian poses: 'My Latin Quarter hat. God, we simply must dress the character' (51). He wishes to find a viable image of authority and a truer form in which to explore the wonder of the everyday world. That form will include interior monologue, but not of the oppressive, immobile sort which has been experienced here. Leopold Bloom, eastern gent, will put it to more humane use before very long.

Stephen's desire, like Joyce's, is to create forms which would capture a multiple self, the self as process rather than product. The development of interior monologue was motivated by a need to save literature from the stock characters of Victorian novels, to prevent the complexities of real persons from collapsing into mere *types*. Such innovations were always most likely to occur on the edge of European culture and in the byways of a large, expansive text: for it was in such places that an author was free to try strange, difficult new things. If Ireland was the laboratory in which the British administration experimented with new social policies, before repeating the more successful ones at home, its writers might also serve as the avant-garde of a new kind of literature. Like other modernists, Joyce often worried that the true potentials of mass literacy were being frittered away. When Bloom reads a *Titbits* story, while seated on the toilet in the next episode, 'it did not move or touch him but it was something quick and neat. Print anything now. Silly season' (84). But Joyce was already on the way to administering the antidote in the counter-newspaper called *Ulysses*.

All kinds of devices are inserted into his prose to slow down the skimming reader – similar words like 'bulb' and 'blub', or even identical ones in sequence like: 'When one reads these strange pages of one long gone one feels that one is at one with one who once . . .' (50). It was the fact that words were read at increasing speed – a speed far greater than that possible in oral delivery – which troubled Joyce and other moderns. The *flâneurs*' languid gait on the boulevards was an attempt to decelerate the modern world, by reducing quick walking to a slow crawl. In like manner poets such as William Carlos Williams devised ways of slowing down the reader by surrounding brief lines with white space on the page, in order to compel the closest of attention for the most seemingly random of utterances:

This Is Just to Say

I have eaten
the plums
that were in
the icebox

and which
you were probably
saving
for breakfast

Forgive me
they were delicious
so sweet
and so cold.

Joyce worried that his own book might be just another of those possibilities discarded by a glib, throw-away culture: 'Who ever anywhere will read these written words?' (60). The reader, even more than the characters, must become the true and only hero, not by modelling a self on that of Odysseus, Jesus, Dante or Hamlet, but by seeking to become more fully a reader than anyone had before in the history of literature. It is the reader, as much as Dedalus, who must learn to decode the signatures of all things, to recognise the traces left by all the varied kinds of life that have passed through the world. And it is the reader who must summon the heroism of a thinker brave and intrepid enough to enter the abyss of the self.

4. Walking

A person's way of walking, whether strut or slouch, reveals a personality. So also with eating. How a man eats an egg, said Joyce, could reveal more about him than how he goes to war. Leopold Bloom appears in *Ulysses* eating – or imagining himself eating – the inner organs of beasts and fowls. The narrative is intimate with his inner life from the start.

The time has gone back from 11 a.m. to 8 a.m. and the coming three episodes will recapitulate the hours passed in the first three. Why? The flashback allows Joyce to make a contrast between the bohemians and this bourgeois. The bachelors ate heedlessly, and compared with their improvisations, Bloom's careful preparation of breakfast is positively sacramental. If anything, he seems to love preparing food even more than eating it, anticipation even more than fulfilment. His thoughtful care contrasts with the approach of his wife Molly, who takes her breakfast in bed, talking as her mouth is full with a doubled-up piece of bread.

Why does Joyce make so much of food, even before his characters have been fully introduced? Stephen felt haunted by the 'dead breaths' and 'urinous offal' at the end of the previous episode; at the start of this one, Bloom enjoys 'a fine tang of faintly scented urine' (65). Compared with Stephen, he is not hag-ridden by the past. Instead, he knows how to consume its offal and inhale its dead air. Where but to the past would a man go to express the 'not yet', to redeem time that seems lost? The past recalls for us all future potentials. It may be our best reminder that the future really does exist. In a work which reactivates lost possibilities of Homer's *Odyssey* and other classics, that understanding alone would make Bloom the central figure.

But is he ever really *introduced*? Hardly. Rather he is suddenly present to us, without any phasing in or narrative explanation. The effect is as arbitrary as a cinematic jump-cut. Who is this man? Why is he here? What on earth has he to do with that tortured poet and intellectual of the previous episodes? It is a technique that will be repeated many times in *Ulysses*, with sudden 'establishing shots' at the start of episodes and sharp, un-explained changes of scene. Those are also devices of the ancient epic whose storytellers, confronted by a familiar audience around a fire or a banqueting table, could assume the intimacy of listeners with their characters and with their world.

A deep knowledge of Dublin in 1904 is assumed by Joyce, but he equally, and even more unnervingly, assumes our intimacy with Bloom. There are no early descriptions of his face, body or clothes. Over the entire book we will learn only a few details (his dark suit, sad face, soft voice, medium height). This blankness en-courages the reader to fill the space with a man of our own imagining as well as Joyce's. The freedom of the interpreter is redoubled, and that may account for the deep sense of involvement with Bloom which most people feel. Although he doesn't know it, Bloom is about to re-enact in the streets of Dublin the wanderings of Odysseus in the Mediterranean. Like the gods and heroes of the Greek classics, he is beyond description, perhaps even beyond impersonation by mere mortals. Whenever I have asked readers to say what Bloom looks like, they almost always end up describing Milo O'Shea, the actor who played the role in a film version of the book.

Bloom is domestic. He is first seen in a kitchen – but from the outset he seems godlike too, able to raise consciousness in a household cat, which can (it seems) talk back to him:

– Milk for the pussens, he said.
– Mrkgnao! The cat cried (65).

The cat already offers an antidote to a puffed-up, self-important humanity, and Bloom knows this. Imagining that he must seem as tall as a tower to her, he thinks that 'they understand what we say better than we understand them' (65). Such empathy for dumb creatures will later be extended by Bloom to inanimate things. This almost god-like capacity to raise awareness in the mutest of objects may also arise from Bloom's loneliness. He has been married for well over a decade to a demanding and rather slatternly Calypso, whose first word, when asked whether she'd like anything for breakfast, is not just a negative but a curt abbreviation of the friendlier cat-speak: 'Mn' (67).

As he walks to the butcher's shop for his morning kidney, Bloom's thoughts turn eastwards. He wonders whether a voyager could travel always in front of the sun (stealing a day's march). So he recapitulates (without ever realising it) not just Stephen's dream of an Eastern

79

gentleman ('Turbaned faces going by', 68), but also his exploration with Deasy of a way of life on which the sun might never set. Unlike Stephen, however, Bloom is never long possessed by any vision, whether happy or sad. He checks his own impulse to wallow in romantic images of the Orient: 'Probably not a bit like that really. Kind of stuff you read' (68). A prospectus for plantations of eucalyptus trees in what was then Palestine briefly reactivates the romantic vision, but yet again he stills it: 'No, not like that. A barren land, laid waste' (73). Because he is regarded by many as a Jew in a Gentile city, this man has taught himself to question every cosy consensus and to adopt the less obvious, less popular viewpoint. For this very reason, he is better equipped than Stephen Dedalus to break free of old thinking.

As he leaves the pork shop, a cloud which Stephen saw that morning in Sandycove begins to cover the sun, inducing in Bloom a feeling of depression. This is reinforced when he sees a bent hag crossing the street with a naggin (noggin) bottle in her clutch: 'Dead: an old woman's: the grey sunken cunt of the world. Desolation' (73). Here is the moment equivalent to Stephen's gloomy vision of the milkwoman. The difference is that Bloom knows how to combat the blues: 'got up wrong side of the bed. Must begin again those Sandow's exercises' (73). It is to demonstrate this more practical wisdom that the book itself has been made to begin again. Joyce has no scruples about conducting his own (or the reader's, or Stephen's) education in this public fashion. Each of his episodes in this singular book will have a very different style. Rather than erase the opening three episodes, he lets them stand as a version of the problem to which Bloom might be the answer. So he depicts the inevitable uplift in Bloom's emotion as he anticipates with keen desire his sizzling breakfast and the chance to be near Molly's 'ample bedwarmed flesh. Yes. Yes' (74).

His reward for such buoyancy is a Homeric vision of a beautiful maiden in sandals (perhaps Joyce's recollection of the June 16 meeting with Nora):

> Quick warm sunlight came running from Berkeley Road, swiftly, in slim sandals, along the brightening footpath. Runs, she runs to meet me, a girl with gold hair on the wind (74).

This moment also compares with Stephen's recovery from the ghoulish memory of his mother haunting his dreams. But in Stephen's case the vision of the girl was brief and wan: 'Stephen, still trembling at his soul's cry, heard warm running sunlight and in the air behind him friendly words' (11) – and that was all.

This episode is titled 'Calypso', for it recalls that seven-year spell in the *Odyssey* which the hero passed in bondage to the nymph. In that tale Odysseus wept on the sea-rocks every morning, mourning his lost home and wife in Ithaca, much as Stephen moped by the rocks around the Martello tower. In both cases, depression led to inactivity. In the case of Hamlet by the cliffs of Elsinore, it was inaction which led to depression. Bloom, however, shows that one need not succumb.

His imagination is lively and, being open to external stimuli, moves quickly from point to point. Stephen cared too little about his environment even to spurn it. Like many Irish, he felt no great investment in a setting which his people did not own. Bloom, as he traces his miniature

81

odyssey to the butcher's and back again, imagines
voyages east, which reminds us that a great deal of the
Odyssey was imaginary too, existing only in its traveller's
head. But somehow, Bloom makes his travelling
purposeful. His interior monologues are quite different
from Stephen's, being outer- rather than inner-directed,
and open to constantly changing stimuli from the passing
street scene. Bloom shows optimism in the midst of
paralysis. His musings on infertility and impotence, on
barren lands and dead seas, link him to the notion of a
lost people: but he resolves before the episode's end to
fertilise and renew his own parched back garden.

Bloom is at his most vital in the world of process, in
motion between two fixed points. A committed wanderer,
he knows that movement is better than stasis. The dream
of an exotic East is resisted by Bloom, who will later warn
himself against equally quaint idealisations of Ireland.
Whereas romantic English liberals like Haines were
seeking an answer to the Irish question, the Irish
themselves (including Bloom) were still trying to find the
meaning of that question. Like him, the Irish were works
in progress. They were each seeking a dream of which
they could not speak – they could only speak of having
sought it. If Bloom endures the disadvantage of a Jewish
image while lacking the solidarity of membership in the
actual community, he is an outsider even more than a
Jew. In that, however, he has much in common with a
people who belong to a nation which does not exist,
except in perpetual potential.

Back at home in Eccles Street, Bloom senses something
afoot. His wife is about to commit adultery. A letter has
arrived in the bold handwriting of her lover, addressed to

Mrs Marion Bloom. Not 'Mrs Leopold Bloom', which would have been more usual on envelopes in 1904. In a nineteenth-century novel, a betrayed husband would already be plotting the exposure of such falsehood, if not violent revenge on his cuckolder. Bloom says absolutely nothing, for he wishes to free sexuality of all traces of possessiveness. Instead of anger, he shows tender lover-like concern for Molly, adjusting the blind by gentle tugs, so that the incoming light will not dazzle her. Compared with such courtesy, her response seems at once crude and imperious: 'Hurry up with that tea . . . I'm parched' (74).

Why is Bloom bringing his wife her breakfast in bed? In today's Dublin such a deed might come naturally to a 'new man', but in the male-dominated city of 1904 it must have seemed an act tantamount to perversion. Perhaps Bloom likes it this way. Some irreparable sadness has caused this couple to divide the home between them, so that they may share a house, if not a life. This is what was called in Ireland a 'silent marriage', the local form of divorce. Bloom notes how he and his wife dislike dressing together, and he seems happy to serve his lady above stairs, if that means that he has the kitchen to himself and the cat. The cat is a less troublesome substitute for Molly, but shares her imperious ways when it comes to subjugating mice who (Bloom muses with the fraternal thoughts of a fellow masochist) 'seem to like it' (66). Of course, there may be method in Bloom's apparent madness. Perhaps he does the breakfast chores so that, as a good but outraged husband, he can more easily lay blame for Molly's infidelity on her later. He treats his trips to her bedroom as reconnaissance missions, to establish what exactly it is that she is up to.

Bloom's preparation of the food suggests that he enjoys playing housewife, a fact confirmed by his anxiety to tidy away Molly's soiled linen, which she has strewn carelessly over a chair. The other letter in the post is for him, from their daughter Milly. From her Molly has received only a card. It seems as if Bloom has taken over much of his wife's mothering role: but the fact that Milly feels the need to send separate communications is itself telling. Bloom reads Milly's letter repeatedly. Aged only fifteen, she has been removed from the home to work in a photographer's shop in Mullingar. She and Molly almost share a name, and can at times seem more like sisters than mother and child. So Bloom, describing his daughter as a wild piece of goods, transfers his fears about his skittish wife on to the teenager: 'Will happen, yes. Prevent. Useless: can't move' (81). The reader may feel the poignancy of such anxiety, knowing that a friend of Mulligan's down in Mullingar has already clapped his eyes on her.

Molly herself reports that her letter is from Blazes Boylan, who will call that afternoon, ostensibly as her concert manager to arrange her singing engagements. Bloom himself is about to leave for a funeral, although he doesn't even know its time. Molly points, as if to a newspaper that may help him, but actually to a book. 'It must have fell down' (77), she says, outraging the niceties of grammar, before rudely searching the text with a stray hairpin until she finds the word which has been baffling her – metempsychosis. 'It's Greek: from the Greek,' explains Bloom: 'That means the transmigration of souls' (77). 'Oh rocks,' she moans, repeating Stephen's complaint about big words which make people unhappy: 'Tell us in plain words' (77). Bloom, quite unaware that he himself is

84

an example of a past Greek life implanted in a new person, warms to his theme.

As he explains, he demonstrates his skills as teacher, trying to make the point ever more concrete: 'Some people believe that we go on living in another body after death, that we lived before' (78). But he realises that 'an example would be better', and so he explains that even an animal or a tree might possess the soul of a dead nymph. Compared with Stephen's heavy self-consciousness, this kind of explanation is tonic. The very fact that Bloom is innocent of the parallel between himself and Odysseus adds to his stature in the book, for heroism can never be conscious of itself as such.

A second layer of irony in this scene may be found in the fact that Bloom's life is a more balanced and sane version of that lived by Joyce's improvident father – mainly because the Blooms were not overrun by a houseful of hungry children.

Molly is no longer beautiful, being past the first bloom of her youth. Bloom 'looked down calmly at her bulk' (76). Nevertheless, in her husband's imagination as he later walks through the streets, she remains lovely, desirable, erotic. Far from resenting his service to her, he fusses over her and tries to devise ever-new ways of pleasing her. These passages may be less a tribute to her pulchritude (at the age of thirty-three) than to her spouse's buoyant consciousness. As Marcel Proust once observed, 'we may leave the love of beautiful women to men without imagination'. Bloom is, however, enough the red-blooded male to take pleasure in the moving hams of the servant-girl next door, as she sways up the street, but he is also something of an androgyne, with elements about

85

him of the dainty housewife: 'in the act of going he stayed to straighten the bedspread' (76).

This tidying of the room, even down to the detail of the door left finally open, might be taken as Bloom sub-consciously 'setting up' the theatre of afternoon adultery for Boylan. He knows that there is an element of 'per-formance' about the rituals of everyday life. If it has to happen, he seems to imply, than it would be better that the place should look well. But the form of delay coded into the gesture ('in the act of going he stayed') recalls also the way in which Odysseus tarried on his travels, spinning a voyage of weeks into many years. In such prolongation of moments of passing pleasure may be found not just a loafing charm but also the bourgeois practice of delayed gratification. The anticipation of fulfilment becomes, in the mind of Bloom (and of Odysseus), the fulfilment of anticipation. To go and stay at one and the same time is not a self-cancelling action, but rather the achievement of a dynamic equilibrium. Bloom's true home, however, is not his house, but the act of journeying.

A similar set of observations might be made of his behaviour in the outhouse toilet. 'Where is my hat?' (83), he asks, as fussy as Stephen is about his. Like Stephen on the beach, Bloom is afraid that he might be spotted by another person as he engages in a private action, but is reassured that there is 'Nobody' (83). Bloom's defecation is a reprise of the act of going-and-staying. As he shits, he reads *Titbits*, joking inwardly that it offers 'payment at the rate of one guinea a column' (83). Here, again, Joyce mocks the seriousness with which writing is taken. But Bloom's little joke is surely conscious and mischievous, whereas Stephen seemed less aware of the implied

86

equation between literature and excretion. If such moments normalise literature, they also raise the status of piss and shit. Bloom, thinking of how his garden needs manuring, can imagine how a waste product like excrement could be made useful all over again. But, most of all, he enjoys the act of delaying his delivery of the columns into the bowl. Yet again, he goes and stays at once: 'Quietly he read, restraining himself, the first column and, yielding but resisting, began the second' (83–4).

Every act by Bloom is countered by its very opposite. His pleasure in restraint and then release recalls Freud's theory that by this means three-year-olds achieve sexual gratification. In truth, Bloom is at many moments childlike: when talking to 'pussens', jumping from point to point in his thoughts, or holding back his motion in the lavatory. But he is also womanly, even coy. His yes may really mean no, his no be a way of saying yes. 'Yielding but resisting' seems a feminine way of taking on the challenges of life in 1904. Godlike yet childlike, masculine and feminine, he seems the very epitome of the multiple self. Whether that balance comes from impotence or from a more positive reconciliation of antitheses remains to be seen. For the present, he appears in the role of ordinary man as artist, someone who has considered making a book out of his wife's colourful phrases by jotting them on his shirt-cuff. Just how many of Nora Barnacle's utterances made it into *Ulysses* is anyone's guess.

Bloom is shown shitting, not in order to shock the reader but rather to dramatise a man who – quite unlike Stephen – feels utterly at home with the workings of his own body. After decades of Victorian denial – a denial so fixated on the body that even piano legs were decently

87

draped in linen lest they prompt obscene thoughts – that could only be refreshing. The body in medieval Gaelic texts had been an image of the nation or state, and its recovery for modern literature might betoken a reconquest of Ireland by its own people. Besides, for such modern philosophers as Wittgenstein, the human body was also the best picture of the human soul. In allocating a different organ to each episode, Joyce wished to build his book into the image of a body, but he had no truck with ideas of the 'body beautiful', preferring to focus on flawed and actual limbs, organs and bones.

His favourite war story concerned a soldier who refused to shoot an enemy infantryman, because the targeted one was defecating near a trench with his trousers around his ankles. Joyce said that there were few more poignant sights than that of a man with his pants lowered. So in the story the nervous marksman held his gun in silent disobedience of the commanding officer, until his quarry had finished the ritual and hitched his trousers back up – at which point he obeyed the hysterically repeated command and shot the man anyway. For Joyce the body was at once dignified and comic, sacred and soiled.

There is a theory, propounded by Adaline Glasheen, that this whole episode is Bloom's self-flattering account of events – with depictions of his sensitivity countered by Molly's coarseness. One could cite many details to bear out the contention that the episode is a parody of Bloom's ideal self-conception, but ultimately, it is unlikely that Joyce would ever have taken such a risk in his opening treatment of Bloom, whom he clearly admired as a character. Before he could mock Bloom's thought processes, Joyce first had to allow his readers to get to know them.

5. Praying

In order to create a protagonist like Bloom, Joyce had to be a hero of the mind, diving deep into his own subconscious for his material. In that way, he repeated something like the manoeuvre performed by Freud, who had the courage to conduct the very first psychoanalysis upon himself. Working at this depth of personality, Joyce had no self to draw upon but his own. Even in psychoanalysis, as in the sacrament of confession, the disclosure of one person's innermost secrets to another had been made in a darkened space: but Bloom's communing with himself is done mostly in daylight and in public places. To each and every detail of the surrounding world he gives that close attention which is the nearest modern equivalent of prayer.

Commentators sometimes say that Bloom's isolation, unlike Stephen's, is enforced because of his Jewish background rather than actively chosen. The truth is that he rather likes to live at an angle to the community. His inner life offers rich compensations for the poverty of social intercourse in a city whose denizens are often more fluent than articulate and where every conversation seems to be repeated many times over. Once again, Bloom's thoughts turn east to the Dead Sea (prompted on this occasion by the Belfast and Oriental Tea Company) and 'the garden of the world, big lazy leaves to float about on' (86), appropriate for an episode titled 'Lotus-Eaters'.

Bloom's first silent encounter is with a boy who collects waste offal and whom he sees 'smoking a chewed fagbutt' (86). Tempted to rebuke him for risking addiction to cigarettes, he checks his own impulse: 'his life isn't such a bed of roses' (86). In the *Odyssey* the travellers ate a lotus-flower and were instantly drugged, forgetting all thoughts of home. Bloom himself might feel tempted to do the same, for he fears that he and Molly are living a tragedy of incompatibility: 'Talk: as if that would mend matters' (88).

He remains androgynous. He watches a fashionable lady alight from a carriage and is frustrated by his colleague M'Coy's talking head and by a passing tramcar, both of which deprive him of the sight of her flashing stockings. The city offers stimulation, but also woeful distraction. For all his kindness, Bloom has only one thought about M'Coy: 'Get rid of him quickly' (88). The ensuing conversation about Paddy Dignam's eleven o'clock funeral might be guessed at, so Bloom readily tunes in and out of it. When Bloom performs for others, he often offers a simplified version of himself in which he is never fully engaged.

Like him, M'Coy is a commercial traveller with a demanding songstress for wife. In theory, Bloom might make common cause with him, but he prefers not to. In fact, he feels quite free to criticise his own weaknesses in the other man. Bloom is intelligent in many ways, but he is insufficiently aware to notice in himself some of those faults which he attributes to others. It might be said that such unawareness is healthy, if the alternative is the marooned self-consciousness of Stephen Dedalus, yet that unawareness may also be hurting Bloom. He is skilled in strategies of avoidance and moves very fast from point to point, briefly facing many of his problems but avoiding a final confrontation with most of his inner demons.

His reluctance to speak with M'Coy is understandable, given the innuendoes with which the other man laces his enquiries about Molly's concert in Belfast, such as 'Who's getting it up?' (91). The answer, of course, is: Blazes Boylan. The arrangement – part shares and part profits – sounds like a dismal description by Bloom of his own marriage. Purging the sexual relationship of all taint of ownership seems admirable, but it is an ideal more easily aspired to than attained. While talking to M'Coy Bloom unrolls a newspaper, only to spot an advertisement that reads like an accusation:

> What is home without
> Plumtree's Potted Meat?
> Incomplete.
> With it an abode of bliss (91).

The unrolling of the newspaper-phallus may indicate Bloom's lost potency, and the ad evokes his incomplete sexual acts at home with Molly. The couple have not had penetrative sex since the death of their baby son Rudy, over ten years earlier. Joyce well understood the ways in which commercial advertisements map the unconscious on to everyday realities, with effects that are not always intended by their makers.

Scanning the hoardings at a street corner, Bloom spots a notice for the actress, Mrs Bandman Palmer: 'Hamlet she played last night. Male impersonator. Perhaps he was a

woman. Why Ophelia committed suicide' (93). No wonder
Bloom is interested, for he is himself something of a female
impersonator. Walking towards the post office earlier, he
had tapped the folded newspaper against his leg in an
attempt to imitate the swaying bottom of the servant-girl
from the neighbouring house: 'How did she walk with her
sausages? Like that something' (87). Bloom may be vaguely
aware that his own feminine element causes problems for
Molly, just as Hamlet's may have driven Ophelia to suicide.
Molly's problem of being married to an androgyne is
projected on to Ophelia, just as the problem of the tragic
Shakespearean hero – how to be at once womanly and
admirable? – is projected on to Bloom.

In the end, Shakespeare could not imagine a successful
male androgyne. In centuries of drag art after the
Renaissance, the feminised male was a figure of ridicule
on the English stage. One of Joyce's motivations in
creating Bloom may have been to reinstate the womanly
man as protagonist. He saw, long before the age of the
Beatles and the Rolling Stones, that a man brave enough
to 'dare' his own femininity, might be, in that very
gesture, an example of the ultimate intrepid machismo –
and so a new species of hero. Bloom's intermediate
sexuality *might* drive a modern Ophelia mad; but, then
again, it might afford her a role as wooer and conquist-
ador. Hours later, Molly will assert that she likes Bloom's
maidenly bashfulness, the fact that he had to be pursued.
If Stephen tries to escape the distortions of a too-knowable
personality by becoming quite literally the boy who could
enjoy invisibility, Bloom is even more triumphantly
indecipherable. That both men are mysterious rather
than available to instant decoders may be the reason why

they alone, this far into the book, have been given interior monologues. For while it is easy to classify mere acquaintances like Mulligan or M'Coy, it is not possible to label or categorise true intimates.

Mention of suicide recalls for Bloom his father Rudolf Virag's death in a hotel room in Ennis. Just as Stephen preferred to sing in an adjoining room for his mother rather than go right up to her dying face, so Bloom did not go into the dead man's room to look at him. The unconscious unity which binds Stephen Dedalus and Leopold Bloom in so many of their actions is Joyce's way of preparing the reader for their eventual meeting. They are very different men on the surface, but deeper down they share three vital characteristics evoked in brilliant phrases by Richard Ellmann: 'passivity in act, energy in thought, tenacity in conviction'.

This episode is a study in various forms of narcotic addiction, beginning with the cigarette-smoking child. Bloom soon passes horses whose heads are crunching oats in nosebags hanging from their necks. They have been gelded, which prompts a self-pitying Bloom to the sardonic reflection: 'Might be happy all the same that way' (94). The nags eating their oats morph into old women, halter-clad in sacred scapulars, approaching the altar of All Hallows Church to take the communion host from a priest. The bread of angels is equated by a baffled Bloom with baby food, however elderly its recipients: 'Shut your eyes and open your mouth. What? *Corpus*. Body. Corpse. Good idea the Latin. Stupefies them first' (99). There speaks not just an anthropologist, trying to understand the cannibalistic rituals of a strange tribe among whom he finds himself, but also the ad man, alert to the seductive power of a repetitive jingle. Later he will equate the ways in which religion and merchandise are sold, as 'pray for us, pray for us and pray for us' becomes 'buy from us, buy from us and buy from us'. Later still, he will consider using advertising techniques to educate Molly.

Sexually aroused by his secret presence at All Hallows, Bloom considers that it would be a nice place to be next to some attractive girl, 'jammed by the hour to slow music' (100). He also wonders, rather provocatively, 'who has the organ here' (100). The psychologist C. G. Jung once marvelled that whenever patients came to him with seemingly religious questions, they were often resolved by a sexual explanation. Although Bloom seems not fully aware of the implications of his own analysis, he feels a sexual frisson in the way the priest, himself feminised by wearing a 'lace affair' (98), and 'holding the thing in his hands' (98), manages with each communicant to shake a drop or two off it, 'and put it neatly into her mouth' (99).

This treatment of the Eucharist might appear mocking, even blasphemous: 'Rum idea: eating bits of a corpse why the cannibals cotton to it' (99). But Bloom really is trying to grasp the meaning behind the ritual. Its effect, he suspects, is to make the lonely receivers feel part of one happy family. Joyce's treatment is not high-handed. The Latin which 'stupefies them first' was employed right back on the opening page of *Ulysses*: '*Introibo ad altare Deï*', the first words of the Latin Mass, 'I will go to the altar of God'. Nor is the description of the communicants a humiliation of religion, so much as a humanisation of it. After all, *Ulysses* will later present many tender, if more homely, versions of the Eucharistic moment, as when Molly, clad in her own 'lace affair', fills Leopold's mouth with the seedcake which she was eating during the first love-making on Howth Hill. And this action is performed by a woman who will assert that there should be woman priests.

If that beautiful moment is the Blooms' own alternative sacrament of the Eucharist, then perhaps Leopold's letter in response to the coy note from Martha Clifford will be his downmarket version of the sacrament of confession. His furtive correspondence with her under the assumed name of Henry Flower is as close as he will come to answering Molly's infidelity with an illicit affair of his own. Martha shrewdly senses the masochistic tendencies of her correspondent, and his brief re-reading of her innuendoes shows just how excited his imagination is by her mock-threats: 'Angry tulips with you darling manflower punish your cactus if you don't' (95).

Bloom is by nature suspicious of official explanations, official policies and official religions. Still, he is impressed by the efficiency with which the cardinals in Rome exercise control through the confession-box, 'and don't they rake the money in?' (100). Molly once told her husband that the INRI legend over the figure of a crucified Jesus meant 'iron nails ran in' (100). (In fact, they said 'Jesus of Nazareth, King of the Jews'.) Other 'nails' will distract Bloom later in the day, when thoughts of his own suffering mingle with his concern about what exactly Boylan may be running into Molly. Many of his words or phrases in this episode remain incomplete ('bread and . . .'), as if to suggest synapses brought on by stress – a recurrent rhythm of expectation followed by disappointment. It is as if Bloom has to keep hinting at and then evading some uncomfortable thought. One of the strangest things about an internal monologue which skips from one

95

perception to another without ultimate development is that there can be no final resolution – just repeated flirtations with a possible moment of clarification.

'Lotus-Eaters' began with Bloom walking 'soberly' (85). No prey to narcotics, he confined himself to such harmless pleasures as the purchase of lemon soap and a prescription for Molly's skin. The proposal of a plantation in the East seems ignoble escapism to him and is not long entertained, though the frequency with which his imagination turns eastward raises the possibility that his true home might be there. His fantasy is that in turning east he might never grow old, but in keeping ahead of the sun's progress defeat time and space.

How to recycle waste is a challenge which dominates both the start and end of 'Lotus-Eaters'. Bloom will be haunted all day by the fear that life may mean nothing, that everybody is like everybody else and everything is like everything else – disposable. Yet the episode which starts with a boy recycling a discarded cigarette concludes when Bloom inadvertently gives a tip on the Gold Cup race to be run that afternoon: 'I was just going to throw it away' (106). The book as a whole constitutes a telling question: how can the refuse of history be integrated into some worthwhile project? The newspaper is no sooner thrown away than it is taken up gratefully by Bantam Lyons – and with it a tip which, though unintended, will confirm Bloom's divine powers when a horse named Throwaway romps home to win.

Joyce's answer to the refuse-of-history question is to reinstate the everyday as the dignified basis of all life. The ordinary, in danger of being forgotten in the intensity of the Great War, is the middle range of experience vindicated here. By simple actions, such as careful tea-making, thoughtful meat-buying, or sensuous street-strolling, Bloom repossesses on a lazy Edwardian day the lost sacrament of everyday life. Because he can really relax and release his being into these moments, he has little need of the deeper narcotics (Mass, alcohol, gambling), whose consumption he watches with the disdainful incredulity of an anthropologist. His musings on the plantations in the East raise also the wider possibility that missionary activity or colonial conquest may be just another type of addiction. Those addictions may be driven not just by a desire for raw materials and markets overseas but also by the need to escape an unutterable boredom and ennui back home. The missionaries and administrators are sent out to challenge the lazy, lotus-eating natives, yet the radical implication of *Ulysses* is that the colonial enterprise itself may be a distraction sought by those who have failed to appreciate and release the exotic elements in their own everyday lives.

Bloom's interest in the languid East is connected to his determination to have a bath in one of the public facilities (there being none back in Eccles Street). The Jews of Dublin were cleaner in their personal habits than most citizens: we recall how Stephen was beyond soap and water as a Nietzschean is beyond good and evil. But Bloom is attracted also by an eastern culture which is more relaxed than its western counterpart. He contrasts the vertical Jesus hanging on a cross with a horizontal Buddha lying relaxedly on his side in the museum.

Now, at the close, but still only in his imagination, he foresees himself in the Hammam (Turkish baths), a reclining Buddha-like figure, but one who can intone the words of Jesus at the consecration of the Mass: 'this is my body' (107). In this godlike role, he is conflating eastern and western religious traditions. This is a further version of self-invention, of how to become your own father: masturbation: 'Yes I. Do it in the bath' (107). Masturbation should not be criticised, however, because in the immortal words of Woody Allen, 'it's sex with someone I love'. As he reclines, Bloom celebrates his private parts, his pubic hair floating around 'the limp father of thousands, a languid floating flower' (107). This is an image of origins, the origin of a new tradition, but Bloom is honest and strong enough to celebrate the limp penis, not the erect one.

If he seems a little surprised by his masturbatory tendency, that may be because he remained unaware of just how sexually aroused he was back in the church. He was only half aware of M'Coy's sexual taunts or of how the Plumtree's ad impinged upon his own domestic situation.

Which raises a question. If the reader already seems to know Bloom even better than he cares to know himself, is that because the reader is actually more caught up in his thought processes than he is? Joyce at certain moments appears to write 'past' Bloom, in a voice which encourages us to see a little more than Bloom can. This is strange, since great literature often prides itself on respecting the mysteries of invented characters, permitting them – as tactful persons permit one another in life – the possession of private understandings and secret spaces. Yet one of the reasons for our feeling so caught up in Bloom's experience is Joyce's persistent refusal to describe him in physical terms. Readers often feel, as they move through the book, that not only have they occupied his situation, but also his telegraph-language has begun to shape the very way in which they process their own thoughts.

But it is a tribute to Joyce's narrative skill that so many readers may burst into laughter during a discussion of *Ulysses* and ask: are we interpreting Bloom's experiences with an even greater degree of intensity than he would accord to them himself? And that is indeed a sobering thought.

6. Dying

At funerals people formally mourn the dead person, while privately experiencing an even deeper sadness for those who remain in the world.

'Are we all here now?' (108), asks Martin Cunningham inside the funeral carriage, before adding, 'Come along, Bloom.' Even though Bloom had politely held back for Simon Dedalus, the 'all' suggests that he may not really count, and the 'Come along' further infantilises, as if Bloom were a straggling child. An old woman peeps into the carriage, which is itself like a coffin. This is a reversal of that scene in the previous episode during which Bloom stared at the female devotees of a holy cult. Now the mockery seems to arise from the onlooking woman, as if she is peeping in at the dead male tradition of Edwardian Dublin which held that only men should attend the final phases of a funeral.

Consistently through *Ulysses* it is men who seem dead and masculinity which is in crisis. 'Extraordinary the interest they take in a corpse,' Bloom thinks about women; 'Glad to see us go when we give them so much trouble coming' (108). Once again, an unconscious double entendre may hint at his sexual problems with Molly. The line also recalls Stephen's rumination on the midwives of Sandymount Strand.

Dublin lacked (and still lacks) an underground transport system, so Glasnevin Cemetery serves in this episode as its 'Hades'. The street scenes, beginning with the woman looking in through the window, are captured almost cinematically, as the carriage moves through the city. At one point, Bloom considers that 'the Irishman's house is his coffin' (139), a witty reworking of 'an Englishman's home is his castle'. By the time he was nineteen, Joyce had lived with his family in eleven different homes, eleven different coffins! The households of *Ulysses* are mostly unhappy: Paddy Dignam's wife is now a widowed mother of many children; Martin Cunningham's is an alcoholic; Molly Bloom is sexually frustrated.

These homes are like burial mounds in which a man is entombed with his holy objects, but there is no social institution larger than the family with which they can identify. They do not feel at ease in the domestic space of womanhood, although Bloom at least tries to be happy there. If Theodor Adorno was right that whoever lives in a house embalms himself alive, then Bloom, the street person, achieves a greater vitality when he is neither at home nor away but in perpetual motion between. By leaving their home-coffins, the men of Dublin can act like risen ghosts, free to explore other options.

'Hades' describes a city of the walking dead, with humans who seem interchangeable with the statues of Dublin. Even before they have travelled far, the male mourners feel trapped in their box-like conveyance. Bloom's love of the witty pun causes him to think of Dignam having 'his last lie on the earth in his box' (139), but this also applies to the men in the carriage. To be boxed is to become an object, the sense of airlessness heightened by the lack of any female company. The men experience a mounting sense of paranoia in the face of death and can only defeat its challenge by numbing themselves to the meaning of the funeral ritual. Bloom's reaction, by contrast, is more composed, because it is both playful and commonsensical. If the rituals as practised by the other men seem perfunctory ('All waited . . . All waited . . . They waited', 108), they become far more real for the man who only half-understands the ceremony but is doing his level best to follow it. For the others, ritual has long ago declined into mere routine, while Bloom is seeking a way to raise such routine to the level of ritual. A descent into the underworld was the greatest test of a hero in ancient myth. Bloom seems to pass it in better shape than any of the others.

Why is he present at all? He scarcely knew Dignam, but he may feel the common Dublin tradesman's need to show his face at a funeral. More poignantly still, he may as an outsider be seeking acceptance in a major Irish ritual from which he cannot decently be excluded. If so, the way in which his joke is interrupted and undercut becomes all the more hurtful. He may even be attending the funeral not just to mourn Dignam but to confront the pain of his own loss of Rudy, a pain unspoken and unshared which may well be destroying his marriage.

As the carriage passes Stephen Dedalus on the pavement, Bloom points him out to his father Simon, 'your son and heir' (109). Irascibly, Simon denounces Mulligan and the low-down crowd his son consorts with. 'Full of his son,' thinks Bloom: 'He is right. Something to hand on' (110). Stephen had earlier thought of his father as the man with his eyes: but Bloom, sad for Rudy, conjures a picture of 'Me in his eyes' (110). His more pressing trouble, however, is Boylan, the very thought of whom provokes mild panic just before he sees him passing in the street. At once Bloom seeks distraction with the stage business of reviewing his fingernails ('The nails, yes', 115). His attempt to deflect his own suffering merely reminds him of the crucifix, already on his mind an hour earlier: Iron Nails Ran In. Bloom's looking at his nails may remind the reader of Stephen's assertion in *A Portrait of the Artist as a Young Man* that the artist is like God, absent from his creation, seemingly indifferent, paring his fingernails. This raises yet again the question of whether Bloom, even in his moment of maximum discomfiture, is indeed godlike, affecting indifference as Boylan struts past, but secretly hurt by the failure of people whom he once trusted to behave better.

'Is there anything more in him that they she sees?' (115), worries Bloom in silent desperation, as he consoles himself with the knowledge that his own body, though softening, is still in decent shape. But the other men sense the chance for some fun, twitting Bloom about 'Madame', her concert tour and whether he will be in the party. Bloom, ever patient, merely smiles politely back at Mr Power's word 'Madame'.

A sighting of Reuben Dodd, pawnbroker, prompts Martin Cunningham to recall that they have all used his services – before his eyes meet Bloom's, causing him to add, 'well, nearly all of us' (117). Bloom tries to recover his composure by telling the story of how the miserly Dodd gave only a florin to a boatman who saved his son from drowning in the Liffey. But he is interrupted, upstaged and edited out by Cunningham, who knows the tale already. In Dublin there are only two kinds of joke – those that were once funny, and those that were never funny.

Bloom's attempt to win credit with a story that shows his own ability to laugh at parsimony has come undone. Perhaps through sheer nervousness, after that failure he now blurts out a thought which, in a calmer state, he might have kept for his inner monologue: that drowning is the best death. The same idea had been suggested by Stephen that morning – and both men feel that the dying man's torment would at least be over fast. Nobody in the carriage speaks, but their air of disapproval is obvious, for the Catholics among the men would prefer a person to have the benefit of the Last Rites. 'But the worst of all', Mr Power then says, 'is the man who takes his own life' (120). Now it is Martin Cunningham's turn to cough with embarrassed concern for Bloom, whose father killed himself, but Power digs himself deeper in. Bloom, however, has already faced up to his father's death that morning and is quite unhurt by the comments. Instead, he is filled with compassion for the suffering of Cunningham, a man who is forever pawning property because of his drunken wife.

The village-like feel of Dublin in 1904 is confirmed by the passing of a drove of cattle and a flock of sheep en route to the seaport for export. Bloom suggests tramlines to the quays for the animals and to Glasnevin for funerals, a practical scheme adopted just one year later. On this occasion, the men agree with Bloom, partly because they fear that a dead body might easily be jolted out of its coffin if the horse-carriage capsizes.

The return of the repressed dead terrifies most Dubliners, but not Bloom, who is amused by more practical worries. Would a nail cut a corpse and cause it to bleed? He knows that the nails and hair continue to grow after death and is at once sceptical and curious about religious values – sceptical about Christian euphemism and evasion but curious about Greek and other funeral practices. He is sardonic about the line 'I am the resurrection and the life', which is praised by another mourner as touching a man's heart. 'Your heart perhaps,' thinks Bloom, 'but what price the fellow in the six feet by two with his toes to the daisies? No touching that' (133). Bloom prefers the homely realism of that Dublin wag who joked, 'Come forth, Lazarus. And he came fifth and lost the job' (133).

While the other men are simply fearful of dying, Bloom is actively curious about the state of *being dead*, about what happens to a decomposing corpse. He ridicules the idea of the resurrection of the body in a mocking scenario of the confusion likely on the Last Day as various buried persons try to reclaim lost organs. However, as has been suggested, he may be a sort of risen ghost himself. His incredulity at some of the language used at the funeral is not based on disrespect for Dignam or for religion. Rather, being something of a literalist, Bloom wishes to strip away all evasive metaphors from the ritual, and to reinstate it at a more honest, everyday level.

A student of metempsychosis, he realises that death may just be the start of another narrative. *Ulysses*, after all, visits the cemetery *before* the lying-in hospital, as if in silent collusion with the famous statue of Parnell in O'Connell Street, which quotes the Chief's famous words 'No man has the right to fix the boundary to the march of a nation' and has him pointing to the nearest maternity hospital. As an undergraduate, Joyce liked to say that 'death is the most beautiful form of life'. Bloom sees death as a challenge which can be surmounted, unlike other Dubliners who simply fixate upon it as part of their mortuary culture. As in the very sentence that introduces him, it is his 'relish' that helps him to confront deadly offal and somehow to consume it.

Yet again he is haunted by a sense of *waste*. He uses the burial of Dignam to organise his own feelings about his dead father and son. The death of Rudy after a few days of life suggests a world without intrinsic value. The decomposition of bodies, gnawed away by rats and water, shows just how cheap life can be. The everyday challenges heroic values, says Blanchot, because it mocks the very idea of value – 'the hero fears the everyday because he dreads meeting in it what is most fearful: a power of dissolution'. Bloom, however, is never more brave than when confronting the possibility that his son's life meant nothing.

Bloom is described as 'chapfallen', the same word used in the graveyard scene of *Hamlet*. Yet his realism is that of Shakespeare's cheerfully sardonic gravedigger: 'Your water is a sore decayer of your whoreson dead body.' Like the coffin-homes of Dublin, the houses that the gravedigger makes 'last till doomsday'. No wonder that Bloom considers that the scene 'shows the profound knowledge of the human heart' (138).

Ever practical and positive, he tries to think of ways of avoiding waste – if persons were buried in a standing position, that would save space. The loss of so much wood with each coffin prompts him to suggest a sliding side-panel, through which the body could be released into earth, so that the coffin might be used again. This was, in fact, a device used often during the Great Famine of the 1840s, but Bloom seems unaware of it: 'Ay, but they might object to be buried out of another fellow's,' he muses; 'They're so particular' (139). That 'They' speaks volumes about his sense of isolation in this scene, even as it reminds us that Bloom is ever the vigilant anthropologist. Yet his vision of a world in which almost everything can be recycled – even bodies helpfully manure the earth – is one he shares with Joyce, who in his book is recycling both the epic and the novel in order to give birth to a new form. A man whose earliest stories appeared next to the manure prices in the *Irish Homestead* knew that columns of prose, like columns of shit, could both recultivate the earth.

Bloom's practicality also causes him to enquire whether Dignam was insured and how his five children will get by. In fact, a whip-round organised by Martin Cunningham will keep things going until matters are cleared. His caustic wit leads Bloom to imagine the different forms of sympathy offered to widows across the world: 'Your terrible loss. I hope you soon follow him. For Hindu widows only' (128). The late Queen Victoria of England had made widowhood fashionable, but her consort had not even been a king, an echo of Bloom's subservient relationship to Mrs Marion.

In this sixth episode, Glasnevin is full of 'bad gas' (130) even as in the third, Sandymount Strand was filled with 'dead breaths'. There is a distinct difference, however, in the way Bloom and Stephen respond. Stephen remains fixated on the dead, but Bloom is able to look through death and find a route back to life. His 'unconsciousness' is part of that wisdom. Without a college degree, he may lack Stephen's erudition but be more familiar with folk wisdom. He knows less than the younger man, but he also knows more. He even knows things which he doesn't 'know' at a conscious, analytic level, so he can be omniscient and obtuse, all at the same time.

Thus, he displays blank incomprehension when confronted by the Catholic ritual. The priest bears a brass bucket with 'something' in it (130). He then takes 'a stick with a knob at the end of it out of the boy's bucket' (131). A technique which makes the familiar trappings of a funeral seem strange, by describing them as if they are being seen for the first time, is one method by which Joyce manages to make everyday banalities seem astonishing. This materialist accounting is all the more striking, given that Joyce would have known the proper word: 'aspergill'. The other mourners presumably know it too, but they are not given interior monologues, being confined to badinage and platitude. Joyce isn't suggesting that they lack inner life, but rather that theirs is much less rich than Bloom's, or else that they have far less to repress and contain at the level of thought. On the rare occasions when Bloom blurts out a thought, he often gets into trouble. If his inner thoughts here were to be made public, there would be outrage.

Among many other things, Bloom (perhaps recalling All Hallows) thinks of the possible excitement of sex among the tombstones, an idea prompted by the phrase 'In the midst of death we are in life' (136). By a lively process of association, he then recalls a day when Molly wanted to have sex at the window of their house. 'She was a finelooking woman,' recalls John Henry Menton, a sentence which her husband might recast in the present tense. The same Menton finds Bloom as indecipherable as Mulligan did Stephen, someone who refuses to present a knowable personality: 'Who is he? What does he do?' (134). Menton cannot understand why Molly would marry 'a coon like that' (134).

Identities are problematic in this scene. The statue of the Saviour over a grave prompted one drunken literalist, during a night visit to the graveyard, to blink up at the Blessed Lord and say 'That's not Mulcahy, whoever done it' (135). This joke, told by John O'Connell, keeper of the cemetery, goes uninterrupted to its hilarious conclusion. There are two ways of telling a joke – a right way and a wrong way. Bloom, though he may lack the skill of the joker, gets the underlying point: the fear, raised by Death the Leveller, that there is no human individuality: 'if we were all suddenly somebody else' (139). Bloom's black suit, amidst so many other suits of mourning, leaves him indecipherable.

If Bloom is a mystery to some of the mourners, a strange man in a mackintosh now troubles all with a similar unknowability. In theory, there are no strangers in Dublin, only friends who haven't met; but nobody seems to know who this man is. Nervously, Bloom wonders whether he or the mackintosh man is mourner number thirteen. The fellow feeling is understandable. They are both inscrutable sorts who disrupt all of the Dubliners' settled codes. The *flâneur* in Dublin cannot remain anonymous for long, cannot savour impersonality in the strangeness of the crowd. If all stories are known and all jokes already told, then the identities of persons should precede them to every meeting. Yet for Bloom the man in the mackintosh poses the same question that he raises for Dubliners: how to savour the strangeness in themselves as a prelude to embracing the stranger in others. If Bloom is a 'coon' to Menton, because of a slightly darker complexion, that can only be because the Irish, troubled by the taunt of racial inferiority, are marking themselves off from those considered closest to them in the scale of inferiority as devised by imperial Britain.

Bloom is a sensitive man, respectful and sceptical both of the culture his people brought and of the culture which they found. In this he will prove himself unlike such national chauvinists as Menton, who revere the native and despise the foreign, or those radicals who admire the foreign and despise the native. For he has transcended the village-like feel of a Dublin in which the man-in-the-mackintosh loves a lady who is dead – that same Mrs Sinico of 'A Painful Case' in *Dubliners* whose lover Mr Duffy mourned her death under a train at Sydney Parade. This wan parody of the plot of *Anna Karenina* of Tolstoy seems deliberate on the part of Joyce – Tolstoy who wrote that everyone's home is a six-foot plot. If in *Dubliners* tales with epic potential were scaled down to mere short stories, in *Ulysses* the material which began as a short story can be scaled up to the proportions of an epic.

One fear that haunts Bloom is that of being buried alive. A possible insurance against that eventuality, he thinks, would be to equip coffins with telephones. The phone, still a recent invention in 1904, accustomed people to hearing a voice without seeing a body – the state of isolation-in-connection. The speakers in 'Telemachus' were not always visible to hearers, nor would they be in some later scenes of this book; but Bloom seems to understand how the phone, with its disembodied voice, is in some ways a rehearsal for death. Above all, however, he mocks Christian euphemisms about dying: 'Who departed this life. As if they did it of their own accord' (143). And he thinks that it would be more practical to spend the money devoted to tombstones on charities for the living. If there must be tombstones, it would be better to have them recount the work people have done: 'I travelled for cork lino' or 'I cooked good Irish stew'. (143) He even suggests gramophone recordings to help mourners remember the dead person's voice.

The impulse behind these musings is Bloom's determination to bounce back into life. If 'a corpse is meat gone bad' (145), then that condition is not always terminal, since cheese is the corpse of milk. Bloom would himself prefer the eastern rite of cremation so that the rats might not devour his body, but the priests are 'dead against it' (145). Drowning may be the pleasantest way to die, but Bloom cannot really believe that death is the end. He is Irish, above all, in his conviction that the dead may not even know that they are dead, but choose instead to continue talking: 'Wonder does the news go about whenever a fresh one is let down' (145). That speculation may have given rise not just to *Cré na Cille* (Graveyard Earth), Máirtín Ó Cadhain's novel of jabbering corpses, but also to the famous passage in Beckett's *Waiting for Godot*: 'All the dead voices. They make a noise like wings. Like leaves . . . To have lived is not enough for them. They have to talk about it.'

Bloom knows that in a funerary culture, death is the ultimate career move and not final at all. In song after song, the corpse (like Joyce's future hero Finnegan) gets up and speaks. A near-death experience, again and again, brought a person back to life. And so it does for Bloom: 'Plenty to see and hear and feel yet' (146).

7. Reporting

'In the everyday, everything is everyday,' says Maurice
Blanchot, 'but in the newspaper everything is strange,
sublime, abominable.' Newspapers, incapable of seizing
the insignificance of the everyday, because their writers
cannot deal with what is hidden rather than obvious,
seize upon seemingly dramatic events, 'replacing the
nothing happens with the emptiness of a news item in
which *something happens*'.

After the quiet of the cemetery comes the noise of the
printing office. After the silent, subjective monologue of
Bloom comes the objective, clinical account as given by a
newspaper in this episode called 'Aeolus'. The paths of
Bloom and Stephen cross, but they do not meet. Each is
given a brief monologue, but for most of the episode they
talk and listen just like other protagonists. Yet, under the
influence of previous episodes, we are somehow aware of
what each man might be thinking even when this is not
reported.

This is a world of mechanism, of trams shuttling to
the terminus and then returning over the same route to
the point at which they started. Likewise with language –
one sentence may easily become the reversal of its predecessor:

Grossbooted draymen rolled barrels dullthudding out of Prince's stores and bumped them up on the brewery float. On the brewery float bumped dullthudding barrels rolled by grossbooted draymen out of Prince's stores (148).

In such a world humans seem to have less agency than machines, so the editor of the *Freeman's Journal*, William Brayden, enters the newspaper office 'steered by an umbrella' (149). This is not necessarily a bad thing in a book which has already deflated the self-importance of humans with the suggestion that objects may themselves have consciousness and life. A door may become articulate, whispering 'ee:cree' (149). As *Ulysses* takes up its earlier attempt to render strange sounds ('seesoo', 'hrss', 'mrkgnao'), the reader may wonder whether any of these could be the 'shout in the street' heralding Stephen's god about to reveal a new order.

The young Joyce was a frequenter of the Dublin Hermetic Society and was intrigued by the notion that things could be endowed with consciousness. You didn't have to be a Theosophist to sense such potentials; writers and artists had similar intuitions. The painter Cézanne, for example, said that the apples he painted were 'filled with thought'. Other modernist artists were moved by the sight of inanimate objects that had suffered rejection. 'This morning I visited the place where the street cleaners dump the rubbish,' Van Gogh reported. 'My God, it was beautiful.' Yeats found a similar poetry in rag-and-bone shop materials, a battered kettle and so on. In his more godlike moments, Bloom's soul seeks to enter some nearby object, and so it imparts speech to a printing machine which is depositing papers on a board:

> Sllt. Almost human the way it sllt to call to attention. Doing its level best to speak. That door too sllt creaking, asking to be shut. Everything speaks in its own way. Sllt (154).

This is the modern form of pathetic fallacy, favoured not just by painters but by surrealist poets, who warned against those who take a merely exterior view of the surfaces of things.

Empathetic with objects, Bloom in this episode proves less deft with people. Stephen has little trouble placing Mr Deasy's letter on foot-and-mouth disease in the paper, but Bloom has a lot more difficulty with his attempt to devise and sell an advertisement for the firm of Alexander J. Keyes. He hopes that the crossed-key logo will touch off subconscious associations with the Vatican and with the idea of Home Rule (since the Manx parliament has such a symbol). This is ironic, given that he is as keyless in his wanderings as Stephen.

Throughout the ensuing scene, men will hand one another matches, touch each other to make a point or a jibe, but nobody will touch Bloom. Somehow, the language of the body excludes him from their easy rapport. Although his speech on the printed page may look like dialogue, Bloom is often talking to himself in a series of separate sentences that are just a spoken monologue. The Irish, stereotypically great talkers, prove less than willing listeners. So Bloom has to insert seven successive conversational sallies, outlining his proposed ad to Mr Nanetti, in the pauses between the clanking of machines.

He displays great tact in feeling his way into the proposal, showing that one sign of a truly good teacher is that he also knows when *not* to teach: 'Better not teach him his own business,' he cautions himself, before saying twice to Nanetti: 'You know yourself' (153). The entire scene suggests that, far from being an ad-canvasser, Bloom would prefer the role of a teacher, or at least an agony uncle on the daily paper:

> Country bumpkin's queries. Dear Mr Editor, what is a good cure for flatulence? I'd like that part. Learn a lot teaching others (151).

This recalls Stephen's perception that he also might be a learner more than a teacher. The episode will later report the young man's avowal: 'Dublin. I have much, much to learn' (183). The two have not met, but Stephen, more and more open to his destiny, senses some promise in the vicinity.

Bloom's brief interior monologues work here to comic effect, showing how he can say one thing, while privately thinking something quite different. Asked whether he thinks Brayden has a face 'like Our Saviour', Bloom is astounded at the cultural insensitivity of Red Murray's question. (In its provincialism it anticipates Taoiseach Liam Cosgrave's statement of the 1970s urging Jews and Palestinians to solve the problem of the Middle East 'by peaceful Christian means'. When told that this would not go down well in Gaza or Jerusalem, Cosgrave merely retorted: 'It'll go down fine in Dún Laoghaire/Rathdown, where my constituents live.') Bloom, on this occasion, is deft enough to change the comparison: 'or like Mario', a famous Italian tenor (149). When Murray mentions two phone calls from the Catholic Archbishop of Dublin, Bloom makes a little joke – 'Well, he is one of Our Saviours also' (150) – while privately wondering whether he will save the paper's circulation.

If the epic contains periodic summaries of its plot, Joyce uses Bloom's descriptions of the 'day-father' to show just how willing his book is to cannibalise itself: 'Queer lot of stuff he must have put through his hands in his time: obituary notices, pubs' ads, speeches, divorce suits, found drowned . . .' (155). Joyce himself is a kind of day-father here, constructing a counter-newspaper that will record a single day. Stephen may flee the prospect of a career in journalism with some distaste – 'He wants you for the pressgang', they warn him about Myles Crawford (171) – but his creator recognised his own journalistic tendency: 'I am quite content to go down to posterity as a scissors and paste man, for that seems to me a harsh but not unjust description.'

It was only in the decade before 1904 that the technology had been at last developed which permitted the publication of papers with news covering the previous twenty-four hours. Joyce was impressed by the penetration of newspapers into the popular mindset, as were surrealist painters who attached pieces of newsprint to their constructs. Yet he was also sceptical of the failure of journalists to take advantage of the full possibilities opened up by the new technology.

When early on he has Bloom wipe his bottom with a page from *Titbits*, Joyce is fretting about the disposability of print, about how much of it is wasted and how much is frittered away. The danger is that newspapers reduce an item of news to mere sensation, so that it is lost to true emplotment and not accorded its full context of cause and effect. The need was to salvage some of the higher potentials, to create a two-way paper in which writers and readers enjoyed a more interactive relationship. One answer might be *Ulysses*, a counter-newspaper which would provide a dense set of background to the day's most apparently trivial happenings. If Bloom was right to raise consciousness in cats and machines, perhaps that could also be done with books and papers. In *Ulysses* Joyce seeks, therefore, to assimilate the considerable repertoire of a newspaper, to do all that it can do *and much more besides.*

This is most obvious in the use of headlines on every page of 'Aeolus'. In a real newspaper, these are usually written last, at great speed and under intense pressure, by sleepy subeditors who did not write the articles themselves. As a consequence headlines are often misleading, highlighting a trivial detail but missing the main point, impoverishing the possible play of meanings in a paragraph or even completely omitting others. So it is here: the playful, sportive headings, far from making reading easier, often challenge and confuse. The episode would be more straightforward to read without them.

Many of the headlines are written in just the sort of telegraphic language out of which Bloom's monologues have been constructed ('Cup of tea soon. Good. Mouth dry.'). The reader may wonder whether Bloom is parodying those headlines in his private thoughts (the ad man cometh) or whether Joyce is using the headlines to initiate a mockery of Bloomian phrases. Like 'Lotus-Eaters' and 'Hades', which warned against the corruptions of language by the institutional church,

'Aeolus' alerts readers to the dangers of mechanical clichés as propounded by journalists. Later episodes will contain similar warnings against the power of academia, medicine, musicianship, law and even theology to distort speech and to corrupt language. With astonishing audacity, Joyce, having perfected his own technique of interior monologue in the early parts of the book, is now issuing a warning, lest it too lapse into just another institution of literature, defined as much by what it excludes as by what it includes. The fear, quite simply, is that his own style will become 'Joycean', as live form degenerates into dead formula. On guard against past masters from the outset, he may be growing suspicious of his own mastery.

Like other great modernist artists, Joyce could never rest easy with a single, personal style, but was constantly seeking renewal. They were willing to risk all that they had gained in hopes of even greater victories. If political radicals sought a constant revolutionising of society, they wanted it in art, sometimes even within a single, evolving artwork. So each figure in Picasso's painting *Les Demoiselles d'Avignon* represents a different style in his artistic evolution, just as each episode in the single text called *Ulysses* is quite different from all others. No style achieved could ever be 'final' or 'official'. In constantly changing, modern art had something in common with the successive editions of a daily paper, each one replacing the previous one (much as the latest edition of the text of *Ulysses* keeps replacing its predecessors).

In the old days, a soldier could escape death by mimicking it, 'playing dead' on the field of battle in order to rise when all was clear, ready to fight again. New forms in art kill off old ones, but not entirely, because they learn how to work elements of the old into the new invention, much as electric light imitated gaslights or as the railcar was modelled on the design of the horse-carriage. The newspaper is, therefore, like the Irish language described in the previous section, forever expiring but refusing to settle into a coffin of complacency, because it is reborn in a somewhat new mode. That is like the way in which *Ulysses* updates past literary classics with a new 'edition'. It also explains why Joyce was terrified that his style of interior monologue might become institutionalised.

Joyce was no lover of masters. 'Material victory is the death of spiritual predominance,' he told Georges Borach. 'Successful states only become colonisers and merchants.' Mr Deasy had early in *Ulysses* provided a distressing example of the problem. Joyce loved the Greeks because of their cultural superiority to the Romans who plundered them; for much the same reasons he admired Ireland and despaired of England. The idea Joyce voiced to Borach is put into the mouth of Professor McHugh in the newspaper office. He says that the British, like the Romans, brought no greater achievement than the water closet: 'But the Greek!' (169). He sees the possibility of a return of a lost possibility, the art of a Catholic Europe:

> The closet-maker and the cloacamaker will never be the lords of our spirit. We are liege subjects of the catholic chivalry of Europe, that foundered at Trafalgar and of the empire of the spirit, not an *imperium*, that went under with the Athenian fleets at Aegospotami (169).

The episode is all talk, with no action; and Professor

McHugh contributes more than his share of the hot air which, circulating through the office, causes doors to blow open and shut. The speech of John F. Taylor about the Irish language develops the Ireland–Israel comparison, with its account of how Moses returned to the 'chosen people' bearing 'the tablets of the law . . . in the language of the outlaw' (181). 'Aeolus' is filled with a sense of missed opportunities: Parnell's failure to achieve Home Rule being matched by that of Moses to reach the Promised Land. J. J. O'Molloy, once the cleverest man at the junior bar, is now down on his luck, and so defeated by life that he wonders whether Stephen will live to see his parable published.

Stephen's 'Parable of the Plums' itself is all about failure and frustration. Two old ladies climb Nelson's Pillar and ejaculate plumstones from its top out on to the street below. Falling on concrete, the stones cannot seed and bear fruit: the very gesture seems masturbatory. The parable reads like one of the epiphanic impasses which might have gone into *Dubliners* and the moral is the same: no paralysed city could be fertilised by such a gesture.

In spite of his search for new form, Stephen has produced yet another national allegory. In spite of his better intentions, he has created another chapter in the moral history of his country. But the parable, like the entire episode, is put into a quite different perspective by the fact of Easter 1916. By the time that *Ulysses* was published six years later, the 'triumph of lost causes' argument no longer sounded threadbare, for a 'hopeless rebellion', centred next to the very site of all this verbalising, had led to the founding of an Irish Free State.

It would not have been immodest of Joyce to see his own book as a gesture appropriate to that moment of independence. Myles Crawford teases Stephen for his failure as yet to produce a major work of literature, but he also lays down a challenge heroic enough to be answered by the book in the reader's hands: 'Put us all into it, damn its soul,' so that the effect will be to 'paralyse Europe' (171–2).

Stephen's failure to trump the methods of *Dubliners* is not final. Even as he dallies in the office, he plays with the idea of new forms leading to new contents for literature. A rhythm may give birth to a phrase, a phrase to an idea. His compositional process is that of an artist who prefers not so much to report feelings as to invent them, to allow his text to take shape at the suggestion of language. So he reworks the poem based on a lyric of Douglas Hyde, which he had composed on the beach that morning: 'Mouth, south. Is the mouth south someway? Or the south a mouth? Must be some' (175).

As with these sounds from a folk tradition, so with the vibrations left by the Irish past. The dead noise of Tara, the ancient Gaelic capital, like the 'dead breaths' on Sandymount Strand, may seem to have been lost, but can be recovered through akasic records in which, so the Theosophists believed, everything is preserved.

Joyce shared the modernists' interest in primitive European art (including that of Gaelic Ireland), because he realised that he and his contemporaries were participants in a new electronic civilisation. As yet they had not got control of technology, making it the servant of humanity. Rather, they had been mastered by it, and the carnage wrought by the repeating guns of World War I was proof enough of that. But Joyce was born early enough to have high hopes for that technology and for the mass literacy which accompanied it. Unlike many other modernist writers, he celebrated elements of popular culture (handbills, advertisements, posters, jingles, radio phrases, newsprint) and incorporated them all into his book. Not for him the later depressive diagnosis of the Frankfurt School, which after his death depicted modern media as forces which achieved nothing better than the manufacture of a dreary consent.

8. Eating

You are what you eat, say the food scientists. Joyce often met the painter Frank Budgen in Zurich restaurants while at work on central parts of *Ulysses*, but he didn't eat a lot himself, being more interested in the white wine. So much of his thinking and talking was done in cafés, however, that it was predictable that he would address the theme of food. It was a pressing concern, anyway, for his Irish generation, whose parents had been born during the Great Famine or its immediate aftermath. Even through Joyce's own childhood in the 1880s and 1890s, the diet of the average Dubliner often lacked basic vitamins, while the city's Jewish citizens had better nutrition.

As Bloom passes Lemon's sweetshop, the fancies displayed seem just another narcotic damaging the health of the poor. He feels caustic towards priests who, having only their own mouths to feed, compel the faithful to increase and multiply in ever-larger families. The results are obvious in the tragedy of the Dedalus household. Dilly Dedalus walks past, looking raggedy and underfed: 'Potatoes and marge . . . Undermines the constitution' (191). In the previous episode, Myles Crawford had belched with hunger, but that did not stop him from heading to the pub at the end. The food priorities of many citizens are all wrong, and the whole corrupt system is presided over by the English monarch, for the proudest boast of Lemon's is that they are 'Lozenge and comfit manufacturers to His Majesty the King' (190).

As Bloom walks past the shop, he is given a handbill:

Bloo . . . Me? No.
Blood of the Lamb (190).

The Reverend Alexander Dowie is on hand with a revival mission to proclaim that Elijah is coming. Bloom's misreading works in telling ways. It mimics the reader's anxious search for the return of a central character after the more general portrayals in 'Aeolus'. It plays on that episode's use of the locale of the 1916 Rising, with its imagery of redemption achieved through the shedding of blood at Easter-time. Most of all, Bloom's quick denial of his possible role as saviour to his people repeats the cautions of Jesus about any claims to be the messiah. Later in *Ulysses*, Bloom will announce a New Bloomusalem, but for the present he is merely godlike at certain fleeting moments – as when he dispenses bread to the gulls over the Liffey, his 'manna' a more kindly version of the Eucharist dispensed at All Hallows. A minute earlier, he had tried to deceive the birds by throwing the handbill in a crumpled white ball on to the water, but they were not fooled. Filled with admiration and compassion, Bloom buys two Bunbury cakes for them.

A rowboat bears an ad for Kino's trousers, prompting Bloom to wonder whether the advertiser pays rent to the Corporation, but 'how can you own water really?' (193). This democrat is all for communal ownership and tries to apply socialist principles, even when it comes to other men sleeping with his wife. His shrewd observation that

'All kind of places are good for ads' (193) leads him, however, to recall how a doctor for venereal diseases advertised on urinals, where some wags had changed the legend POST NO BILLS to POST 110 PILLS. As if by nervous reflex, Bloom worries whether Boylan may infect Molly. He distracts himself by considering the matter of 'parallax' – how the relative position of two objects changes, depending on the vantage point assumed by the observer. But that merely returns him to the painful thought of his marriage: if Molly and Boylan are the two objects, Bloom must be the observer of the parallax.

Bloom can seem like an eccentric but only because he has a deeper than average understanding of reality. The city is filled with actual eccentrics suffering from personality disorders. Cashel Boyle O'Connor Fitzmaurice Tisdall Farrell has the affectation of walking only on the very edge of pavements and outside all lamp posts. Mrs Josie Breen, of whom Bloom has been fond since their youthful days, complains of her husband Denis, who will be like Farrell soon. Denis has seen the ace of spades walking upstairs in his home and is threatening litigation, following receipt of an obscene postcard which said simply 'U.P.' ('You pee up' looks like a coded taunt against a man who may prefer to lie under his wife during love-making). These colourful eccentrics are a consequence of the repression of a life policed so thoroughly by church and state. They are extreme versions, perhaps, of ordinary people, a reminder of what can happen to those who fail to express themselves in more usual ways and so fall out of the human community. There is a manic quality to their responses which troubles Bloom. Breen is now determined to go to law over an obscure slight, unlike Bloom, who has endured so many jibes uncomplainingly.

Acting out is one response to repression; keeping things in is the other. If the healthy person is one in whom every internal impulse is balanced by an external one, this raises the question of a pathological element in Bloom's monologues. The first extended monologue in the book, Stephen's in 'Proteus', is anything but healthy in its level of self-obsession; and 'Aeolus', by mocking Bloomian telegraph-language, opened the possibility that even his monologues might contain a satiric element. This episode, 'Lestrygonians', contains more dialogue than most, yet the exchanges prove inconclusive compared to the richness of Bloom's musings. Could it be that Joyce sees that richness as a direct result of social repression? If the tragedy of interior monologue is the poverty of its social occasions, then it might be better not to have quite so rich an inner life.

The very fluency and depth of Bloom's inner consciousness may work against a fuller participation in the social world. This hint was taken further by Brian Friel in his play *Philadelphia, Here I Come!*, where a character is played by two actors, Private and Public. Private is witty, debonair and fluent, while Public is tentative, uncertain and gauche. However, in the end, Private undermines Public with his corrosive mockery and put-downs, until the social man is left stuttering and dysfunctional.

Admirers of the interior monologues as one of Joyce's great technical achievements have overlooked the element of self-repression which they contain. Franco Moretti has suggested that there is a necessary link between

127

advertising and the stream of consciousness: whereas the former sends out stimuli to the brain, the latter organises them into some kind of flow. But it may well be that advertising is itself an agent of repression, driving tractable persons back even deeper into themselves. 'Lestrygonians' is filled with Bloom's thoughts about ads, all the more deliberate and conscious in one of the earliest fictional ad men. But on other occasions his monologues can read like a compulsive blather, blocking out and controlling more painful thoughts, much as a person might switch on a radio to distract from a sadness.

The satiric potential of interior monologue may arise from our sense of the comical nature of the compulsive babbler, the one who talks aloud to himself or herself, even in the guise of addressing company. A century before Joyce, for example, Jane Austen created a rather similar effect in the character of Mrs Elton in *Emma*. At a strawberry party given by Mr Knightley, she cheers herself up with the following performance:

The best fruit in England – everybody's favourite – always wholesome – These the finest beds and finest sorts – Delightful to gather for one's self – the only way of really enjoying them – Morning decidedly the best time – never tired – every sort good – hautboy infinitely superior – no comparison – the others hardly eatable – hautboys very scarce – chili preferred – white wood finest flavour of all – price of strawberries in London – abundance about Bristol – Maple Grove – cultivation – beds when to be renewed – gardeners never to be put out of their way – delicious fruit – only too rich to be eaten much of – inferior to cherries – currants more

> refreshing – only objection to gathering strawberries
> the stooping – glaring sun – tired to death – could bear
> it no longer – must go and sit in the shade.

Carol Shields has tartly observed that it is not at all clear to whom these scattered, telescoped remarks are addressed, 'to the wind, perhaps, or to readers – who can feel Jane Austen winking in their direction'. Much the same might have been said of Bloom if he had not so fully internalised that type of voicing.

Mrs Elton is, of course, acting out whereas Bloom seldom feels such a need. An even closer analogy to his monologues can be found in the secret diary kept by Theobald Wolfe Tone during an extended sojourn as a clandestine emissary in Paris in the 1790s. It demonstrates the same cryptic and cutting eloquence found in some of Bloom's wittier asides. For instance, this is Tone on Edmund Burke:

> Sad. Sad. Edmund wants to get another 2,000 guineas
> for his son, if he can: dirty work. Edmund no fool in
> money matters. Flattering Gog to carry his point. Is
> that *sublime* or beautiful?

Like Tone, Bloom is a self-critical monologist. In a city where consciousness is constantly invaded by headlines, handbills or ads, he is astutely aware that you 'never know whose thoughts you're chewing' (217). *His* sense of identity is fluid and unstable. He returns to the image of water, which nobody can own, in the attempt to reconcile himself to what Molly is about to do: 'Could never like it again after Rudy. Can't bring back time. Like holding water in your hand' (213).

The noonday devil grips Bloom at one o'clock, the worst time of the day, he considers, as he lapses into a kind of depression. The bourgeois world has lost its enchantment and declined into mere mechanism. In 'Aeolus' gestures were self-cancelling, as people blew 'hot and cold', and the trams clanked backwards and forwards. But things seem no better here in a world of people. The sight of police constables with their flushed well-fed faces debouching from College Green nauseates Bloom, giving rise to the subversive idea that the best moment to attack them would be during their feeding-time. Bloom is caustic about their motives for serving the colonial authorities: 'Prepare to receive soup' (205). But it is also the mechanical, unthinking nature of their drill which depresses him and leads him to wonder whether anything is worth doing:

> Things go the same; day after day: squads of police marching out, back; trams in, out. Those two loonies marching about. Dignam carted off (208).

The likely birth of a child to Mina Purefoy later that day can hardly compensate for Dignam's death. It merely suggests a self-cancelling quality to a human life in which no one is anything in particular.

Seeing the mystic poet George Russell on the street causes Bloom to contrast the meat-eating police with the vegetarian Theosophist who edited the *Irish Homestead*. One aspect of that journal's campaign against paralysis was its advice on how to improve the diet of ordinary families. Bloom is, however, sceptical of the vegetarian code: 'Only weggebobbles and fruit. Don't eat a beefsteak. If you do the eyes of that cow will pursue you through all eternity' (210). Nut-steaks are fraudulent imitations, fooling nobody. A man of balance and sanity, Bloom is irritated by the dreamy, cloudy poetry produced by the vegetarians of the Irish revival, while admitting that you couldn't squeeze a single line of poetry out of the over-fed police.

Yet it is part of Bloom's equilibrium that he often proceeds to embrace a code which he has just appeared to reject. The man who refuses to beget another Rudy will soon visit Mrs Purefoy, offering sympathy during her confinement in the maternity hospital. The man who fears Boylan's sexual conquest of his wife also facilitates it by keeping well away from Eccles Street for the rest of the day. So now, with a sort of inevitability, the person who began the day cating with relish the innards of animals turns against meat-eaters.

Why has this change come about? Perhaps he has been troubled by the cannibalistic images of flesh-eating in All Hallows Church, the line about the Blood of the Lamb, the ad for Plumtree's Potted Meat? Whatever the reason, he is appalled by the rows of men guzzling meat in the Burton restaurant. 'See the animals feed . . . men, men, men' (215) becomes in his mind the plaintive rhythm: 'Eat or be eaten. Kill! Kill!' (216). In Glasnevin Cemetery he had felt some sympathy for animals, even rats, as they made short work of a human corpse (meat gone bad). Now he feels a kind of sympathy for food – especially when others are eating it.

Bloom is keenly aware of the curative as well as the harmful effects of certain foods. Earlier he had mused that the first man to pick a herb to cure himself had a bit of pluck. Now he praises the audacity of the first person to eat an oyster. The risk was worth it, as the shell was neither empty (like Deasy's) nor crushed (like Stephen's), but filled with life. Ever the apostle of self-help, Bloom wonders who was the first distiller. This obsession with firstness reflects Joyce's awareness of his own programme in writing *Ulysses*: but, coming from Bloom, these ideas also suggest that he sees both a symbolic and a practical meaning in all forms of food.

His distaste as he looks into the Burton may not be for meat-eating as such, but for the group nature of the activity. He had felt a similar reservation about the rows of female communicants. After all, this is a man who preferred the solitary ritual of tea-making and kidney-cooking alone in his kitchen. In fact, he may have enjoyed the preparation even more than the eating. His revulsion is against waste, against the fact that so much food is dropped or left on the plate. If Stephen was nauseated by inhaling the breaths of the dead, something even more distressing is enacted here before Bloom, who may not know whose thoughts he is chewing but can recognise a lack of self-respect in the way these people eat their food: 'A man spitting back on his plate: halfmasticated gristle: no teeth to chewchewchew it' (215). The morning newspaper itself becomes waste once read and discarded, but it can also function as a placemat. Once again, many forms of waste can be recycled, as the paper could even be read again by another, while being used in that way.

'Not here. Don't see him' (216), Bloom's eyes tell him. His agitation is linked to thoughts of Boylan. If the distaste is for the group eating of meat by men, Bloom may be seeing before him an awful vision of Molly's possible sexual partners. As soon as he was introduced in

132

the book, Bloom was shown to put food to different uses from those made of it by the bachelors in the tower: they enjoyed their power-relations with the milkwoman, whereas Bloom was unafraid to serve his wife, above him upstairs. His orderly consumption was at variance with Molly's stuffing of a folded piece of bread into her mouth. In the *Odyssey* the men tear at their meat, and Antiphates eats one of Odysseus' men for supper. Bloom may simply want more control over the eating process.

It is the scavenging nature of a creation in which everything feeds off everything else that disgusts him. But *Ulysses* itself spits back half-masticated gristle, each time it summarises and reprocesses earlier material – rather like the dog mentioned here as eating its own vomit. The vegetarians in their food but also in their poetry lack bodily solidity (the very element which *Ulysses* celebrates by its itemisation of each organ of the body). Joyce recognises that the processes of life run through decay, death and transformation: if newspapers can become food-holders, then waste really can be turned to use. For the present, however, Bloom turns vegetarian with a cheese sandwich and a glass of Burgundy wine in Davy Byrne's pub. He takes pleasure in cutting the sandwich into slender strips, which he now eats 'with relish of disgust' (220), because of the flavour of the cheese. He has already reconciled himself to the fact that fine flavours come from the earth. Since food affects our moods, he reasons, even matters of peace and war may depend on someone's digestion.

Bloom's lunch is modest. He doesn't fritter away money on drink, which makes him different from many other men in Dublin. The episode is concerned not just with food but with money – Kino's trousers at eleven shillings and so on. Near the end, Nosey Flynn and Davy Byrne discuss where Bloom got the wealth which allows his wife to eat plovers on toast. Flynn is convinced that Bloom must be a secret member of the Protestant freemasons. It never strikes him that Bloom's financial comfort may be due to simple prudence. Davy Byrne knows this and recalls that, although Bloom has often drunk in his pub, never once has he done so to excess.

At Bloom's lunch a minor miracle occurs. As he contemplates two flies stuck together on the pub window-pane, he is reminded of his first tryst with Molly on Howth Hill and of the pleasure he felt in receiving seedcake from her mouth, 'warm and chewed' (224). If Molly, in a sense, inseminated Bloom, that was how he liked it. On that occasion he had no objection to chewing another person's thoughts or half-masticated meal: 'Hot I tongued her. She kissed me. I was kissed' (224).

The wine and its effects recall Bloom to his sensory life and to that moment of ecstasy. Indeed, many of his thoughts of past happiness with Molly are linked to pleasant food. But his depression will not completely lift:

> Me. And me now.
> Stuck, the flies buzzed (224).

He amuses himself, however, with a caustic meditation on a possible conversation between Nosey Flynn and one of the Greek goddesses in the National Museum. The goddesses' quaffing of nectar seems a far cry from the more homely scenes of eating and disgorging just witnessed. This reminds Bloom to see whether the statues really have organs for the discharge of food and drink.

Passing a blind stripling, he wonders whether the lack of sight has left his other senses more acute, giving him stronger senses of smell and taste. He helps him cross the street, a prefiguration of the moment when later he will assist Stephen. Empathetic as ever, he wonders how the blind man might conduct himself with a woman, or what kind of dreams he has. Bloom is heading for the National Library to research material for his planned advertisement, when he comes suddenly upon the straw hat and tan shoes that can only betoken Boylan. The paragraphs of his monologue, long and detailed up to this moment, break up now into short units of nervous, staccato sentences. Far from being a stalker of his enemy, Bloom, covered in confusion, feels like one who is being stalked: 'No, didn't see me' (234). Eventually, he finds a stage prop to become the focus of his distraction: 'His hand looking for the where did I put found in his hip pocket soap lotion' (234).

This is an interesting sentence. Together with the last line of the episode 'Safe!' (234), it suggests that Bloom can still find a resting-place in thoughts of Molly for whom the soap was purchased. He still loves and wants her, even if he cannot summon the courage to conceive and possibly lose another Rudy. That sentence moves from a third-person-singular description, through a direct state-ment made inside Bloom's own head, back to objective narration. Joyce is now so confident of his ability to render interior monologue that he can switch it on and off in mid-sentence. But the effect is to reinforce our sense that, despite his panic, Bloom somehow partakes in this writerly omniscience.

As the 'parallax' motif suggests, Bloom is a man open to many perspectives, more so than any other character in

135

the book. He feels instinctively what it's like to be a woman like Josie Breen, a bar-room cadger like Flynn, a blind piano tuner. At one point in the episode he even imagines the communication between pigeons in the air above Dublin streets as they decide which citizen to target with their good-luck droppings. During his progress through the city centre, the sun shines directly overhead on Bloom, as if he were indeed illuminated.

If the nineteenth-century novelist often wrote omnisciently, Joyce seems less concerned to stake such a claim than to create an equivalent figure inside the text. Whatever his limitations, Bloom knows far more about what is going on than anybody around him. If he is accepting of Boylan's tryst with Molly, where then does the notion of Bloom as victim come from? If he refuses to be possessive of his wife, then he may have more agency than anyone else in *Ulysses*. Yet again, out of a moment of disadvantage and discouragement, he suddenly appears as a man possessed of secret power. The art of everyday living demands that a person has the wisdom to process a potentially negative experience in a different way, transcending the problem rather than being limited by it. Organ by organ, page by page, Joyce is intent upon his creation of a new species of man.

9. Reading

Reading was often the last thing on Joyce's mind when he visited the National Library. Like many Dublin libraries, it was used more for talk than study. In the hour covered by the 'Scylla and Charybdis' episode, although lots of writers are discussed, nobody commits the grave, unsocial offence of opening a book. Like other modernists, Joyce was rather cavalier about books, but he loved leaflets, postcards, advertisements and newspaper cuttings, eventually capturing their codes for all eternity in his own non-traditional book.

The beautiful reading-room in Kildare Street served University College students mainly as a pick-up place. In the words of Pádraic and Mary Colum, it was 'a handsome place in which to read, to view each other, to converse in the portico below, to make the encounters that permitted couples to walk together to their quarters'. For Joyce his desk there functioned also as a poste restante, 'but he was not nailed to it' scoffed his classmate Con Curran. Curran recalled how exchanges with him were really just interruptible monologues conducted by the brilliant youth in full flow:

For anything approaching serious talk he preferred the company of one to many, and even then . . . you were reduced to the docile recipient of his earlier meditations, sententiously delivered . . . He did not debate . . . irony, wry humour, grotesquerie, courteous evasion, or silence – each in turn was enlisted to build up an impregnable defence against intrusion on the inner sanctuary.

Joyce was socially unsure and these performances were a shy person's revenge. Stephen suffers from a similar sense of grievance, having been excluded from the invitation to that evening's literary gathering: but the record shows that, for a youth of his age and inexperience, Joyce enjoyed much patronage and support, being asked to review in the *Daily Express* and to place stories in the *Irish Homestead* as well as a poem in *Dana*. Moreover, in both 'Aeolus' and again here, Stephen is regarded far more highly by other intellectuals than he seems to realise. Depression, rather than belittlement by others, is the source of his low self-esteem.

The scene is Stephen's delivery of the set piece on *Hamlet*, promised earlier in the day to Haines (who misses it). Being wilful, Stephen will not always perform on cue, and he fears that Haines would cheapen his wisdom by writing it all down in a book. As other people come and go throughout the discourse (images of the 'wandering rocks' to be negotiated by the traveller in the *Odyssey*), Stephen has to struggle to keep his audience's attention. Such entrances and exits characterised many Greek symposia, posing a severe test for the speaker, who had to appear serenely untouched. This all seems demeaning, yet Stephen comes across here as a far more confident figure than the morose, largely silent youth of the opening episodes. However, he feels himself now what he accused Wilde of being, a jester at the court of his intellectual inferiors, someone who is being literally 'put on'. As he outlines his theory, he overhears himself (as Hamlet overheard himself) saying things, and he also begins to tire of his self-appointed role as brilliant soliloquist.

One way out of such boredom is to make the listening characters more interesting by playing games of distortion with their names and personalities. Stephen mangles many pseudonyms (W. K. Magee, aka John Eglinton, becomes Mageelinjohn), recognising such pen names as the defensive tactic of timid men who fear to become themselves. Douglas Hyde is mentioned as 'the pleasant little branch' (An Craoibhín Aoibhinn), a pen name he may have used because his own surname pointed all too painfully back to Cromwell's invading soldiery. George Russell's own pseudonym, AE, derived from the word 'aeon', thereby giving rise to the pun 'A.E.I.O.U.' (243), since Joyce owed him not just cash but gratitude for his first real literary break.

The pseudonyms often conflate the identities of real and fictional persons, the oddity being that the made-up ones seem somehow more real. They also evoke the idea of a literary 'ghost' or a ghosted story. The fabrication of 'Mageelinjohn' combines the first- and third-person elements to be found also in the narrative voice of the book. A sudden shift, well into the episode, from narrative prose to dramatic form is Stephen's attempt to see whether another genre would serve his purpose better, picking up on his resentful feelings of being 'theatricalised' by Haines in the tower and by the journalists in the newspaper office. But, mostly, the form derives from those stage

directions in which Stephen prompts himself: 'Smile.'
(235). The brief irruption of the dramatic form also reminds the reader of the many other genres in which this
book might have been written but which are excluded
from this particular text.

Joyce's main motive is to show just how many of the
aspirations of the Irish Literary Revival come to fruition
in *Ulysses*. By the time that Eglinton says 'Our young Irish
bards have yet to create a figure which the world will set
beside Shakespeare's Hamlet' (236), the job is already half
done. Or when George Sigerson is quoted as remarking
'Our national epic has yet to be written. Moore is the man
for it' (246), Joyce wants us to think 'Good idea, wrong
writer'. A reader might easily conclude something
similar, when Yeats's high-flown review of Lady Gregory
is (mis)quoted: 'The most beautiful book that has come
out of our country in my time. One thinks of Homer' (278).
In such a fashion did *Ulysses* supply the critical apparatus
by which it might be interpreted.

Augusta Gregory had indeed attempted to normalise
the epic. She was an Anglo-Irish aristocrat, retailing
stories about ancient warriors, designed (in her own mind,
at least) to appeal to a mainly peasant audience. In her
dedication of the Irish edition of *Cuchulain of Muirthemne*
to the people of Kiltartan, she confessed that she had
removed material 'they would not care for', to protect the
native culture from the sneers of professors at Trinity
College. In evidence to the Committee on Intermediate
Education in 1899, Trinity don J. P. Mahaffy had said it
would be a mistake to encourage the study of Gaelic
literature, as Robert Atkinson (Professor of Old Irish at
Trinity) declared that many Irish-language texts were

unfit to be left in the house within reach of his daughters – if perused, they could cause a shock from which the young ladies might not recover for the rest of their lives. Mahaffy was allergic to *any* epic of Irish provenance, for it was he who remarked, after the printing of *Ulysses*, that Joyce's work proved that 'it was a mistake to set up a separate university for the aborigines of the island, for the corner-boys who spit into the Liffey'. That visceral response was tell-tale. Different as they were, *Cuchulain of Muirthemne* – a novelised epic – and *Ulysses* – an epic rewriting of the novel form – offered a splicing of genres which disrupted the codes of both the novel and the epic in ways that jarred on the nerves of the classicists at Trinity College.

Ulysses is, in fact, a parody of *Cuchulain of Muirthemne*. It is an epic with an urban setting rather than a rural one, a proletarian rather than an aristocratic audience, and a pacifist rather than a militarist ethos. The boy-deeds of Cúchulainn were an Irish Telemachiad, repeated in the opening episodes concerning Stephen. In the Gaelic tale, Setanta kills by accident the hound of Culan and offers himself as substitute. The Abbey Theatre, whose logo was a picture of Setanta with hound, is mocked here in ferocious parodies of Synge's Hiberno-English style. Yet the maturation of Setanta to become 'the hound of Culan' (Cú Chulain), is a perfect illustration of Stephen's perception that in *Hamlet* 'the boy of act one is the mature man of act five' (272). Joyce's project of becoming himself-his-own-father requires that he bring his younger and older selves into connection, so the narrative logic at the heart of the Cúchulainn saga is exploited for its full psychological possibilities. For Setanta sought a surrogate father as surely as does Stephen.

Stephen's theory is that a writer tries to illuminate life's problems in a book; he uses Shakespeare's *Hamlet* to solve his problem with his own father. The interlocutors in the scene are surrounded by books, which strike Stephen as 'coffined thoughts' placed in 'mummy cases' (248). If Nietzsche was right to say that every word is an epitaph on an emotion, the hard-cover book almost seems to mimic a coffin, making the Library an equivalent of the graveyard visited in the sixth episode or of Sandymount Strand in the third, where Stephen was troubled by having to breathe 'dead breaths' (63). The conversation of the other litterateurs is second-hand, smothered by quotations from past authors. Even in Ireland, a natural home of epic and oral poetry, the old spoken energies are ebbing, as talk gets corrupted by a multi-clausal writerly style, immobilising itself with endless citations.

The men's literary debate refers to the 'leaves falling' (247) of mature Ann Hathaway, Shakespeare's abandoned wife, as a corrupt text. Stephen finds writing as deathly as did the Bloom who wiped his bottom that morning with a copy of *Titbits*. So he refuses at the end to publish his own theory, for to do so would be to embalm it. Joyce concurs by mocking the commodification of the hard-cover book through his presentation of HELY'S Sandwich-board men. Writing, once given asylum in books, is now (in the words of Walter Benjamin) 'cast out onto the street by advertising'. By a further twist in this process, Joyce seeks in *Ulysses* to return the energies of everyday speech from their natural habitat in the street back into the hard-bound book.

The Library is the intellectuals' Hades, which for Homer was the place to tell the story of Achilles' funeral and of Odysseus's return. It is, as much as any cemetery, the archive of a community, its librarian playing the same role as John O'Connell, keeper of the graveyard at Glasnevin. If Hades, 'the safe-depository of tales, the treasure-house of myth', gave Odysseus the opportunity to access the source of Greek common memory, then the men in the National Library should be able to tap into ancestral energies as surely as did Bloom in the graveyard. But that is not quite how things pan out.

Mr Best, assistant librarian, suggests that *Hamlet* is a reflection of Shakespeare's private life – as *Ulysses* may be of Joyce's. Mr Lyster, head librarian, echoes Goethe on *Hamlet*: 'the beautiful ineffectual dreamer who comes to grief against hard facts' (235). This is also the Celtic version, masterminded by Yeats, who saw in many of Shakespeare's plays a clash between a triumphant but prosaic efficiency and a doomed but poetic complexity. Claudius or Hamlet? Bolingbroke or Richard? The story always seemed to Yeats a version of what England had done to the Irish, who (like Hamlet and Richard) got all the best lines, but lost out in the real world of facts. The 'triumph of failure' motif from Wilde to the Easter Rising meant that the Irish had evolved a language to cope with and even celebrate failure, but none at all for dealing with success.

Joyce was deeply aware of the debate and, through Stephen, makes his addition to the Celtic Shakespeare, reading his own 'note of banishment' into all the plays from *The Two Gentlemen of Verona* to *The Tempest* (272). But he accepted Edward Dowden's version of a pragmatic, wealth-accumulating Shakespeare not averse to the main chance. ('Khaki Hamlets don't hesitate to shoot' (239) must have had some resonance after British soldiers had opened fire upon an unarmed crowd on Bachelor's Walk in 1914.) The dreamy boy of act one had, Joyce acidly noted, become a killing machine by act five. Caught between the whirlpool of abstraction and the rocks of material danger, Shakespeare combined the spiritual and the worldly, much as Joyce himself blended high theory with a respect for everyday practices. If Matthew Arnold had urged the English to complicate their practical mercantilism with an Irish sense of poetry, Joyce was taking a lead from John Butler Yeats who urged the Irish to combine Protestant practicality with Catholic imagination.

Shakespeare was a priceless connection with the lost Catholic element of Europe before the Protestant Reformation took hold in England. His Elizabethan language, as much as his Stratford religion, was more available in the Ireland of 1904 than in England, because all these traditions had lingered on in the colony – not least the lost oral energies of Merrie England. So, Haines's arrival with his phrase book may signal a search not so much for revivalist Ireland as for a 'lost' old England of the sort lamented also by Mr Deasy. But for Stephen, Shakespeare is also a deracinated modern exile, who seeks to make a home in the midst of disorder and who attempts to solve the problem of a faithless wife by his own absence.

This is the wisdom offered by the story of Scylla and Charybdis – the healthy mind must not submit to either extreme, but entertain both possibilities in a mode of openness. Likewise, a viable marriage is something more than the coexistence of each partner in opposition. The key to the genius of Socrates or of Shakespeare, Stephen holds, lay in their successful mediation of a troubled marriage. His own rather hostile view of Ann Hathaway as a sexual opportunist in the manner of a Queen Gertrude casts Shakespeare as an Odysseus, leaving his wife as the Greek wanderer left Penelope. That hostility could derive from a covert aggression by Stephen against his own mother. He is clearly seeking to resolve not just his shame about an inadequate father but also his anxiety about failing to pray for his dying mother. Paternity and maternity seem linked in his mind, with the ghost as mediator.

The episode as a whole suggests that all binary oppositions – England and Ireland, Aristotle and Plato, Mulligan and Russell – are perfectly useless, unless one learns how to position oneself at some point in between. The Moore/Martyn combination is presented as a joke-version of the guru/adept relationship – one that will be more seriously fulfilled between Bloom and Stephen. Bloom has exactly those qualities of balance sought by Stephen, for the previous episode has shown him neither carnivore nor vegetarian but something between those extremes. Masculine is no more the true opposite of feminine that is heterosexuality of homosexuality. All seem to converge in a third phase, that of pansexuality.

Fathers in every sense are hopeless. Father Shakespeare is no more than 'the chap that writes like Synge' (254). Insofar as he has value, it is as a warning against misplaced ideas of paternity. Far from being the progenitor of English literature, he 'was made in Germany, as the champion French-polisher of Italian scandals' (263). Shakespeare wrote *Hamlet* in the months after his own father's death, and the hero of that play was as uncertain of his lineage as Joyce was of his. A father is just a necessary evil, but paternity may be nothing more than a 'legal fiction' (266).

If fathers are unreliable, that is only because mothers are too: 'If others have their will Ann hath a way. By cock, she was to blame' (244). The line used by Ophelia to clear her innocence instead rebounds on Shakespeare's Stratford doxy, who causes her husband to anticipate even in his own humiliation the future married life of Leopold Bloom: 'Forgot: any more than he forgot the whipping lousy Lucy gave him. And left the *femme de trente ans.* And why no other children born? And his first child a girl?' (277). This is far from the 'muscular' Shakespeare propounded by the robust imperialist Trinity professor, Edward Dowden. Instead, this is a passive, sensitive male overborne in a field by a wealthy older woman. Shakespeare, after his escape from Stratford, went on to create a whole series of memorable heroes and heroines, all united by the trait of androgyny. Yet the womanly man of his plays is always tragic.

Three hundred years later, Joyce saw other, more positive possibilities, which had been hinted at by John Eglinton in essays of 1910 and 1916 on the need for a comic hero, an Irish Quixote. This would be a figure who lived his androgyny not just in heaven ('in the economy of heaven, foretold by Hamlet, there are no more marriages, glorified man, an androgynous angel, being a wife unto himself', 274), but also on earth in the figure of Bloom, who passes between Stephen and Mulligan near the end of this episode. It is at this moment that Stephen decides to part with Mulligan, as he recalls the premonitory dream of an eastern male, inviting him to a different way of life:

'Street of harlots after. A creamfruit melon he held to me. In. You will see' (279).

If Stephen as soliloquist cannot really converse, then any guide whom he meets will have to work less by direct statement than by implication. Mulligan has sensed in Bloom a rival for Stephen's goodwill, so he projects onto Bloom his own desire for Stephen: 'Did you see his eye? He looked upon you to lust after you' (279). Bloom is described by him as Greeker than the Greeks, an intended slur, which of course stands in utter contradiction of Mulligan's earlier aim to Hellenise the island. Perhaps that statement back in the tower, along with his Wildean paradoxes and his ejaculations ('my love'), were all coded overtures to Stephen. If so, they are now firmly rebuffed.

The emerging relationship between Bloom and Stephen is an interesting variation on a classical theme: the willingness of an older man, wise in the ways of the world, to advise and protect a callow but talented youth. This might well be the love that dare not speak its name – or is *that* paternity, the legal fiction but necessary evil? Earlier Mulligan had twitted Eglinton about Shakespeare's sexual proclivities as revealed in the sonnets, asking 'Whom do you suspect?' (259) – a phrase that will later be used on 16 June to throw into question the paternity of Bloom's two children. As in the newspaper office, Bloom and Stephen do not meet. Their paths, as yet, are set on parallel quests, much as Telemachus, seeking news of Odysseus, actually if unknowingly repeats his quest. Such male-dominated narratives omit a female perspective. Even the androgyny explored is that of men rather than women – but female androgynes (Gerty and Molly) will appear in due course. As

147

characters, they will be open to the objection made by Stephen against the boy-women of Shakespeare's London stage: that their life, thought and speech 'are lent them by males' (244). Specifically, here, by Joyce.

As Joyce rewrote past works, he must have been aware of how each of these classics had world-historical importance, despite their lowly enough origins. George Russell understood this better than most. He is evoked here in tones of some mockery as a Theosophist. (When Gogarty was invited to one of his meetings, he asked, 'Would my mother be raped by a mystic?'; and he and Joyce hung a pair of bloomers on a brush in the Hermetic Society offices to mock the sexual repression of some leading members.) But he is also permitted to speak some of the profoundest truths of the episode. Mulligan's fear that Bloom may become a new guru to Stephen heightens his mockery of the Theosophists, to whose ranks the young Joyce was strongly attracted – after all, Bloom's kindness to animals and openness to reincarnation are part of the tradition epitomised by Russell.

The story of Jesus survived, like that of Odysseus, Dante's pilgrim or indeed Hamlet, because it contained wisdom and succour. Russell therefore says that 'the supreme question about a work of art is out of how deep a life does it spring' (236). The infant Jesus and mature messiah had much in common, as did Telemachus and Odysseus, or the young Dante and the older exile. Stephen demonstrates the continuity and discontinuity between a past self and a present one, between a past text and its replacement in the process of entelechy: 'I, I and I. I' (242). Entelechy is that which actualises potential, much as *Ulysses* is the further fulfilment of the *Odyssey*. The term is

Aristotle's, to describe the completion of what a being was meant to be. This raises once again for Stephen the question of those events which might have flowed from an earlier moment, if history had worked out somewhat differently: 'Here he ponders things that were not: what Caesar would have lived to do had he believed the soothsayer' (248).

The openness of each moment in the past provides Stephen with an image of creation and creativity. Although the connection between fathers and sons is more a matter of biological accident than psychological affinity, the possibility exists also that people create new life without realising that that is what they are doing: 'What links them in nature? An instant of blind rut. Am I father? If I were?' (267). The mystery of all human life is that of continuity within change. Simon Dedalus steals matches from Dublin pubs but fritters away pounds on drink, while his eldest son nicks slips of paper from the Library but buys drinks for people whom he privately despises. The mole on a human body remains the same, even as its constituent molecules change utterly over the years, much as the paradigms of epic repeat themselves with each retelling: 'though all my body has been woven of new stuff time after time, so through the ghost of an unquiet father the image of the unloving son looks forth' (249). This has implications for the future too, for the moment of creation is one in which past, present and future come together. *Ulysses*, though set in 1904, is written at the mercy of all those later moments of its enunciation from 1914 to 1921. It may tell even more about the present in which its lines are composed than about its actual subjects, just as Stephen's portrait of the author of

Hamlet reveals even more about himself than about Shakespeare: 'So, in the future, the sister of the past, I may see myself as I sit here now but by reflection from that which then I shall be' (249).

The son who repeats his father, like the text which recycles an epic, should not be a mere copy. For every true father is repelled by the image of other males of his blood, seeing in them botched attempts of nature to repeat himself. But nature, like the moles on a human body, never does exactly plagiarise itself. Stephen's theory describes not only the bad father Simon, who has his eyes and his weaknesses, but also the future instructor Bloom, who sends a lordling to woo for him by proxy (Boylan) and assumes a sort of Don Giovannism on Sandymount Strand. The true guru will often work more by instinct than deliberate example, being innocent of the wisdom which he himself communicates. In a similar fashion, Joyce may be quite unconscious of *some* of the wise teaching in his book. For all his modernist mentality, Stephen shares in the Victorian view of Shakespeare as someone who shows us how to live: 'he passes on towards eternity in undiminished personality, untaught by the wisdom he has written or the laws he has revealed. His beaver is up. He is a ghost, a shadow now, the wind by Elsinore's rocks' (252). But the Bard of Avon's ghostly presence pervades many scenes of *Ulysses*, as injunctive in its way as old King Hamlet.

Two methods of education are put to the test by Stephen's theory. The first is Socratic, based on the method of '*solvitur ambulando*', discoursing while walking. Socrates allowed his students to try out ideas, to learn from their own mistakes, to go wrong in order that later they might go right. Stephen believes that even the errors of a genius like Shakespeare are never mistakes but 'portals of discovery' (243); and that the critical interpretation of Shakespeare as an English pragmatist went astray in the imperial decades of the nineteenth century before being set to rights by artists like Walter Pater and Yeats. This is another version of the 'triumph of failure' argument, pioneered by Wilde and Pater, then reimported into Ireland by Yeats and by the rebels of 1916, before being codified for all time by Samuel Beckett. The method of Socrates was as far as possible to get other persons to speak the truth: but the rich old irony here is that Stephen must do most of the talking himself. Bloom, in fact, is far more Socratic, acting like a sort of chemical element placed in a solution to bring out the truth through his effect upon others. Like Socrates, he, being godlike, knows far more than he seems to.

The second method applied by Stephen is Scholastic and derives from his training with the Jesuits. The Scholastic submits and defends a proposition, which can then lead to 'disputation' in the medieval style. Unlike the Scholastics, however, Stephen doesn't believe in his own theory, preferring to follow the example of Oscar Wilde who subverted his own *Intentions*, another classic 'symposium', by having its main sponsor admit that he no longer believed the case he was advancing with such brio. Stephen, likewise, may be seen to triumph in his intellectual 'failure', by detaining an audience of elders with a theory in which he doesn't really believe. His refusal to publish it may be due in part to his contempt for what he has created; or it may, more likely, imply a scornful rejection of his immediate audience of intellectual

151

inferiors by an artist who saves it cannily for publication here in *Ulysses*. One thing is clear: his cleverness is wholly redundant in his situation. The theories of Aristotle and Aquinas taught at school and college do *not* solve the problem of his relationship with his father. Russell was right at the start of the debate to say that *Hamlet* brought eternal wisdom: 'All the rest is the speculation of schoolboys for schoolboys' (236). Stephen himself feels deformed rather than illuminated by a Jesuit education which is no practical help to him in facing life's challenges: 'What have I learned? Of them? Of me?' (276).

Immediately afterwards, he senses a new presence, 'feeling one behind' (279), and makes way for Leopold Bloom. It is at this moment that he resolves to break with Mulligan, false friend and fake intellectual, and is haunted once again by the premonitory dream of the strange eastern man holding out a melon in the street of harlots. He leaves the Library: 'Life is many days. This will end' (276). In fact, Stephen all through *Ulysses* seems constantly in the act of leaving – land, tower, school, friends, newspaper office, now the National Library. But for anyone in *Ulysses*, 'going' is an act which is fraught (like the 'sinkapaces' taken by the librarian who goes back and forth on his own two feet). If Odysseus dallied long about returning home, so does Stephen about leaving, and so does Bloom about every single move he makes. *His* eastern quietism and ability to immerse himself in the everyday may hold the ultimate lesson for Stephen as agonised intellectual: 'Cease to strive' (280).

10. Wandering

From the interior world of *Hamlet*, *Ulysses* turns to mostly exterior depictions of life in the city streets. It moves also, in a manner that must have been baffling to early readers, from a focus on Stephen and Bloom to a focus on peripheral characters, each of whom might have been central in a different kind of book. Cubist painters, at the time Joyce wrote, were challenging the idea that the subject of a painting was more important than its background. Similarly, in *Ulysses* anyone could be a hero, anyone might be given an interior monologue. The episode is cut up into nineteen sections, some of which describe the same moment from different angles, as when Molly Bloom throws a coin to a begging one-legged sailor. This is also a cubist technique, recalling paintings in which apples or wine bottles were seen from many aspects and diverse planes. Ways of seeing were as important to Joyce and to the cubists as the thing seen.

Some have read the episode as a map or guide to *Ulysses*, with each section representing one or other of the episodes. Joyce was certainly a lover of guides. 'If that fellow was dropped in the middle of the Sahara,' said his proud father when James was only six, 'he'd sit, be God, and make a map of it.' But a map of a book only half written? 'Wandering Rocks' was mostly composed near the end of Joyce's labours, but is inserted in the centre of things, being at once a baffling maze and a reassurance to the reader that the author *is* in control and that the work will finally be finished. This is, however, yet another moment when the reader is required to take full command of the act of interpretation. He or she may feel lost in a labyrinth, which is exactly how Joyce wants readers to feel.

Why is it all so complicated? All through the book, Joyce has worried about the brutal fashion in which his own narrative, like the plot of history, negates real potentials which once existed. By focusing on the city as a whole, he allows it to stake its claim as an entity, but he also restores the claims of many secondary characters on our attention. At the same time, false leads abound – a pot boiling on a stove contains shirts, not the food hoped for by a hungry young Dedalus child; a man named Bloom turns out to be a dentist, not Leopold; a watch is 'reset', but only in a pocket. These confusing leads, in which inevitably too much energy is invested and thereby wasted, are the opposite of real potentials. Joyce seeks to capture not just the openness but also the randomness of life, something which it is almost impossible to do in a neat narrative.

The episode is framed at both ends by accounts of a progress through the city by church and state, by Father John Conmee and the Viceroy. Conmee is accorded interior monologue and the Viceroy isn't, as if to suggest that at least this colonial administration lacks a significant inner life. Conmee travels on public transport, the Viceroy in a splendid cavalcade. E. M. Forster observed that in India military officials travelled first class in trains, feeling only the need to rule over a people, but missionaries went in third-class carriages, because they had to know the mentality of Indians, if ever they were to make a counter-claim on their souls.

Conmee, whose very name hints at self-deception, is permitted to expose his own shortcomings through his inner voice. Once again, interior monologue works to satiric effect and to the discredit of the soliloquist. Although an ordinary Irishman, he bears himself like a missioner, bound for the less fashionable north side of the city as on a voyage among the heathen. He compares himself to St Peter Clavier, a fellow Jesuit who worked to save souls of 'black and brown and yellow men' (285). Conmee fancies himself a liberal, holding that unbaptised souls are not necessarily lost. He has read and admired a book, *Le Nombre des Élus*, which says that the number of God's chosen elect may be higher than people say: and to Conmee it seemed 'a pity that they should all be lost, a waste, if one might say' (286). This holy priest is all for restoring possibilities that have been ousted. After all, this view will emerge in the later 'Oxen of the Sun' episode as the very basis of Catholic opposition to contraception: nobody has the right to remove a potential life from a narrative.

Names are repeated *ad nauseam* in Conmee's discourse, and always cumbersomely, with their full titles attached: Mr David Sheehy MP. That alone might serve as a retrospective justification of the variation of names in the previous episode, which prevented boring repetition of lines like 'John Eglinton said'. Here, however, it is linked to the new sense of respectability, so fragile and precarious, of an emerging Catholic upper-middle-class Ireland, still unsure of its rule, needing constantly to coach itself on how to act, as if not yet fully convinced of the truth of it own existence. Passing schoolboys, when requested, post a letter for Conmee – see, the system is working! But the words in which the Jesuit reminded himself of the need to post it recall British military cliché ('lest he forget', 281) and the invincible regionalism of his Catholic class ('That letter to father provincial', 281).

The obsessive and finicky use of titles is the tell-tale sign of a toadying culture. Conmee is heroicising himself, as a knight of Ignatius Loyola, by imagining his every action in the objectivity of a third-person narrative, Caesar-style. In fact, the narrative voice is neither fully inside nor outside his head; rather it produces phrases and gestures attached to him by formula, as if he is impersonating the sort of Jesuit he thinks he ought to be. The suggestion is of a man who feels himself caught between a role and a self, not fully at home in either. Joyce was only too well aware of the painful pretensions of this new bourgeoisie, trying to keep up appearances on a little recent wealth. By the time he was writing 'Wandering Rocks', the old deference towards this class and their British overlords had been shattered by World War I and by the Easter Rising.

The Rising is the great, unmentionable fact which hovers behind so many episodes of *Ulysses* – the setting of 'Aeolus' near the Post Office which provided its head-quarters; the 'triumph of failure' motif in that episode and in the Library scene; the blood sacrifice theme of 'Lestry-gonians'; and the Viceregal cavalcade here. Joyce knew well the personalities of the upper-middle-class Catholic constitutional nationalists blown away in 1916. But he also felt that he himself had been, in a prior sense, blown away by them. For no 'nice girl' from that social group would ever marry a boy like him from Cabra, a lad such as he was in his final college years. He was an acceptable and amusing presence at parties of the Sheehy family, where he did his parodies of the Queen in *Hamlet.* Hanna Sheehy's advanced ideas of suffragism, shared with her husband Frank Skeffington, conditioned his portrait of Bloom's androgyny, even down to the detail of his being given a female as well as male name, Leopold Paula Bloom. But the young Joyce had also called himself a socialist artist: and in an essay titled 'Home Rule Comes of Age', he had proposed that little good would come of that group's take-over. As early as that essay, written for a Triestine news-paper in 1907, he had painted a devastating portrait of a local elite collaborating with a colonial occupier. 'The Irish parliamentary party has gone bankrupt,' he lamented:

> For twenty-seven years it has talked and agitated. In that time it has collected 35 million francs from its sup-porters, and the fruit of its agitation is that Irish taxes have gone up 88 million francs and the Irish population has decreased a million. The repre-sentatives have improved their own lot, aside from small discomforts like a few months in prison and some lengthy sittings. From the sons of ordinary citizens, peddlers, and lawyers without clients they have become well-paid syndics, directors of factories and commercial houses, newspaper owners, and large landowners. They had given proof of their altruism only in 1891, when they sold their leader, Parnell, to the pharisaical conscience of the English Dissenters without extracting the thirty pieces of silver.

'Wandering Rocks' is a remote-lens view of ordinary citizens moving through the maze of the Edwardian city, but it frames their struggles within the prevailing regimes of Christ and Caesar. Stephen's inability to give his starving sister money is shocking. It is understandable if not forgivable, because he does not want to get sucked back into the family's cycle of poverty. Yet even his own father, with less ready money to command that day, gives something. Molly's donation to the crippled sailor is probably tainted by bad conscience. However, the pervasive feeling, as through the entire book, is of a people under intolerable economic pressure.

The various sections of the episode might be placed in any other order, for their randomness is part of their point: but the fact that Joyce went to such trouble to invent a Viceregal procession and to top-and-tail the chapter with Conmee and the Viceroy suggests an anxiety on his part to dramatise those twin forces that repressed Irish life. In such a context, it's hardly surprising that Mrs M'Guinness, a pawnbroker, should have 'such a queenly mien' (282). Like the morning milkwoman, she is just another example of the Gaelic *aisling* gone wrong.

As Father Conmee proceeds on his mission along Malahide Road, he passes a field of cabbages, 'curtseying to him with ample underleaves' (287). The motif of the raised skirt will be repeated moments later, when a young couple emerge guiltily from a hedge and the woman lifts her skirt to remove a twig. The raised skirt will become a leitmotif recurring through the rest of *Ulysses*. But that line about curtseying cabbages reads like an insolent mockery of Conmee's complacency and self-regarding imperiousness. It is paralleled by a sentence recording in even more ambiguous style a formal salute to the Viceregal cavalcade: 'From its sluice in Wood quay

wall under Tom Devan's office Poddle river hung out in
fealty a tongue of liquid sewage' (325).

There is a sense of resentment bubbling not far below
this city's consciousness. If its skirts are lifted only a little,
much trouble is nonetheless brewing. The surrealists
sought to disclose the unconscious, and in this city that is
symbolised by the sewers. From one of them, Tom
Rochford has rescued a man overcome by gas, and as a
consequence he is a hero. But in this episode and in this
book, almost anybody might be, even the reader finding a
way, Odysseus-like, through the maze. The surface calm
of a provincial Edwardian city on a sleepy summer's
afternoon is deceptive. Not far beneath is a stress on poor
sanitation, widespread debt, much unemployment and
economic frustration among the workers, but also among
sections of the middle class.

There may be yet another reason why the Viceroy has
no lines of interior monologue: to suggest that he is
completely subsumed into his role, a *type* rather than a
person, one who cannot aspire even to the bogus glamour
of being dispossessed of personality. Very few passers-by
respond to him. Some who do notice mistake him for the
Lord Lieutenant or Long John Fanning, city sheriff.
Others treat him with indifference, coldness, or the
stroking of a nose. The barmaids at the Ormond, who
seem to look on in admiration, turn out at the start of the
next episode to have been simply assessing the clothes
and mocking the vanity of their male wearers. The
predominant feeling is that the Viceroy himself may be no
more than a passer-by, someone disengaged from the
society around him. If the smug Catholic upper middle
class was blown away by the rebellion, the uninvolved

British rulers are also shown to have been off guard and out of touch with a people whom they claimed to be helping. Both Stephen and Bloom are untouched by the governmental cavalcade.

For Dublin is both a colonial and an anti-colonial city, in which these forces are not just opposed but also sometimes interpenetrated by one another. The intimate enemy may offer many bribes, from Haines's cigarettes to an efficient tram system, but all the time citizens will find their own ways of withholding consent. Cashel Boyle's rebellion against church and state may take the form of walking outside lamp posts; Bloom's is to recreate everyday life as a form of resistance to heroic narrative – making good tea as opposed to insincere communion; creating a useful advertisement rather than theorising emptily about art; giving five shillings (beyond expectation) to the Dignam fund, instead of holding forth about love. In a city where everyone, from rulers to ruled, appears to be marginal, the sense of being an outsider which he suffered from in the earlier scenes suddenly seems quite normal for all: as if this is more like the true state of things in a society yet to be made. If Bloom emerges now as representative of many other citizens, he also becomes a version of the reader, excited by but also anxious to decode the private signs all around.

The Dublin of 1904 might be a collection of villages, but it had been well and truly penetrated by the English language and the British presence. There was no 'native quarter' left, such as might have been found in an Arab or African city, which a romantic visitor like Haines could enter in search of a *frisson*. Nighttown, to be dramatised later in 'Circe', was largely a creation of British soldiers, their doxies and some local dissidents. It was hardly a version of an 'elsewhere' or of a Dublin Unconscious. Even the Gaeltacht of the western seaboard seemed to offer the young of Stephen Dedalus's generation a performance of Irish-speaking rather than the real thing. The only zones of alterity left were inside the human head, a place into which you were driven, where you might *think* many things which you could not necessarily *say*. 'Wandering Rocks' shows a city in which the facts were mostly brutal, and the dreams consequently unreal. But there would be no final fusion of the *is* and the *ought* in a vision of redemption until the later episodes of *Ulysses*.

Already, even in 'Wandering Rocks', there are hints of that potential. The streets are the dwelling-place of the collective: and the street people, many of whom are unhappy at home, are enthusiastic users of public space. Although it was a colonial capital, the ruling Anglo-Irish aristocracy was present in Dublin only for a short 'season'. For the greater part of the year, its members were in the countryside or in London, so that citizens could feel that the streets really did belong to them. For Joyce a city was the true repository of a civilisation, especially in the era of the civic bourgeoisie, who (like the more socially minded members of the Anglo-Irish aristocracy) knew how to sublimate private display for the sake of public good in libraries, museums, and art centres.

This blend of entrepreneurship and idealism, designed to translate the private-personal into urbane art, is the project underlying *Ulysses*. The streets teach good lessons, encouraging people to look after one another, to care for the weak (the blind stripling or crippled sailor). Even the eccentricity of a Cashel Boyle provides a defence against anonymity, allowing citizens a strongly personal signature, so that they might remain colourful to themselves. The fear of conformism, of getting lost in the crowd, has produced in Cashel Boyle O'Connor Fitzmaurice Tisdall Farrell an extravagance of manner, whereby self-esteem is saved through the fact of being noticed by others, not for the meaning of an activity but simply for being 'different'. Such persons, in a city of connected villages, recall the 'characters' more easily articulated in a rural world. For the appeal of *Ulysses* is as much to the past – Dublin as a sort of pastoral community – as it is to the future, the uncreated forms of a new kind of urban space in which a person could simultaneously enjoy the benefits of an organic community and of the metropolis. The colour of Dublin life in 1904 may have been rather similar to that ascribed by George Simmel to the *polis* of ancient Athens, in which 'a people of incomparably individualised personalities were in constant struggle against the inner and external oppression of a deindividualising small town'.

The procession traced by the Viceroy recalls in some ways the funeral cortege of Paddy Dignam, and this gives it a deathly quality as if its power has all but gone. That, in turn, has led commentators to assume that the hour between 3 and 4 p.m. is the sleepiest part of this day, when nothing much happens. But Joyce knows differently. If this is a false calm, he subtly alerts the reader to much that is happening beneath the textual surface, even at the level of plot.

In Thornton's shop Boylan presumptuously sniffs and fondles fruit, as if forbidden, making himself too much at home, as he will soon be too much at home in Eccles

Street. He lies nervously but brazenly that the fruit is for an invalid. He looks down the shopgirl's opened blouse at her breast, likened to 'a young pullet' (292). This is all the interior monologue given to him in the entire book. 'It is', as Richard Ellmann writes, 'as if coarseness had no consciousness.' No wonder that the packed peaches are blushing. Molly, also nervous and guilty before their assignation, throws her coin to the sailor. Father Conmee has money but refuses to give alms (as Stephen refuses his sister), whereas Bloom gives generously to the Dignams. Public opinion seems suddenly to turn in his favour. M'Coy says that there is much kindness in the Jew, while Wyse Nolan praises his giving nature. Most of the characters in this episode were real people in Dublin 1904, yet Bloom, the invented one, turns out to be the most complex and the most memorable. The real, by contrast, are 'flattened', as if Joyce were seeking some form of revenge on a city which seemed to have no use for him. Yet such is the subtlety of his protagonist that the zone between the real and the factual is boundaryless.

The more time elapses in the book, the better Bloom shines. While Stephen at a bookstall studies a volume designed to advise him on how to seduce a lady, Bloom considers purchasing *Sweets of Sin* in hopes that it might interest Molly. As he scans certain passages ('Frillies . . . for Raoul', 303), he plans to use the text as a sort of code which will let Molly know that he is aware of what's going on – whether in dismay or in fascination is not quite clear. In an earlier passage in this episode, Lenehan had jocularly recalled a night in a carriage at Glencree, when Bloom had been so busy studying the stars that Lenehan had time to feel his young wife's 'orbs'. This is Joyce's

ULYSSES AND US

joke at the expense of all systematisers, who are prone to
miss the homely things happening under their very nose
(perhaps even a warning against those who would over-
systematise *Ulysses*). Theory is only one thing; practice
something very different. At the book's end, Bloom will be
joined in his star-gazing by Stephen, as both men share a
piss under Molly's window.

Of course, Bloom may have known exactly what was
going on in the carriage at Glencree, finding another
man's interest in his wife as fascinating as he finds the
Boylan caper. It's no accident that, just after Lenehan
opines that there's a touch of the artist about Bloom (yet
another of his developing links with Stephen), he is seen
studying a work of pornography. The 'blooming stud' –
Bloom's, as well as Master Dignam's – may be too small
for its designated hole (323), a possibility raised also by
Lenehan's mocking reference to 'pinprick' (301). Once
again, however, out of an unpromising scenario in which
'the lad stood to attention anyhow' (301), Lenehan is
forced to sing the praises of the maligned and wronged
man. Boylan, who has now taken Lenehan's place as
usurper, will win a victory as empty as Lenehan's. His
secretary, meanwhile, is reading *The Woman in White*,
but finds it filled with too much mystery: 'Is he in love
with that one, Marion?' (294). It looks as if Miss Dunne,
without ever quite realising it, is displaying some
prophetic powers.

Bloom's own semi-divine powers are confirmed by his
discarded handbill ('Elijah is Coming!'), as it floats,
seemingly meaninglessly, along the Liffey waters out into
Dublin Bay. This seems yet another false lead. However,
it will later become clear that Bloom could be the prophet

164

of a new dispensation (so the handbill *did* mean something) and an inadvertent prophet at that (since a throwaway remark of his leads to a winning tip on the Gold Cup). Potentials which appeared to be lost are never really gone. This could be why Stephen, at the bookstall, is so taken by the eighth and ninth Books of Moses: for these were 'lost books', which left the peoples of the Old Testament with only half-knowledge of how to resolve their crisis. They were believed to contain prophetic wisdom. Stephen may hope to find in them a self-understanding which his own earlier training couldn't give, even though he came upon these books by accident in a bad translation on a bookstand for cheap cast-off texts.

In an episode so devoted to the random, all systems are suspect. These are the moments in which Stephen resolves to leave Ireland, having been warned by his music teacher, Almidano Artifoni, against succumbing to depression and self-torture. 'I, too, was convinced, when young, that the world was a beast,' he says in Italian (293). Advised to stop sacrificing himself, Stephen plans to go, but not to take up the singing career recommended by Artifoni. In the maze that is Dublin, some paths can be followed; others will not be taken. Even a hero comes, as in the epic, to a moment of choice; and Joyce also, at the centre of his tale, must explore the *what if* moments. Although there is a great deal of dialogue in the episode, the talk is so inconclusive that not much is advanced by conversation.

The patterning of the episode can seem at once systematised and chancy, just like *Ulysses* as a whole. For example, John Parnell is depicted playing chess in the Dublin Bakery Company, but he disdains to look up from the board at the Viceroy, for he can recall how the English destroyed his brother. Of course, all the people in this episode are like figures and pawns making circumscribed moves on a chess board. Conmee, like a bishop, moves diagonally. The Viceroy is like a king-piece caught up in an endgame, on no account to be moved in a way that would expose him to attack, but given protection at every turn. Now, however, because he has been foolishly placed out in the centre of things, he may have to take the consequences. Ordinary people are, of course, the pawns.

Joyce 'knows' the near future in a book set in the recent past. Just as the Books of Moses telescope future and past time into their own moments, so the Rising of 1916 may be seen as latent in the conditions of 1904.

If Joyce is sardonic in his treatment of the Viceroy, he is utterly sarcastic about the way in which Haines, unable to find a native quarter to enter, must settle for buying Douglas Hyde's *Love Songs of Connacht* and for sampling real Irish cream. Already, the demeaning overlaps between Irish Studies and tourism are being noted, as a group of English visitors progress past Trinity College. Such touristic activity will lead, like Haines's notebook, to a sentimentalising of that backwardness which Stephen, like most of his compatriots, wishes only to extirpate. When told that Stephen intends to write something in ten years, Haines says rather caustically, 'Seems a long way off . . . Still, I shouldn't wonder if he did after all' (321) – another of those remarks which recall the reader to the book now in hand. Stephen feels very hurt because he hasn't been invited to the literary soirée; but already the 'answer' that is Ulysses has begun to take shape in a tale which will come to a climax when Bloom, intuiting but not knowing his sense of grievance and exclusion, will invite him to his own home instead.

The brief vignettes of this episode have been described as filmic and so they are, like those early movie 'shorts' which show a coin being thrown or people taking a book in hand, just to demonstrate how movement rather than mere stillness can now be rendered on camera. But the shards are also like the fragmented sections of a recovered bardic poem; it's not at all clear just what order they might be placed in (a problem also with elements of the eighth and ninth Books of Moses). While offering to fill out the wider social panorama, 'Wandering Rocks' as a collection of shards which do not amount to a linked narrative is a paradigm of the refusal of *Ulysses* to become a novel. Each fragment has limited levels of meaning but each is pushed away from the structure of sequential plot towards a form of simultaneity. No longer is it just the previous twelve or twenty-four hours which weigh on the minds of the characters. Now there is a further condensation down to the 'quiet hour' between three and four o'clock, on the dailiest day in a sun-drenched city of Edwardian paralysis. What is celebrated, amid that paralysis, is the random, uncontrollable circulation of bodies through the streets.

11. Singing

The opening pages of 'Sirens' have been called an overture, that introduction to a musical piece which puts listeners in the mood with examples of melodies to follow. Walter Pater had said that all the arts aspire to the condition of music, and Joyce wished to see how close he could bring language to pure melody. In this episode, he uses music to continue his tests at the limits of language.

Some of the early paragraphs read like finger exercises in musical scales, ringing changes on the same set of words:

> Miss Kennedy sauntered sadly from bright light, twining a loose hair behind an ear. Sauntering sadly, gold no more, she twisted twined a hair. Sadly she twined in sauntering gold hair behind a curving ear (331).

The repetitions and inversions underscore the redundancy of Miss Kennedy's self-caressing gesture; but the whole episode is, also, about the many different ways of playing the same limited set of notes. It should be remembered that the Irish had become English-speaking only in the previous two generations. Their discovery of the expressive potentials of English still had the freshness and excitement of surprise. Joyce was not the only one to deviate from the approved routes of standard grammar, for J. M. Synge had noticed on the Aran islands a similar tendency in people who continued to think in Irish while using English words: 'She plays continual tricks with her Gaelic in the ways girls are fond of, piling up diminutives and repeating adjectives with a humorous scorn of syntax.' This sort of playing with words is something which Joyce also does much of the time.

After the Great Famine of the 1840s and the rapid shift from Irish to English in most parts of the country, people felt as if they had been set down in a strange place with only a smattering of the new language, so they had to improvise. The early experience of any foreign language is mainly musical, a matter of pure sound, before meaning supervenes. In that transition there will be many loan words, such as 'bothered' for 'deaf' (used here of Pat the waiter). Simon Dedalus may say that Italian is the only language to sing songs in, but it sounds romantic to him because he knows scarcely a word of it. Even in 1904 the Irish were still learning to master English, so some of the sentences in the episode read like parodies of a school primer: 'Bald deaf Pat brought quite flat pad ink. Pat set with ink pen quite flat pad' (359). The barmaids, Douce and Kennedy, make great play with two things: their use of impressive figures of speech ('with the greatest alacrity') and their ability to read, an accomplishment which they make sure that the men in the bar can witness and admire.

That feeling of being suddenly confronted by the challenges of a new language is, of course, the experience of most readers as they work through *Ulysses*. Often the reader is expected to decode material without necessarily enjoying full knowledge of who is speaking. This is also true here of Bloom who listens to songs and voices coming from a nearby room. Such disembodied voices were becoming commonplace by 1904 in the age of the electronic recording. These voices connect also with those episodes of *Ulysses* which lack a named narrator. The overall effect is to make the reader feel as if he or she has been set down in a zone at once familiar and strange, like a Robinson Crusoe placed suddenly among the denizens of a modern city.

A spoken word sometimes poses a problem, for the same sound can denote more than one word: 'Blew. Bloom is on the rise' (329). But writing the words down confronted Joyce with the fact that a single choice must be made. He always asked that passages of his book be read aloud, because the reciter could supply with an appropriate vocalisation the rich play of possible meanings. In doing as much, he may have recalled the bardic tradition of Ireland before 1600, when authors had their texts performed by a professional reciter to accompaniment by a stringed instrument. Yeats had already attempted to revive the tradition by commissioning Arnold Dolmetsch to make a psaltery, whose thirteen strings might be plucked in time to the recital of his poetry. If the *fili* of Gaelic Ireland felt no need to make a choice between words and music, their detachment from one another after 1600 was something that Joyce regretted, another possibility 'ousted'. 'Sirens' is really an intensification of an attempt throughout *Ulysses* to apply musical techniques to all kinds of scenes: the monologues of Gerty and Bloom in the next episode are like a duet, just as Stephen's in the Library was an aria.

The laments for the dead in songs like 'The Croppy Boy' were also bardic in their suggestion that somehow the land might be redeemed by human self-sacrifice. However sentimental their appeal, Joyce knew that such lyrics helped to restore a national sentiment that came to a climax in 1916. The men gathered around the pub piano partake in a cult of death. They feel that they are like ghosts, 'Down Among the Dead Men'. Ben Dollard self-pityingly has 'the fat of death' about him; and even Boylan is 'dressed to kill' (371). No wonder that the piano is likened to a coffin. Like Gerald Ward in the Viceregal cavalcade, the men are 'killed looking back' (331); and the barmaids conclude that they are idiots. By their sheer presence, the two barmaids affect all that the men do: they may caress their hair, as if internalising the male Other, but they also despise men like Ward for being so easily manipulated. Such men are all in danger of commemorating themselves to death.

The barmaids affect gentility, describing the imper-tinence of the servant boy as 'most aggravating' (332). They stand beside the 'reef' of their counter, their shoes and stockings cracked and dirty like the unseen fishtails of beautiful mermaids, while their satin blouses shimmer. As 'Bronze by gold', they are described in terms of coin-age, with Joyce cynically pricing their respective blouses (two shillings and ninepence, two shillings and seven-pence a yard). They are employed not to sell their actual bodies but rather the image of them. Lacking a focused sexuality of their own, they cast a vaguely sexual aura over everything they contemplate. So a man's greasy nose causes Miss Douce to go into peals of laughter at the thought of being married to him. Yet there seems to be fascination amid her repulsion, for she is left feeling all wet. The panting and sighing of the barmaids produce many false orgasms, by way of anticipating Boylan's real one that afternoon. Teasingly, the maids play with the desires of the men in the bar, unlike the more honest Molly, who will refuse to play sexual games that do not satisfy her.

The musical performances through the episode allow Joyce to reprise some of the situations of Romantic opera. Miss Douce withdraws a satiny arm from an admirer's grip and says, 'Don't make half so free till we are better acquainted' (358) – and the flirtatious phrase might come from any of the songs rendered around the piano. She enjoys her sexual aura. In the passage which begins 'A baton cool protruding' (369), she becomes in effect the conductor of this all-male orchestra. As her hand lightly touches and slides down the knob, she becomes a version of Molly arousing Boylan. But the sexuality of the barmaids is all virtual, as when Lenehan asks one to lift her dress and whack a garter against her leg, another use of the 'raised skirt' motif. The Sirens, protected by the counter which is their coral reef, are not real come-ons: and so Bloom checks his tendency to bask in their winsome smiles, for he knows they do that for all men. Likewise, he can imagine Molly's last look in the mirror to survey her appearance before she answers the door to Boylan. As always in such scenes, Bloom has more empathy with the woman than with the man.

In the *Odyssey* the song of seduction and danger was sung by the women, but here the singers are all men. It is they who assert their masculinity, rather strangely, by singing high notes. (Back in 'Lotus-Eaters' Bloom had wondered whether becoming a gelded castrato might be one way out of his problems.) As Bloom maps a letter to

Martha Clifford on the pad, he thinks he may accompany it with a present: 'Play on her heartstrings pursestrings too' (354). If the female body is an instrument to be played on by a man, this may explain why men do all the singing here. But they must learn how to play the instrument properly. Returned now to the problem of sexual synchrony with Molly, Bloom wonders whether it may be caused by the fact that men and women have different techniques: 'They can't manage men's intervals' (364). The sad implication is that Boylan can play the instrument better than the appointed husband.

If sex is Molly's escape from this impasse, music is Bloom's. It creates social solidarities between the men in the pub (where Bloom is described as 'married' (347) to Richie Goulding who sits beside him) transcending the individual with an oceanic feeling. That note of solidarity, implicit in the call-and-response duet, comes all the more poignantly in a book of lonely monologues. Dedalus's *fermata* closure of a song produces the word 'Siopold!' (356), a conflation of Leopold, Simon and Lionel (whose part Simon sings), as if to suggest a collective orgasm in which individual identity is quite unimportant. That representation of a chord solves the technical problem posed in 'Wandering Rocks', of how to depict various events in a mode of simultaneity, but at a cost of some violence to Bloom's sensitivities, since it is really Boylan's sexual climax which is reached in the crescendo. Bloom, nonetheless, feels himself bathed in sound, just like the moment at the close of 'Lotus-Eaters' when he reclined luxuriously in bath water.

Yet music can also effeminise men, leaving them robbed of their virility – as in Homer's tale. If Odysseus

173

was the true singer of the tale, the Sirens are false ones, threatening to trump his song with their versions, all rooted in the past. To continue to sing of the *Iliad* around a coffin of old battle lyrics would be to become becalmed, at a standstill on the windless part of the island, repeating the same old ditties over and over. Odysseus counters this by a wily resolve to keep on moving, and so does Bloom, who resolves to 'get out before the end' (370). Prior to that, however, Odysseus advises his men to protect themselves by wearing earplugs, while he, more audacious in the leader's role, will tie himself to the ship's mast before listening to the sounds. Like Bloom checking his own impulse to bask in the barmaid's smiles, he is scientific enough to want to experience a pull in order to know precisely what it is that he must resist. The Sirens, still close to ancient mythology, want to draw their victims back into the past: but their outmoded art offers little benefit to modern-day people, among whom only the elite are still given the chance to listen to it (e.g. opera). Bloom, like Odysseus, is not really beguiled by all this music of an earlier time. Listening to the rebel song of 1798, he prefers to ask, 'Who fears to speak of nineteen four?' (368). He knows that the worship of the past in Ireland is often just a way of excusing and escaping the mediocrity of the present.

Although Bloom doesn't sing, he plays in his own way in the Ormond orchestra. If Odysseus was tied by a band to the mast, he tries to distract himself from the arrival of Boylan at the bar by performing stage business with an elastic band. He extends the band repeatedly, as if playing notes on the slack and tautened string, in order to deflect the embarrassment he feels in proximity to his cuckolder.

It might not be fanciful to see in that elastic an image of the stress placed upon his marriage. Eventually, of course, it snaps, raising a doubt as to whether that marriage can survive. There is a touch of male hysteria all through the episode, to be found also in the way in which Bloom shortens words and phrases, like a man in shock.

Joyce never directly describes the act of sexual betrayal, leaving it to the reader and to Bloom to imagine what may have transpired. Yet he drops many hints that Bloom could be conniving in the whole affair, beginning with the observation at the start of the day that his back garden, lying fallow, needed to be fertilised. Lenehan asks for the garter-trick as if it were somehow connected with Boylan's intentions for the afternoon, but he also enquires about the plot of the novel which Miss Kennedy is reading: 'Did she fall or was she pushed?' (340). By some sixth sense, he intuits that Bloom may have contributed to the moment. Bloom may himself derive more pleasure from imagining the scene than Boylan from the actual performance. So it is that, mysteriously here, Bloom plots to earn five guineas from his ad, which would allow him to buy petticoats for Molly, whether as a reward for her escapade (which may even 'jump start' their marriage) or merely as a distraction from Boylan is never made clear.

Molly is herself a figure of some mystery to the men. 'Irish? I don't know, faith. Is she, Simon?' (347), asks Ben Dollard, who finds her hard to pin down. Bloom himself marvels at the unknowability of all married couples, much as Homer did. He would love to have a healthy son and notices how Simon doesn't always recognise his own eldest boy; yet he himself has noticed the similarities

175

between them, most of all their fecklessness. Suddenly, he recalls the scene at the Library:

> I could not see. That fellow spoke. A student. After with Dedalus's son. He might be Mulligan. All comely virgins. (369)

Bloom's interest in Stephen is quite paternal. Listening to the song of the Croppy Boy, he thinks of his lost son Rudy: 'Too late now. Or if not? If still? He bore no hate' (367–8). This leaves open a possibility of recovering their marriage. Although Bloom can at one moment feel that all is lost, turning down the frieze on a doiley in a gesture which reverses that in the morning when he straightened Molly's bedspread, his use of water imagery suggests acceptance of what has happened between her and Boylan: 'As easy stop the sea' (351). Hours later, Molly will use the same image of the sea to explain her adventure, so this line in 'Sirens', which seems to record their sundering, carries also a suggestion that the Blooms are married not just in law but in the profound depths of a shared imaginative life. If neither is possessive, and both can celebrate life's flow, they may yet have a future together. 'Sweets to the sweet', Gertrude's plaint for Ophelia, may be a reference to the sweets of sin, the happy final outcome of an extramarital fling which brings the couple back together.

Hamlet, though mentioned only indirectly – as when Bloom 'ungyved his crisscrossed hands' (357) – is relevant here. If this is the moment when Bloom resolves to take decisive action, it recalls the third act of the play, when Hamlet does the same thing. The play-within-the-play occurred in the Library chapter here, with the idea of a performance creating emotional responses to the moment of imminent crisis. 'Sirens' evokes ideas of betrayal, with Boylan in the role of usurping monarch. Bloom wishes to watch closely both Boylan and barmaids, but prefers not to be seen while doing so, just like Polonius spying from behind the curtain in *Hamlet*, hoping to find out the real state of things. Polonius is killed in Shakespeare's play and Queen Gertrude offers 'sweets to the sweet' to a dead Ophelia. The masquerade of femininity offered by the barmaids is the sort against which Hamlet rails in his complaint to Ophelia, as he, a womanly man, tries to make her more manly in her womanhood, much as Bloom has sought to do with Molly. The prostitute who crosses Bloom's path at the end is introduced to suggest that he hasn't always been faithful himself. Bloom's refusal to take revenge on Boylan is deeply moving. In a more traditional novel, his cuckolding would have led to pistols at dawn and possible death. The moral value of self-restraint pressed all the more strongly on Joyce after the violence of World War I, whose lesson was that past slights should not be taken over-seriously.

'Music hath charms to soothe a savage breast.' Bloom is more keenly analytical about its pleasures than most people would be. Music melts all listeners into a shared orgasmic flow, one that is more communal than individual – and he seems to like it that way. It is hardly surprising, then, that Molly is presented as a communal fantasy more than a distinct person. It may be that quality which attracted him to her in the first place, his desire for that which was already desired by other men. The rhythm of sex, like the rise and fall of the sea-tides, produces desire and then forgiveness, a sound to be heard in the seashell thrown up on the beach (though what is heard is really the pulsing of the listener's own blood). At the end, the episode resolves itself into a summary of its own keynote sounds, as at the beginning.

Part of Bloom's fascination with sounds is rooted in his desire to demystify music. Earlier, he had been sceptical of the seductive power of Latin – now at the words '*mea culpa*' in 'The Croppy Boy', he mocks it again. He is also sharp enough to recognise that the creaking sound made by Ruttledge's door at the newspaper office is not music: 'no, that's noise' (364). Equally, a melody that attracts may be spoilt by poor lyrics. Even performances that please call for close attention to enhance the pleasure: 'instance he's playing now. Improvising. Might be what you like, till you hear the words. Want to listen sharp' (359). Bloom worries that music works too much through a single sense, a concern which might be shared by readers who note the rather caricaturising effect of phrases which repeatedly distort the narrative for the sake of music-related puns.

Music can be further demystified by the recognition that many songs would fall quite flat if reduced to mere numbers. If 'Martha' were reduced to 'seven times nine minus x is thirtyfive thousand' (359), such musemathematics wouldn't work. Any arrangement or permutation is possible, but the actual performance, though delimiting, is the only test of art. The beauty of good music is that you can hear it many times with added pleasure – like reading *Ulysses*. At its best, it may evolve new forms, which work in surprising ways; but the sentimental songs performed around the piano by tired men will not generate such meanings. These men want to retreat into a past which will allow them to forget the unhappy present. Bloom knows, however, that the only justification for going back to earlier art is to reactivate potentials in the past which might answer present or future needs.

The new forms of which he dreams could emerge in unusual ways – a 'sllt', 'mrkgnao', a shout in the street, even in the notion of an emergent nation whose noise might lead in time to newer forms of music. Bloom imagines how the minuet played in the big houses of aristocrats must have sounded ('one: one, one, one, one, one: two, one three four', 364) to the starving peasants eating dockleaves: and he is sarcastic about the rhythms and their meaning: 'look: look, look, look, look, look: you look at us' (364). Recognising, however, that there is music everywhere, he hopes to be the bearer of a more democratic form of the art.

And so he is. His monologues have the improvisational quality of jazz. They are the sounds of the city, a city not centrally planned but made up of additions and accretions, as its composers go along. Bloom celebrates music as an art which can mediate between the physical and spiritual to the point at which those opposites merge. He wishes to move beyond the addictive element – 'thinking strictly prohibited . . . fiddle-faddle about notes' (372) – and one way of doing that is to materialise sound. So he considers the separate instruments in homely terms that may help to democratise music by bringing it closer to the facts of daily experience. The piano is really just a 'muffled hammerfall in action' (339), when tuned by the blind stripling. The sawing of a cellist is compared to a toothache.

In the end, Bloom's scepticism wins out over his fascination. Although music attracts, it is finally too irrational for a man as measured as he. He resolves to get out before the end because he has grown suspicious of the false solidarities created by the music. His perception is that, like the All Hallows communion, such rituals have their beauty but only at the cost of insulting the intelligence. On a more banal level, he is about to fart, after taking a gassy drink; and he is too considerate to fart in the bar, alongside other men. Although he decides to leave before the performance is finished, in a sense he completes it himself, by emitting a tuba-like fart while he reads Robert Emmet's speech at the shop window outside.

12. Drinking

'Good puzzle would be cross Dublin without passing a pub' (69), mused Bloom in 'Calypso'. 'Cyclops' is set mainly in Barney Kiernan's pub at Little Britain Street and dramatises why Bloom is right to be sparing in his use of alcohol. Licensed premises, like many other public spaces in those days, were almost always 'men only' locations. The separation of genders in Dublin 1904 was well-nigh absolute. Women sought from the curates of the local church some of those consolations which men sought from the curates of the local pub. But the all-male ambience of pubs was conducive to maudlin self-pity, outbursts of aggression and outright hysteria, especially after much drink was taken. 'Poor little Willy Dignam' (391), lament the boozers in this scene, their emotion well in excess of their accuracy, before using his death to vent their personal frustrations: 'Is that a good Christ?' (391). They are as sentimental as the men in the Ormond – but now it's an hour later, 5 p.m., and the day's alcohol is taking effect.

The narrator is never identified, in keeping with the theme of 'anonymity' which dominates the episode. He is the 'nameless one', the title of a poem by James Clarence Mangan which Joyce knew by heart. In the *Odyssey* the hero, confronted by the one-eyed monster Polyphemus, pretended that his name was No-Man (Outis), and blinded his antagonist with a burning stake. Much of the reportage here makes satiric play with the anonymous way in which British parliamentarians refer to one another as 'the Member for Bolsover' (rather than use a personal name); but there is no hiding place in anonymity for Bloom, the man who is both Outis (no man) and Zeus (a god). By the episode's end, he will have gone from hero to zero, but not before he has had to brandish a burning cigar at a nationalist zealot, the Citizen (a character based on Michael Cusack, founder of the Gaelic Athletic Association in 1884). The puniness of that cigar as a weapon, when compared with the burning stake, may seem to reduce Bloom; but his littleness is the true condition of his greatness. Joyce uses the incident to suggest that violence is not only wrong but deeply pretentious and that no disagreement can justify killing or injury.

Who is the nameless narrator? A collector of bad debts and someone, therefore, with many connections in the Dublin Castle regime. In a city of chronic borrowers, he is a busy man and his calling leaves him impartially suspicious of all around him. He is never properly introduced, but his garrulous tone assumes treacherous intimacy with his listeners from the outset. He is ferociously critical of Bloom, who has no interior monologue in this section. However, the reader, having come to know Bloom well, can infer what he might be thinking and is likely to take a protective and corrective approach. The malicious narrator is tolerated by the other drinkers, who have reason to fear his sharp tongue and possible future power over them.

The overly critical attitude towards everyone assumed by the debt-collector gives him something in common with John Stanislaus Joyce. Joyce's father worked in such a job for a time and had the nameless one's gift for the colourful phrase, as well as the same bipolar oscillation between hauteur and vulgarity:

> he could fascinate indefinitely with stories told with consummate art, one neatly fitting into another. And these stories would be of a perfectly drawing-room character till suddenly, as if taken unaware, he would slip into the coarse vein and another side of his nature and vocabulary be revealed.

This is the sort of oscillatory technique to be found throughout 'Cyclops', which alternates between a demotic blather, adopted by the main teller, and interpolated rhetorical sections in a second voice, done in a style of Celtic heroism, pompous journalese or bureaucratic report.

Such an oscillation is by this stage characteristic of *Ulysses* as a whole, a version of the constant discrepancy between the richness of interior monologue and the banality of the actual dialogue which breaks such sections up. The negative feelings which the reader will have about all the sections of fustian in this chapter ('In Inisfail the fair there lies a land', 378) may have further implications, inducing a revised and even more caustic view of interior monologue. Those interior monologues, like the patriotic riffs here, are to be seen as more immobilising than their speakers realise – poor compensation at the level of mere rhetoric for a failure to act in the world. The narrow-gauge nationalists blame Jews for the woes of their country, thereby excusing their own failure to take a more purposeful, more intelligent action: and Bloom, as if becoming a little frustrated with his own interior monologues, starts to blurt out things in conversation which might earlier have been contained at the level of thought.

The debt-collector seems to know certain aspects of Bloom a little better than he may know them himself. Bloom's self-proclaimed interest in every passing detail of life is proclaimed excessive here, after he holds forth on the dangers of violent exercise. 'I declare to my anti-macassar,' says the narrator, 'if you took up a straw from the bloody floor and you said to Bloom: *Look at, Bloom. Do you see that straw? That's a straw.* Declare to my aunt he'd talk about it for an hour so he would and talk steady' (410). This voices the reservations which some readers will have felt about the density of interior monologue in earlier sections, where there seemed at times to be a line devoted to every passing second. Not even Joyce could have sustained such a rate; and, from now on, there will be more gaps in time between episodes but those episodes themselves will be less exhaustive.

The use of Celtic heroic narrative in some riffs here represents another possibility once rejected but now re-turning: that Joyce might have had resort to *Cuchulain of Muirthemne* rather than the *Odyssey*. The citizen's hound, Garry Owen, recalls for us the tale of Setanta, hound of Culan – but the turgid prose and absurd epic boastfulness will make every reader glad that Joyce kept well away from Celtic heroics. The juxtaposition of such passages with contemporary journalistic accounts of boxing matches between English and Irish contestants is a typical surrealist technique, developing the counter-newspaper tactic first explored in 'Aeolus'. Dubliners, who profess to be appalled by British cruelty ("They believe in rod, the scourger almighty', 427) nevertheless show a vicarious taste for such violence in the sporting ring, especially when their pet lamb lashes out at the Saxon.

Joyce employs these juxtapositions to suggest that newspapers are merely carriers of the latest forms of folklore. If he wanted to mock inherited models of the English novel, Joyce also sent up all the old Gaelic forms. Here he combines the oral traditions, jokes and snatches of song of a people who might never have committed such things to print themselves. The oral culture is known only in shreds and radiant fragments:

> The curse of my curses
> Seven days every day
> And seven dry Thursdays
> On you Barney Kiernan,
> Has no sup of water
> To cool my courage,
> And my guts red roaring
> After Lowry's lights (404).

– but the rest, which remains unsaved, must be inferred (rather like Bloom's missing monologue here). Accordingly, the gaps in later sections of *Ulysses* mimic those in Cúchulainn and Celtic legend. Joyce has found a way of capturing the instability of Irish literary tradition, but in a form of juxtaposition which makes it available also to the audience interested in modernist art.

The England–Ireland boxing match between Percy and Myler morphs out of another riff describing the execution of Robert Emmet, at which an Oxford undergraduate (possibly Haines) steps forward to claim the hand of Emmet's love, Sarah Curran. The implication is that the

Act of Union was really more a rape than a marriage of equals, and that Haines is a modern-day version of the British officer who stole away Emmet's beloved – a take-over of the independence movement on the terms most favourable to the British. (If England feels these days like a penitent thief, as Haines said, that fact doesn't stop the thief from robbing yet again.) The outpouring of popular hysteria surrounding the hanging links with the sentiment felt by the self-pitying men during the singing of 'The Croppy Boy', suggesting a masochism in the Irish temperament, a strange love of occasions of pain. The cult of 'blood sacrifice', which was promoted in England by writers like Rupert Brooke during World War I and given a particular definition in rebel Ireland after 1916, may explain Joyce's obsession with the theme.

A scene set in Little Britain Street indicts an Ireland which is hardly its own authentic self so much as a not-England – just as England appears to be a not-Germany, with the royal family singing 'Ehren on the Rhine'. The nationalism of modern Ireland is portrayed as a neurotic reaction to Englishness. By the 'ingenious device of national parallelism', Gaelic sports like football can be presented as the antidote to soccer and hockey; the kilt is worn instead of trousers; a convocation of political activists calls itself a Dáil instead of Parliament. The Citizen denounces English landlordism but re-enacts it in forcing the eviction of a tenant. He denounces the 'syphilisation' (421) of his old enemy but often seems intent on building a replica at home.

He laments the deforestation of Ireland. Given that the woods sheltered rebels and rapparees, they might be felt to have symbolised the lost Unconscious of the nation, those secret places in which forbidden but vital instincts were still expressed. But the Citizen's way of restoring those forces is a lot less effective than Joyce's own more radical uncovering of the subconscious. The wedding-list composed entirely of the names of trees (Miss Blanche Maple, Miss Timidity Aspinall, Miss Liana Forest) is written in the best style of provincial English journalism rather than in any daring new form. The founder of the GAA is simply a man determined to prove that the playing fields of Rugby and Eton can have their Irish counterparts. The lost nation which he seeks is really a lost projection of an idealised English identity, for the real Irish nation lies beyond such clichés, in a different place altogether, in the consciousness of Stephen Dedalus and Leopold Bloom. 'What is your nation if I may ask,' says the Citizen, to receive Bloom's reply: 'Ireland, I was born here. Ireland' (43). He knows that a nation is no abstraction, but the reality of the same people living in the same place. 'If that's so, I'm a nation,' says Ned, 'for I'm living in the same place the last five years' (430), a rare enough achievement in the Dublin of 1904.

The Citizen rants in the language of *Cathleen Ni Houlihan*, the play by Yeats and Gregory staged in 1902, that 'we want no more strangers in our house' (420); and, in saying as much, he shows himself to be no different from Mr Deasy, the Orange bigot who similarly blamed a dishonoured wife for Irish misfortunes. He also, like the Citizen, spoke out against the Jews. Once again here, Bloom knows and feels a lot more than anyone else. With his wife in the arms of another man, he is enduring the reality of a condition around which the others merely theorise. This is the moment when he feels impelled to wag his fiery cigar, in a gesture which speaks even more of his personal than his racial predicament:

> – And I belong to a race too, says Bloom, that is hated and persecuted. Also now. This very moment. This very instant. (431)

He is talking about injustice, he insists, not about any New Jerusalem – but it's no use:

> – Force, hatred, history, all that. That's not life for men and women, insult and hatred. And everybody knows it's the very opposite of that that is really life.
> – What? says Alf.
> – Love, says Bloom. I mean the opposite of hatred. I must go now. (432)

All through that scene the men have been toying with Bloom's raw nerves, brazenly enquiring about Molly's concert tour, forcing him into slips of the tongue about his wife's admirers/advisers. The rant against strangers in the house is designed to test him further, as when the joker Alf Bergan produces a newspaper account of a faithless but pretty wife in the lap of a soldier, while the wealthy husband arrives home 'just in time to be late' (420). The suspense which drove the 'Sirens' episode was based on the possibility that Bloom might belatedly tackle Boylan at the bar, but that would have been a submission to the formulas of melodramatic novelettes. So Joyce's attack on cliché all through this section serves to establish Bloom as the more dignified protagonist.

The men in the bar really are neurotics, in the sense that for them Irishness must be in all respects the opposite of Englishness, and masculinity the opposite of femininity. (The bipolar style of the narrative helps to expose this Manichean thinking.) For them, a womanly man who goes shopping for baby food is intolerably subversive of the prevailing heroic code: so abject, indeed, that he may be undergoing something analogous to the monthly menstrual cycle of women: 'Lying up in the hotel Pisser was telling me once a month with headache like a totty with her courses' (439). They believe that such a fellow would adorn a sweeping-brush.

The challenge which Bloom poses for Irish society is radical. He is neither completely masculine nor completely feminine, but pan-sexual. His life is an illustration of the truth that a businessman is not necessarily the opposite of a bohemian (since his touch of the artist enhances his skills as a purveyor of ads). So also in the zone of religious practice, he is a non-Jewish Jew who has been baptised by both Catholics and Protestants.

As a liminal person, Leopold Bloom disrupts the complacencies of all the settled codes with which he comes into contact. 'Is he a jew or a gentile or a holy Roman or a swaddler or what the hell is he?' (438), asks a baffled Ned. He isn't even a cousin of Bloom the dentist, but may be responsible for Arthur Griffith's idea of Austro-Hungary as a model for Ireland. Ultimately, the word 'Jewman', when used of him in disgust by the drinkers, is a code for their own insecurity in the face of so complex a personality. Bloom is, in effect, all that they have rejected in themselves, including the more vital implications of the Christian tradition. Convinced that he has won money on Throwaway but is meanly refusing to stand a round of drinks, they quickly convert him into a Jew, 'all for number one . . . cute as a shithouse rat' (443) – but the abstemious Bloom has no inkling of what they are thinking. When the Citizen continues to taunt him, Bloom finally decides that he *is* a Jew. He adds, 'Your God was a jew. Christ was a jew like me' (445).

After his enforced silences and social tact during the day, this statement has the quality of a prophetic utterance, not of a man seeking a fight but of one simply speaking his truth. Moments earlier the Citizen had disparaged him as the new messiah for Ireland; but now, that same Citizen gives credence to the mocking title by throwing a biscuit tin at Bloom with the cry, 'I'll crucify him so I will' (445). To have spoken of love as a prelude to saying that he would have to leave (as Bloom did minutes earlier) is to have repeated a telling scene in the life of Jesus, a womanly man who was himself Jewish-Christian and who also served as a scapegoat for local frustration. In the final paragraphs of the episode, Bloom is borne away by Martin Cunningham in a chariot, enveloped like a baby in the womb in a prophetic cloud, as he ascends unexpectedly into the heavens, like a shot off a shovel.

It is at this weird but beautiful moment that the two opposed discourses – the heroic-monologic *ought* and the banal-conversational *is* – so long kept opposed in *Ulysses*, finally fuse. The missing flood of feeling which the reader has supplied in the absence of a Bloom monologue flows like a strong tributary into the river of that fusion. Compared with Bloom's beatific ascension, Paddy Dignam's seems a less convincing blending of styles, for in his case lingering everyday concerns (such as his missing second boot) stick out too obviously from the account of his karmic drift. As regards Bloom, it is not so much that he is further estranged from Dublin by his assumption into

heaven as that he is himself the agent of its transformation into a heavenly city, a place touched at last by
the 'divinity' of his presence.

If this epic is inadvertent, so also is this 'god'. In
'Sirens' Lenehan had said 'see the conquering hero
comes' (340), in order to introduce Boylan, but instead
Bloom had walked in. Whenever the possibility of his
prophetic status had been raised, Bloom had been quick
to disclaim it. This is a tradition well established around
all hero figures and religious founders. Odysseus's refusal
to give his name to Polyphemus provides the model, for
when he's bold enough to state his name later, serious
trouble ensues. The Buddha had warned that, if you meet
the Buddha on the road, kill the Buddha. Nor did Jesus
ever claim to be king of the Jews. As we've seen, heroism
can never be conscious of itself as such.

Unlike the religious founders, Bloom's role is not to
teach any great truth in words, but simply to embody a
way of being in the world. At times, his direct attempts to
explain something can seem comic, even ludicrous, as in
his attempt to outline the scientific causes of an erect
penis when a man is hanged. That attempt is laughed to
scorn by drinkers who deride his jawbreakers but feel
even more threatened by his desire, so unusual in Dublin
bars as to appear revolutionary, to reconcile theory and
practice, to link the intellectual and the everyday. The
lives of the men in the pub are devoted, like those of most
other Dubliners from the Jesuits to Mr Deasy, to keeping
such categories absolutely separate. Any androgynous
internationalist who tries to reunite them – especially
when drink has been taken by men busy being not-
English and not-female – has his work cut out for him. In

this episode Bloom makes many practical points of the sort he restricted to the level of thought in earlier scenes, but here he displays less adept social skills. In the kingdom of the one-eyed, the two-eyed man is in mortal danger, if only for looking and sounding omniscient.

Joyce once told Frank Budgen that the narrator of 'Cyclops' was a secret admirer of Bloom; and in the final phase of his account he shows Bloom ascending into heaven. It is as if, after discharging his bilious invective, the narrator is suddenly freed of all that negativity and is co-opted, in spite of himself, into a heartfelt tribute to a godlike human. Such a transformation occurs also at the close of 'The Dead', when a previously cynical Gabriel Conroy was drawn into a silent hymn to his snow-clad nation; and again, at the end of *A Portrait of the Artist as a Young Man*, when a Stephen who had angrily repudiated all patriotic feeling announces his intention of forging the uncreated conscience of his race. This seems to be how the inadvertent epic works – the nay-sayer is suddenly revealed as celebrant. The more the barflies denounce Bloom as a 'mixed middling' (439), the more convincing this man seems in his blend of many attributes to be the spiritual representative of the present and future community.

As a young man, Joyce felt impatience with religious instructors, not for what they taught so much as for their refusal to practise it. 'Cyclops' reads like his last desperate attempt to see whether what he learned as a child could be made real and incarnate in a worldly protagonist.

13. Ogling

Two hours are lost between the previous episode and 'Nausikaa', a huge span in a book whose earlier sections minutely documented every passing moment. During this interval Bloom and Boylan were visiting lonely women – Bloom to comfort Mrs Dignam, Boylan to take his pleasure with Mrs Bloom. At the start of the next episode, Bloom will visit another woman, Mrs Purefoy, at the lying-in hospital.

In the *Odyssey* the encounter between the grizzled old traveller and the king's beautiful daughter is narrated with the same delicacy and tact shown by the couple for one another. Here Bloom's encounter on Sandymount Strand with Gerty MacDowell is free of all speech, yet he muses afterward that it was 'a kind of language between us' (435). If Homer's reader/listener is expected to supply the unspoken feeling, the two interior monologues do so here – Gerty's in what Joyce called 'a namby-pamby jamsy marmalady drawersy style', Bloom's in a more blunt, matter-of-fact idiom. The episode develops the notion of a male/female duet suggested in 'Sirens', even down to verbal echoes of the formula ('Big he and little she', 487; 'Her high notes and her low notes', 488), with both voices blending for a time in mid-episode.

Gerty opens the episode, and with her comes a shift from the macho-heroic language of 'Cyclops' to a dainty exercise in the feminine mode. Joyce sardonically contrasts the masculine tone of Irish Revival writing and the increasingly feminine character of popular culture, which such writing sought to challenge. This is a difficult feat in a land of whose people Synge could mischievously comment that 'every healthy mind is more interested in *Titbits* than in *Idylls of the King*'. But in some aspects at least, Gerty's monologue is revivalist – in its love of aristocratic values ('Had kind fate but willed her to be born a gentlewoman', 453) and in its insistence on the racial quality of her beauty ('as fair a specimen of winsome Irish girlhood as one could wish to see' with eyes of 'the bluest Irish blue', 452–3). She follows old Gaelic superstitions (cutting her hair for luck in love on the appearance of a new moon), as well as the latest advice offered to young ladies in fashion magazines, the modern form of folklore.

T. S. Eliot, Wyndham Lewis and Ernest Hemingway, as well as many other modernist males, saw their art as a counter-move to the feminine–commercial code of popular magazines. They called for an end to the idea of 'poetry for ladies' and a return to what they would consider the harsh, surgical modes of modern life. Joyce's mockery of Gerty's anxiety to convert herself into the fetish recommended by such magazines is a contribution to that programme, but something even more subtle seems to be afoot here: a conflation of masculine and feminine modes, via Bloom, the man brave enough to admit his own femininity.

Gerty is on the beach with her friends Cissy Caffrey and Edy Boardman, looking after children at eight o'clock in the evening. Just as the men in 'Sirens' were constantly aware of the onlooking barmaids, the young women here are aware of the watching Bloom, so their whole demeanour becomes a sort of performance. The cry of baby Boardman seems to carry the promise of new forms of language: 'a jink a jink a jawbo' (450) being 'I want a drink of water'. But Gerty will have no truck with such creativity, for her days and hours are spent carefully repeating only approved phrases. Watching the Caffrey boys build a tower in sand, she recalls that an 'Irishman's house is his castle' (450), but Jacky resists 'improvements' imposed by Tommy – an image of how the Irish are resisting all Tommies, the generic name for British soldiers. Bloom has already displayed a strong motherly streak earlier in the day, and now he is contemptuous of the young women for giving an empty bottle to the baby, who will surely fill up with wind.

Gerty has no desire to be become the mother of children. Although describing the Caffrey boys as 'darling little fellows' (450), later she considers that they are just 'as bold as brass' (462). Her father is an alcoholic and her mother has taken to her bed, leaving Gerty to cope with the mess. It's hardly surprising that, like many girls of the time, she has considered escaping all this by adopting the life of a Dominican nun. Like most of the characters in *Ulysses*, she is not in full possession of herself or of her world. By the late nineteenth century, there were far fewer women in the Irish workforce than there had been before the Great Famine. Most of them had mastered literacy, but they could seldom find paid opportunities to use their skills. Marriage was one obvious answer, but not all young women could hope for it. Her experience tells Gerty that it isn't necessarily an answer at all. Bloom will later fret over the possibility that the boredom of a home life without a child may have driven Molly into the arms of Boylan. In a book of unhappy families, the portents for Gerty are not good. Perhaps this is the real reason why she chooses blatantly inappropriate men as fantasy objects – Reggie Wylie, a mere boy, still far too young for her, and Leopold Bloom, a middle-aged pater-familias, rather too old. Her lack of a partner may be, in many respects, a liberation, even if she feels obliged to maintain an attractive appearance for men.

Does she know that Bloom is masturbating as she lifts her skirt and reveals more and more of her legs to him? The Roman candles of a nearby fireworks display are bursting in the sky, to add to the effect of tumescence and detumescence which Joyce sought in the climax of the exchange. Close by, a group of men are worshipping the exposed body of the Blessed Sacrament at Our Lady Star of the Sea church in Sandymount. Gerty's colour is blue, like that of the Blessed Virgin, and she exists in that climate of ambivalence which surrounded Our Lady in *A Portrait of the Artist as a Young Man* – on the one hand, the lovely virgin beckoned with extended arms, while surrounded by flowers whose buds opened invitingly, but on the other hand, from the self-same altar priests preached their bans on sexual or sensual fulfilment. Joyce voices his protest through Stephen in the Library scene, when he has him complain about the figure of the Madonna 'which the cunning Italian intellect flung to the mob of Europe' (266). In many ways, Gerty may see in that Madonna an image of controlled sexuality: if Mary had a child without having sex, then Gerty here has sex but without the risk of giving birth to a child. Non-penetrative sexuality may suit her, and Bloom, just fine. The poet Donald Davie once described the night-streets of

Dublin as saturated in sexuality, but that was because of the heavy petting engaged in by couples in doorways, before they returned by bus to their families' respective houses. When Gerty walks away from the encounter at the very end, Bloom notices that she doesn't look back, perhaps the sign of her ultimate control.

But who has final power in this scene? Bloom wishes to see but not be seen, so she seems happier with the overall situation. Gerty is not worried that Bloom might be masturbating: in fact she is excited to think she had raised the devil in him. She holds to the view that anything short of full penetration is permissible outside of wedlock: 'there was absolution so long as you didn't do the whole thing before being married' (476). She is advanced enough to believe that there ought to be women priests who would understand female needs. At one moment she denies that Bloom's action is sordid: 'But this was altogether different from a thing like that' (476). Her aim is a more rarified romance, a world away from prostitution, 'the fallen women of the accommodation walk beside the Dodder that went with the soldiers and coarse men', and she prefers that she and Bloom should be 'just good friends' (474).

Although their silent exchange occurs in the gathering dusk, it could hardly be classified as an exercise in the Celtic Twilight mode. Gerty will not turn into Yeats's glimmering girl, who led Wandering Aengus through hollow land and hilly land. And Bloom himself will prove even less dainty than Gerty on the subject of prostitution. In the depressive aftermath of their encounter, as he copes with feelings of self-disgust, he wonders whether Molly could have charged Boylan for his pleasure: 'All a prejudice. She's worth ten, fifteen, more, a pound' (481).

Gerty works hard to seem like the ideal wife, while not actually being one. Molly, though not ideal, is actually a wife. Bloom seems to be using this moment as a rehearsal for his eventual return to Molly, for it is remarkable how often Molly recurs in his thoughts after he has climaxed. The episode reveals him as uncircumcised, a non-Jewish Jew, but also as a still potent male. The very foreignness which led to his suffering in 'Cyclops' has worked to his advantage here, as Gerty is moved by a face which she considers the saddest in the world: 'Why me?' he will ask afterwards, before imagining the answer: 'Because you were so foreign from all the others' (496). The truth is that Gerty would not be a suitable partner for Bloom. She wants a manly man who would crush her to his body and she is critical of the brazen-faced female cyclists whom he fancies. In fact, her friend Cissy, who likes to wear her father's clothes, to whistle out loud and to walk in large strides, seems far more compatible in her gender style – another opportunity lost in *Ulysses*, when she cheekily asks Bloom the time but has to leave the conversation un-developed. Strangely, Bloom's watch has stopped at the time of his cuckolding, presumably because, in his distraction, he forgot to wind it.

The climactic moments of the episode, when both arias merge, are entirely musical, as the Roman candle explodes:

> and it was like a sigh of O! and everyone cried O! O! in raptures and it gushed out of it a stream of raingold hair threads and they shed and ah! they were all greeny dewy stars falling with golden O! so lively! O so soft sweet soft! (477)

Neither Gerty nor Bloom is in complete control at this

moment, as the demarcation between both individuals grows fuzzy. In the ensuing paragraph it appears that Joyce alternates in certain lines between her genteel version of the scene ('a little glance of piteous protest') and his more blunt idiom ('At it again'), before returning to her euphemisms about the flying bats ('and little bats don't tell', 478). Joyce shows amazing technical audacity by moving so swiftly in mid-paragraph from one performer to the other.

In 1982 when Irish radio broadcast the book, there was intense debate among the producers as to which voice, female or male, might utter certain lines. Was 'What a brute' so obviously Bloom's? Or Bloom imagining Gerty's horrified response? Or Gerty taking some pleasure in his guilty look? There was no doubt, however, that it was Bloom who spoke the lines of astounded recognition of her limp:

Tight boots? No. She's lame. O! (479)

That line proves Bloom to be the poet that, so far, Stephen has just played at being. It stops and starts four times, as if in re-enactment of her limp: and at its end her orgasmic sound of all those repeated Os is uttered just a single time, now more quizzical than ecstatic. Three pages later, that open innocent O has been replaced by the more worldly-wise grunt of Ah!, to capture Boylan's moment of satisfaction in Molly's bed:

He did. Into her. She did. Done.
Ah! (482)

Gerty's monologue never really concludes, but is simply interrupted and displaced by Bloom's, which very rapidly begins to list anaemia, squints, female periods and all the other illnesses with which the body beautiful mocks our ideals for it. The still body of Gerty seemed beautiful, but when it moved, a flaw was revealed. Joyce was always suspicious of static portrayals and of men who fantasised about the female body in this way. Consider how Gabriel Conroy, looking at his wife in profile halfway down a stairway as she listens to a singer in another room, decides that he would call the scene 'Distant Music' if he were a painter – the remainder of 'The Dead' is an account of how this fetishist receives his come-uppance, as his wife Gretta restores her body to a real world of process, suffering and lost love.

Joyce sought to cultivate the actual body rather than the 'body beautiful'. If Gerty's monologue is incomplete, neither is her frame perfect. Like *Ulysses* itself, she is an Irish beauty, but one with a deformation. As in all encyclopedic narratives, *Ulysses* must contain an image of its own flawed formation. Bloom partakes in the same sense of incompletion, writing I AM A in the sand with a stick, but then erasing the sentence, because he knows she will never return and the moment has gone.

If Gerty's style is generally flowing, Bloom's is staccato, a return to his usual telegraphic language of the summarising phrase. But some of her phrases, as in the sacred litanies, are Bloomian; and Bloom's single, breathless sentence at the end of his monologue reverts to her style ('O sweety', 458), before a conclusion which blends both. The episode has been built on apparent contrasts between the two protagonists that often resolve into an underlying unity. If Gerty blushes under his gaze, under hers he colours like a girl; if after his climax, she promises 'an infinite store of mercy' (478), he comes in time to appreciate 'small mercies' (479). And so on. The light/dark antitheses in the opening paragraph of the episode are developed through all that follows.

The entire scene is a 'rewrite' of one in *A Portrait of the Artist as a Young Man,* where Stephen discovered his artistic vocation. If on Dollymount Strand all was scaled up as the young man saw a vision of a 'birdgirl', here an older man sees the 'seabird' Gerty scaled down eventually to the status of a cripple (the word is unavoidable here). Stephen, faced with the brazen gaze of a girl who raises her skirts well above the water in which she wades, runs back into the sandhills with a cry of 'Heavenly God!', whereas Bloom simply experiences a sexual pleasure. At Dollymount, with his option to create, Stephen makes art out of reality; on Sandymount, reality is created out of art. The art in this case is that of popular magazines (for which Bloom works and which Gerty reads) and of *The Lamplighter* – the sky reminds Gerty of a setting from a novel of that name.

Popular culture holds the key to these moments. The girl on Dollymount Strand returned Stephen's gaze brazenly, because no nice young lady would enter the waters unaccompanied in the Dublin of the turn of the century; but also, more piquantly, because that was how she appeared in the cigarette-box card on which Joyce based this scene. Stanislaus Joyce took a malicious pleasure in citing this as a possible source for the key scene in which his brother was supposed to have embraced his vocation as a writer. How Stannie would have chortled at the much more recent revelation by Katherine Mullin that the scene in 'Nausikaa' is based on another kind of risqué entertainment, the 'mutoscopes' of

Capel Street mentioned by Bloom. These were machines, operated by a male who entered a booth and cranked a handle. As he did so, young women in the picture showed off their legs by raising their skirts for the cameraman until the viewer – in Bloom-like fantasy, watching without being watched – reached his satisfaction. The whole episode is, in short, an assimilation of this entertainment.

Bloom is discomfited by the clammy after-effect, not to mention the revelation of Gerty's limp. He engages in some quite uncharacteristic moments of misogyny, as if to mask his self-disgust: 'A defect is ten times worse in a woman. But makes them polite' (479). Then he decides that he might still enjoy sex with such as Gerty: 'Curiosity like a nun or a negress or a girl with glasses' (479). This reveals something more than a passing moment of misogyny. Bloom is trying to differentiate himself from the negro, much as Dubliners all through *Ulysses* have tried to map blackness on to one another, mainly it must be said on to Bloom. This now is his act of resistance. Attracted by the racialised Irish beauty of Gerty, he wants to impatriate through her eyes of bluest Irish blue. For this womanly man, the female image can be both a desired partner and a version of the desired self. Because of this, Bloom has fixed his gaze upon Gerty rather than on the more suitable manly woman, Cissy Caffrey. Only when her limp reveals that Gerty is a 'curiosity' does he blacken her.

Even in this gesture, Bloom is trying to feel himself 'normal' vis-à-vis Gerty, a flaw being (he says) ten times worse in a woman than in a man. Earlier Bloom had been dubbed a 'coon' (134) by Menton, 'that whiteyed kaffir' (435) by the Citizen, and 'a bloody dark horse' (435) by Joe Hynes. Evolutionary theory had often placed the Irish a few notches above the negro on the ethnographic scale, with the same prognathous jaw, shallow forehead and thick lips. Back in 'Cyclops', the drinkers in Barney Kiernan's, for all their coarseness, voiced common cause with Africans being defrauded of their resources under the lash of colonialism. It is because the Irish had something in common with Africans that they were fascinated by black-and-white minstrel shows and some desperate souls among them felt compelled to differentiate themselves from people of colour. Whenever a man like Bloom embraces his own womanly element, the female within him cries out for proof that he is, despite this, reassuringly male. After the androgynous styles of long hair and coloured clothes worn by 1960s rock bands came the short hair and strict black outfits of the 1970s punks. Bloom's outburst of racism and misogyny may have similar roots in the personality of a man who feels that he has already conceded too much.

Gerty's monologue reads at times like Bloom's male fantasy, but that could simply be because of the real woman's near-total submission to the world of male desire, coded into product advertising and women's magazines. In the end, such performances of an essential 'femininity' suffer from the same defect which Angela Carter found in all pornography. It purports to describe an ideal relationship between men and women but has nothing to do with actual female desire and everything to do with the man's, being therefore no better than 'a manual of navigation written by land-lubbers for land-lubbers'. Or, as Stanislaus Joyce put it so pithily, in the final analysis men always blame women for being exactly what men have made of them.

Gerty's very anonymity is the source of her high-voltage attractiveness, since it allows Bloom to read whatever he wants into that empty space. It is to protect his own anonymity that he erases I AM A and resolves not to return. Once more Bloom decides not to be decipherable. Thus, the episode recalls Homer's fairytale in which Nausikaa, the king's daughter, never once spoke in the city except to say 'farewell, stranger' to the wanderer, whose name she didn't ever learn; and Odysseus will never speak of her again but pray to her as to a god who has given him life.

Gerty may be more wily than she seems, using the performance of femininity as a screen behind which an alternative set of values – women priests, non-genital sexuality – can be developed. Sex and chastity are not necessarily opposites for her or for Bloom: and what is celebrated at the close by the voice-music is exactly the sort of theosophical masturbatory practice mocked by Mulligan as a case of 'everyman his own wife'. Gerty's problem, however, is rather like that of the nationalists in 'Cyclops': her rebellion is doomed because it is trapped in the very codes which it opposes.

Bloom's quietism seems a preferable mode. His poetic success with a line like 'tight boots' is as inadvertent as the epic that is *Ulysses*, as undeliberated as his success in throwing a stick and making it lodge firmly at the first attempt in the soft sand: 'If you were trying that for a week on end you couldn't' (498). Sometimes, Joyce is suggesting, people achieve great things without attempting anything much at all. Bloom, even as he appears to be rendering homage to Gerty, is already filled with thoughts of how this stick-in-the-mud can come to terms with

Molly. Gerty herself seems to intuit as much: 'Perhaps it was an old flame he was in mourning for from the days beyond recall' (475). And she's right. For no sooner has Bloom forgiven the Citizen's attack ('Perhaps not to hurt he meant', 496) than he is rewarded with a vision of Molly in her Turkish slippers and pyjamas. This is his daylight version of that moment anticipated only dimly in Stephen's forecasting dream of his rescue by Bloom. For all the randomness and humiliation of the moment, events are taking shape nicely.

14. Birthing

Set in the National Maternity Hospital, Holles Street, 'Oxen of the Sun' is the episode in which Joyce's book is finally born, in that its author can now sense that it will take a definite, living shape. Its succession of styles mimics the slow evolution of the English language from Anglo-Saxon to American slang, and its plot-line suggests the nine-month gestation of the foetus in the mother's womb. Early on, Bloom is admitted to the hospital by Nurse Callan ('infare under her thatch', 503); and near the end the child Stephen is born ('outflings my Lord Stephen', 554), emitting the cry of the arriving babe. All that action is metaphorical, of course. In literal truth Mrs Purefoy is the one who gives birth to a boy, after her painful three-day confinement, during the latter stages of which she is visited by Leopold Bloom.

Why are Bloom and Stephen in a maternity hospital at all? There is something a little unlikely about their presence. Bloom has just spilled his seed on the beach, and Stephen has yet to create a significant artwork. Both practise the very forms of birth control which they denounce – and are rebuked accordingly by the narrative voice, which asks, in the case of Bloom, whether he has not at home a seedfield lying fallow. Thwarted in his attempt to achieve fatherhood with a growing son, Bloom recalls a night long ago with the prostitute Bridie Kelly, who 'dare not bear the sunny-golden babe of day', with the result that 'there is none now to be for Leopold, what Leopold was for Rudolf' (541).

Here for the first time in *Ulysses*, an objective narrative voice, not Bloom's, clearly identifies the traumatic effect of the loss of Rudy. Yet, even as he sits with the increasingly drunken medical students in the hospital waiting-room, Bloom is paternal and considers that his companions might be his sons. Perhaps he has come out of kindness to Mrs Purefoy. Earlier that day he had admitted that he could never bear the pain of childbirth. He may also have come out of a desire to share vicariously in the pleasure of the birth as a prelude to facing that experience of hope and fear with Molly one more time.

Because sons were crucial in that patriarchal world, Stephen returns as the main focus of an episode, yet he is surrounded by an atmosphere of frustration and depression. Bloom's sixth sense has alerted him to Stephen's melancholy and brought him to the place where he is consorting with the low-down crowd denounced earlier by Simon Dedalus. It is almost as if Bloom intuits that he could play the protective fatherly role which Simon has in some desperation abandoned. Bloom looks on his friend's son, feeling 'sorrow for his forepassed happiness' (510). Part of Stephen's frustration is his own lack of creativity, a parallel to Bloom's lack of procreativity, for he needs more than 'a capful of light odes to call your genius father' (543). In a truly radical sense, that depression will be finally lifted not just by Bloom's kindness but by the flash of insight in which Stephen learns that he can immortalise his ordinary rescuer in a great book.

The medical students, awaiting the birth, debate whether, when a choice has to be made, the life of the mother or the child should be given priority. Stephen asserts the primacy of the child, perhaps because he believes in the superiority of art to nature (since he is the child-artist of the Dedalus family), or maybe just because this reflects orthodox Catholic thinking at the time. Bloom, still pondering Rudy, is unsure. Art, in Stephen's scheme of things, seems to be produced mainly by men who feel envious of women's birthing power and who therefore seek a compensatory act of creation. Many men in *Ulysses* are intimidated by the centrality of woman to the life-giving process. The jocularity of the students around the table has a hysterical quality, as if they are un-nerved by the procreative power of the nearby women. Even the narrative voice takes refuge from this challenge by jerking from one style to another, from Mandeville through Pepys to Dickens and beyond, no one style of which takes root.

There is something masturbatory about this wastage; and the jerking from one style to the next is made possible by refills of drink, except for Bloom who 'spills' his life-juice one more time, pouring it furtively away. Stephen and Bloom, alone among the inebriated students, refuse to join in the nervous mockery, for they understand that the deed of the Purefoys seems dignified and purposeful in comparison.

With badinage afoot, Mulligan inevitably enters the picture. He joins in pretend-outrage against the practice of contraception, which sees 'the nuptial couch defrauded of its dearest pledges' (526). Implying that Bloom may be impotent, he rudely asks whether he is in need of professional help. That isn't Bloom's problem, of course. His real problem is one which he shares with Mulligan, Stephen and the noisy students – a fear of the female. On Sandymount Strand, Bloom baulked at a first-hand encounter, wishing to see Gerty but not be seen by her. In that he was like the followers of Odysseus, who were allowed to look upon but not touch the sacred cattle of Sicily. The equation between women and cattle emerged as far back as the reference to the morning milkwoman as 'silk of the kine' and in Milly's joke about Mullingar women as 'beef to the heels'.

Joyce told Frank Budgen that the crime against the ancient gods was the sterilisation of the act of coition. One form of this sin, as Stephen freely admits, is the nightly act of masturbation: 'But, gramercy, what of those God-possibled souls that we nightly impossibilise, which is the sin against the Holy Ghost, Very God, Lord and Giver of Life?' (508). That sounds like a return in Stephen's mind to his thoughts in the Dalkey classroom on how Julius Caesar and Argos are 'not to be thought away' but 'lodged in the room of the infinite possibilities they have ousted' (30). All day he has been troubled by the loss of possible lives, plot-lines, voices, wondering whether there might be some narrative device in which those potentials could be retained.

His annoyance with Mulligan derives from his sense that the other man is far too willing to see people and potentials die. Mulligan's ideas of creation and creativity are at root trivial, flip, dismissive: 'I see them pop off every day in the Mater and Richmond . . . It simply doesn't matter' (8). But for Stephen it did and it does: if Bloom wants Rudy's life to have meant something, Stephen desires no less for his mother. Joyce agreed, saying to a friend that he could not understand households without children: 'To leave nothing behind, not to survive yourself – how sad!' Which is why he has Stephen send the rather strange, suggestive telegram to Mulligan, with its line from *The Ordeal of Richard Feverel* by George Meredith: 'The sentimentalist is he who would enjoy without incurring the immense debtorship for a thing done' (255). This isn't just a reference to the fact that Mulligan has enjoyed life in the tower without paying his share of the rent. It is also about sex without procreativity.

All through *Ulysses* Mulligan as medic has adopted a brazenly materialist approach to human life, whereas Stephen has sought a balance between the spiritual and the physical. Mulligan's obsession with the body is a sort of 'panic reaction' after decades of Victorian denial. Ultimately, such a fixation on the body, either in pleasure or in disgust, suggests a lack of balance: Mulligan is in complicity with those censorious critics of modern art who had grown so used to life without the body that they could see the body only when it was restored.

For Joyce as for Stephen, the denial of the body began long before the Victorian era. 'For too long were the stars studied and men's insides neglected,' said Joyce: 'An eclipse of the sun could be predicted many centuries before anyone knew what way the blood circulated in our bodies.' Stephen suggests that Christians made a terrible error in denying the material reality of the host at the consecration of the Mass. In bitter parody of this exclusion, he offers here his own false consecration, which may be placed alongside Boylan's raising of his 'chalice' in the Ormond or Bloom's 'this is my body' in the bath: 'Quaff ye this mead which is not indeed parcel of my body but my soul's bodiment. Leave ye fraction of bread to them that live by bread alone' (510). On Sandymount, the merely spiritual worship of the host in the sacred monstrance was contrasted with the merely physical pleasure taken by Bloom in the display of the human body. But the division between the two types of experience remained absolute – so absolute that one could add both to the growing list of fake consecrations in *Ulysses*.

For Stephen body and soul must be placed in equilibrium; in the same way the child born of human bodies and the art that comes out of human minds should not be treated as distinct. Appalled by the Pope's assertion of the Immaculate Conception of the Virgin Mary, Stephen insists on the physical reality of lives lived in the world. He rails against 'a pregnancy without joy, a birth without pangs, a body without blemish, a belly without bigness' (511). Both the Catholic belief in transubstantiation and the Protestant doctrine of consubstantiation are wrong because they deny the material nature of the human body. At the core of Joyce's analysis is a simple enough reservation, focusing on the use of the word 'labour' to describe a woman's confinement. Where once labour and work were done under the sign of creativity and play, in the 'developed' Judaeo-Christian world play and labour were disconnected and the sex act was reduced to the level of work, without the utopian longings which once gave it greater meaning.

The forbidden slaughter of the sacred cows is punished in the *Odyssey* by the thunderbolts sent by Zeus, leading to shipwreck. Only Odysseus is saved, because of his pious refusal to eat forbidden food, much as Bloom pours away the unnecessary drink. In *Ulysses* that shipwreck is telescoped with the slaughtering, for it is the traditional styles of written English which are both slaughtered and wrecked in Joyce's treatment. The anthology on which he based many of his parodies was made by William Peacock. Designed to illustrate Darwinian notions of evolution, it was a smug selection of the best that had been thought and said over the centuries in which English developed as a modern literary language. Such anthologies were often brought to places like colonial India or colonial Ireland, to be studied there by native elites who might learn by imitating English masters how to assimilate themselves to the project of the British Empire. Like readers of this episode, students were asked in exams to identify the author of an 'unseen' passage, or to make an educated guess based on the period style of the sample. Versions of these anthologies, first tested in the colonies, would in time be brought home to Britain, for use in classrooms to initiate scholarship boys and girls from the lower orders in the classics of civilisation.

Joyce's aim was to escape being 'captured' by such systems and to produce a subversive reverse anthology of his own. He knew that the imperial mindset was obsessed with anthologies, often as a way of refusing to know a native culture in all its depth and rigour, when its turn came to be anthologised. Too often anthologies of Indian or Irish writing contained only brief, exemplary extracts of major classic works. If anthologies of both British and native art were used by the imperial powers on the periphery of their global holdings, what Joyce attempts here is a radical inversion of the whole process. One of his objects right through *Ulysses* was to make his book unassimilable to such an anthology by refusing to settle into a single 'hallmark' style. In many ways this episode marks the end of his involvement with writerly tradition, for what will follow in *Ulysses* and *Finnegans Wake* is a medley of voices, more oral than written. In 'Oxen of the Sun' no one style seeds and fructifies. Each achieves only a temporary control, more a matter of fashion than substance in the flow of time. Most are masturbatory with a self-caressing vanity which gives no lasting life.

By aligning so many styles side by side, Joyce makes the reader keenly aware of just how little any one style can do, how much more is excluded rather than included by it. Like the unfertilised ovum, most of these styles do not blossom. It's notable that neither Chaucer nor Shakespeare is given this derisive treatment; and that the parody of John Henry Newman is so straight-faced in tone and content as to be a form of homage. By far the greatest contempt, however, is reserved for the more recent styles of late nineteenth-century realism, with their claim to engage more fully with the actual flow of life than did any previous type of writing. No style is more anti-aphrodisiac than that of the day before yesterday, and Joyce is merciless in his dismissal of immediate forerunners. *Ulysses*, however, remains tender towards ancient art, such as Homer's, because it usually draws attention to its own artifices.

By the close of the episode, the new Purefoy son is born. The thunder has clapped, terrifying Stephen, who is comforted by Bloom. Like Homer, Joyce felt that thunder was a sign of the anger of the gods at blasphemy by mortals. When a visitor to his Parisian apartment during a thunderstorm pointed out to a cowering Joyce that his own children were not one bit frightened, he complained rather sourly that 'they have no religion'. Stephen is told by Calmer Bloom (who sounds like a character in *Pilgrim's Progress*) that the noise is a natural phenomenon, but he isn't mollified, 'for he had in his bosom a spike named Bitterness which could not by words be done away' (516). Yet in the time which he is about to share with Bloom, he will achieve a sense of consubstantiality of a kind that may sometimes exist between a younger adept and an older teacher. It is Mulligan of all people who senses that Bloom may possess unusual spiritual powers. Gazing transfixed at a bottle of Bass ale, Bloom should not have his reverie interrupted, warns Mulligan, who knows the procedures of Theosophy: 'It is as painful perhaps to be awakened from a vision as to be born' (545).

Bloom welcomes the thunder, knowing that much-needed rain will water his parched garden. But for Stephen it evokes real fear. After all, he had said that God might announce a new phase with a shout in the street – perhaps the thunder, perhaps the cry which he emits after being 'born'. His anxiety may be just a nervousness about newness, or that old fear of his own creative moments which lies hidden in his terror of the feminine.

'Oxen of the Sun' moves from the chaos of language at its opening ('Hoopsa, boyaboy, hoopsa!', 500) to the chaotic medley of words and phrases at its conclusion. The main action might be read as a version of the Last Supper of Jesus with his apostles, in which case the medley of languages would be a sort of Pentecost with its tongues of fire. The working of these analogies is rather strange. Bloom is personally ennobled by each analogy made between himself and Jesus. Yet from a broader perspective it appears as if Joyce were mocking the key sources of Judaeo-Christian culture. If *Ulysses* explores the apparent breakdown of that civilisation after World War I, ending with an American apocalypse, then it may well be an attack on *everything.*

A biblical narrative that comes out of chaos and returns to chaos suggests that evolutionary optimism offers little hope. Some interpreters of *Ulysses* have sought relief from this bleak view in the idea of formal symmetry to absolve themselves of the burden of discovering a meaning in a text which they fear has none. As Jesus refused to say that he was the prophet foretold, so *Ulysses* offers a challenge as difficult as that held out by any sacred text. Nevertheless, Bloom is cast as the latest incarnation of Odysseus, Jesus and Hamlet. So, it is no great surprise that in the midst of all the American slang at the close – sometimes dubbed the 'afterbirth' or placenta that issued forth following the birth of the book itself – the line '*Ut implerentur scripturae*' (561) appears suddenly in Latin, 'that the scriptures might be fulfilled'. For earlier classic texts also described a world of flux in which people come from chaos and return to it.

Those crackling voices at the close, like tongues of fire, portend a new order, perhaps even the 'afterbirth' of literature to be found in 1922 in the cacophony of voices on the radio when the dial is moved from station to station. The clap of thunder at the centre of the episode is the godlike voice foretold by Stephen to Deasy: 'a black crack of noise in the street there' (558). Hence his fear. But the new language will be found to have been latent in the old, just as elements of this episode carry fragments from

215

some previous ones and shards of some future ones. The crack of thunder may even have been foreshadowed by the creaking of Ruttledge's door in the newspaper office.

The succession of styles is also a self-parody, a mockery by Joyce of his own succession of daredevil feats from one episode to the next. Like an impetuous general who is never satisfied, Joyce has to keep risking what he has just won. He has to recreate within a single text the triumph of style over style which took centuries, much as the fashion system allows each new form of clothing to replace its predecessor without any one becoming official. This notion of endless upheaval and self-reformation represents the inner life of the bourgeoisie, as attiring its members in the togas of ancient Rome or the costumes of old Greece could never do. For what is true of the fashion system is also true of the modernism which Joyce embraced: it must make war on official versions but never become official itself. In that process of unceasing change, the creator of a new art must, nonetheless, keep measuring it against the very greatest works, for that is the only way to ensure success. Yet 'success' too must be somehow eluded.

As the storyline advances ever faster towards the conclusion to *Ulysses*, the display of successive styles blocks easy access to the detail. Aware that all of literature is in some sense a parody of actual life – a mock-up of the real thing – Joyce once again tries to raise doubts about the expressive power of any medium. If we all live at the mercy of our chosen styles and language, then Gerty MacDowell may be no more abject than anyone else. By now, Joyce has grown sophisticated enough to raise doubts about the very medium through which these doubts are expressed.

If, as he once told Stuart Gilbert, the style really is the subject of his book, then a question arises: is a classification system the content of scientific knowledge, or a mere means for gaining such knowledge? Do the forms of each episode of *Ulysses* arise from the content, or are they simply imposed from the outside in ways that make them seem more real than the material on which they are imposed? The mockery of previous styles might suggest that Joyce in the end is hardly any better than Mulligan. Able to paint moustaches on Mona Lisas but not really creative himself, he can ransack the wardrobe of literary history and play every previous part except his own. The difference, however, is radical: Joyce's self-theatricalisation is knowing, not abject. Because of that he is able to evolve consistently new forms. By telling one story – the conduct of the students and Bloom in the maternity hospital – he shows us another – the evolution of English literature – appropriately citing John Bunyan's notion of an allegory which personifies something other than just the author himself.

By the close, the participants other than Bloom are blind drunk and so is the language. Already halfway to the technique of *Finnegans Wake*, Joyce has put English to sleep, revealing the deeper idiom of dreams. As he told Harriet Shaw Weaver, 'This area of experience cannot be rendered by the use of wideawake language, cutanddry grammar, or goahead plot.' But the chaos at the end leaves the reader feeling abandoned, as if he or she will have to go ahead to the next episode to find out what really happened at the close of this one. Joyce enjoys that bafflement: 'where's that bleeding awfur?' (556). The failure of the author to clarify seems like a dereliction of

male authority, but Joyce is actually disparaging bourgeois notions of ownership in *Ulysses*: ownership of texts
as well as wives, of plots as well as children. If the other
men around the table are the lost 'seeds', who may be
Bloom's children, then any one of them could be a
counterpart to Rudy.

By the 1880s evolutionary theory, derided by Joyce in
the episode, proclaimed the need to cull Ireland's population by emigration, early death and reduced fertility –
and the survival thereafter of the fittest. The unfit who fell
are epitomised by the dead Rudy; and the episode asks
why one child of healthy parents succumbs while the
other one prospers. Uncertainty about this implants in
Bloom a sense of guilt which he should not feel (it is no
more the father's doing than the mother's when a child is
weak), a guilt deepened by his painful sense of contrast
with Theodore Purefoy, prolific father. Gaelic culture, like
the Book of Genesis, celebrated fertility and the heroic
manhood which made such increase possible. But it also
voiced repeated anxieties about a crisis in virility which
could lead to the erasure of the race. Brian Merriman's
late eighteenth-century Gaelic poem *The Midnight Court*
is a meditation on such fears, but so also in *Ulysses*, which
wonders why Irish women prefer the 'lustful half-men'
(527) to the ponderous testes of more traditional heroes.
Back in 'Cyclops', Irish womanhood was shown preferring English to Irish males who must face either the
gallows or emigration.

Joyce answers these humiliations with a sustained
attack on the English tradition epitomised by Haines who
carries a phial labelled POISON ('dope is my only hope',
539). This suggests that the strain of running an empire

has driven British men mad, but Ireland seems little better off with its population in rapid decline since the 1840s. 'Oxen of the Sun' is troubled by intimations of a desperation that may become general, as the robust males die out or quit the land, leaving only masturbators and seed-spillers. Stephen's own ambition to create major art has itself fallen victim to the prevailing culture of contraception: his 'capful of light odes' recalls the very image of a condom.

But he at least may be saved, for he knows that the energy of life is its desire for form and that such an energy can triumph in the end. He tells his scoffing companions: 'we are means to those small creatures within us and nature has other ends than we' (508). The very way in which the form of *Ulysses* is taking shape in Joyce's hands illustrates the underlying point: the future is exciting to precisely the extent that it is unknowable. Much of that form was not foreknown by its deviser, who was less an 'awfur' than a medium for the tongues of fire that burned in his head.

It's now 10 p.m. and entire hours are being lost between episodes. Not that Joyce is tiring; rather he is implying that, as the book nears its climax, it comes upon the inexpressible. If the ship is wrecked, a signal may yet be sent by Odysseus atop the wreck, giving rise to the possibility of rescue. Moreover, during the aftermath of such a disaster, the solution to old problems may be found only in the new world. For centuries Gaelic poets like Dáibhí Ó Bruadair had lamented the *longbhriseadh* or shipwreck of their land, often in the baroque style of the Counter-Reformation. Their reaction to the Protestantising of their culture was akin to Joyce's. He exempts Chaucer and

Shakespeare from his parodies in this episode, but he suggests that when the old meanings were taken away, only the husks of a tradition remained.

If Stephen crunched the shells of Deasy's collection underfoot in 'Proteus', as prelude to a new order, Joyce grinds down the shells of English literature in 'Oxen of the Sun'. Like Ó Bruadair, he uses at times a deliberately redundant, over-learned language, already obsolete, as a mark of his inner despair and of his protest against the world which is taking cultural value away. Terrified by the possibility of apocalypse, he engages in endless catalogues and inventories of those worldly things which still remain. But he holds on to them, as a man being driven by turbulent waters towards a wreck clings onto fragments from the once-proud barque. 'It is a common practice in the literature of the baroque', says Walter Benjamin, 'to pile up fragments endlessly, without any strict idea of a goal, and in the unremitting expectation of a miracle.'

Before there is a birth, there must be a death. That is why Ulysses must proceed, as noted, from graveyard to maternity hospital. Only in death is the spirit freed; and only after death, adds Benjamin, does the body come into its own, with its parts enumerated as in an anatomical dissection. The 'epic of the body' can only be lamented after a death has occurred. The elegy for a decent, dead old Ireland in the hopeless case of Paddy Dignam (whom they have taken the liberty of burying) is to be replaced by Stephen's new song, hard, rebellious and proud. In baroque art everything is wrecked before the new god can be announced: 'there is no turn of events which the baroque style would not conclude with a miracle'. That miracle will come when least expected and from one who might not be thought capable of offering such deliverance.

The new art calls also for a different reading of the old texts. And it is at about this point in the book that the old genres to which it might be likened – epic, Bible, play, novel – fall away to reveal a wholly unprecedented, possibly monstrous, form. Mina Purefoy's three days in the womb/tomb of Holles Street demonstrate how a death can lead to a resurrection; just as Joyce's glee in destruction has its strongly creative side, with an ending in a new Pentecost. If an anxiety about fertility and creativity shadows this episode, despite all of Joyce's playfulness, that is because he voiced in 1907 the fear that his country – as he had known it – might be about to disappear. That was an exile's fear, and one that he shared with many creators of wisdom narratives. A major motive for embarking on *Ulysses* in 1914 was the desire to record that world. Lest it soon be dissolved. But that was a project Joyce shared also with those Gaelic poets who, writing out the *longbhriseadh* of their people after 1600, found themselves asserting the death of a culture in the most buoyant new forms. So it was for Joyce. Like them, he couldn't go on, but he did anyway.

15. Dreaming

'Cannot the dream also be applied to the resolution of some of life's fundamental questions?' asked Sigmund Freud. Advertising in *Ulysses* has already provided one answer when Bloom's half-conscious fears and hopes were mapped on to a visible sign: 'What is a home without Plumtree's Potted Meat?' Joyce's fellow surrealists in Zurich and Paris knew exactly how to use dreams to release the transformative energy present in everyday life by directing that energy against all the censors and barriers which blocked it off.

This art, which turned all the promises of modern life against the limitations set by such a life, had flourished since the mid-nineteenth century. The loss of many cathartic public rituals – from sacred ceremonies in churches to ghoulish market-square hangings – had led a people who had fewer outlets for emotion to develop many private neuroses, tell-tale symptoms, and nervous tics. Artists, like analysts, began to investigate the personal phobias and problems that people tried to keep private. Joyce's notion of 'epiphany', although it has ancient links with the Christian feast of the manifestation of Jesus to the wise kings of the East, is also a fairly obvious version of the medical 'symptom'.

Freud held that we meet some of our worst potential moments in dreams, so that we may confront the fear and sleep more deeply afterwards. So it is in 'Circe' where Bloom undergoes many humiliations before he can enjoy a more positive wish-fulfilment, which can also go with dreams (like being the prophet of a New Bloomusalem). Alongside the fantasy elements in 'Circe', however, may be found real events of the plot-line of *Ulysses*, events which did actually happen in the brothel, such as the attempt by its madam to cheat Stephen and Bloom's timely rescue of the young man. The episode takes the form of a dream play in the course of which – according to the form's pioneer, August Strindberg – 'the characters are split, doubled, multiplied; they evaporate and are condensed; are diffused and concentrated; but a single consciousness holds sway over them all – that of the dreamer'. In this scenario humans mutate into animals and back again: Bloom becomes a pig; men become women, as Bloom becomes the whoremistress, Bella; and so on.

Why is a dream play necessary at this point in the book? Because even in the candour of their own interior monologues characters have engaged in self-deception. Beneath the apparent richness of their materials there was often to be found a deeply troubled or unhappy consciousness. Much that had been repressed or denied in the daylight hours can be brought to the surface at night. So this expressionist play about hidden impulses is also an examination of some of the sicknesses (and more positive yearnings) which lay behind the monologues.

But there is another reason for staging a dream play now. It permits Joyce to dramatise the consciousness of a multiplicity of persons who appeared only briefly in previous episodes. Here, each can have a moment, even if their situations seem to be projections from the mind of Bloom.

223

There was also a more national logic to Joyce's use of a play at this juncture. If the Abbey Theatre sought to put on stage what Synge sarcastically dubbed 'a purely fantastic unmodern ideal breezy springdayish Cuchulanoid' world, the fundamental realities of life were often quite the opposite. Joyce's artistic rendition of the undergrowth of that world is a development of his earlier critique of a theatre in thrall to the 'trolls' of narrow nationalism, a theatre that wilfully ignored the lives of 'men and women as we meet them in the real world'. If the National Theatre idealised everything, here was Joyce's counter-truth, notably about what it would really be like inside the head of a husband who had 'a stranger in the house'. This was the alternative theatre staged nightly in the kips of Monto, Sundays included (when the Abbey was decently shut). That staging went on a few hundred yards from the Abbey door, as a far more popular, more vulgar and more expressive counter-attraction. Of course it offered its customers (like readers of 'Circe') many of those elements for which Yeats had castigated the vulgar commercial theatre: music-hall songs, vulgar scene-painting, and actress-whores. Joyce often said himself that the music hall, rather than poetry, was the true 'criticism of life'.

The lesson wasn't lost on the Abbey. Just four years after the publication of *Ulysses*, Sean O'Casey in *The Plough and the Stars* adopted many of the devices used in 'Circe': the whore in the pub, the heavy drinking by distressed men, the singing of vaudeville songs. But Joyce himself, of course, had adapted elements from a famous play of 1893 about prostitution, *Mrs Warren's Profession* by George Bernard Shaw. If Bella Cohen keeps a son at Oxford from her profits as a whoremistress, Mrs Warren

224

maintains her daughter as a student at Cambridge on the same basis. The theme of prostitution had been adumbrated by Joyce in many earlier references in *Ulysses*.

The shape of *Ulysses* as a whole is becoming ever clearer. If it was 'born' in the previous episode, this is the one in which Shakespeare will finally be trumped – that is, paralysed. Confident now that he will manage his narrative to a conclusion, Joyce uses 'Circe' to respond caustically to the censorship of the 'Nausikaa' episode by the United States postal and legal authorities. Growing in audacity and power, he mocks the censors with scenes of absolute obscenity. Because the episode was completed during the final phase of the Anglo-Irish war, he also offers an attack on the Anglicisation of Irish life, via the brothels, the soldiers who patronised them, and the English songs which they made current. Joyce joked that 'Circe' was the most realistic episode of *Ulysses*, but he was stretching realism to the limit, as one way of responding to charges of obscenity.

Shakespeare is mocked not so that Joyce can replace him as the Great Writer, but in order to question all notions of mastery. So *Ulysses* cannibalises its own earlier episodes here, as it has already cannibalised Homer, the Bible, Dante and Shakespeare. Back in 'Proteus' Stephen had asked: 'who ever anywhere will read these written words?' (60); but now Joyce knows that the book will be completed. Joyce always advised writers to welcome chance: 'in writing the good things will come'. *Ulysses* is unusual for a major work in that its strategies changed as it was written, by way of the writer's reaction to the reception of earlier episodes, and with no clear sense of the total conception until the final phase was written.

In 'Circe' the book itself becomes drunk and teases the reader by lifting its skirts to reveal many secrets. A lot is still hidden, however, even as much is revealed about the lost hours of Leopold Bloom and others. Joyce is investigating how the traditional forms of drama have been utterly altered by his own discoveries in the sustained interior monologue, much as the art of painting would be transformed by abstract expressionism. The prevailing idea here is that *everyone* might be given a soliloquy as a sort of spoken thought, not exactly an interior monologue, but rather in the manner of the surrealists exchanging their private dreams and soliloquies with absolute frankness.

There is, therefore, a lot of back-tracking to earlier moments of *Ulysses* which are then reprocessed in this new dramatic form, to see just how differently they might appear. Joyce, however, teases us by withholding the more conventional sort of interior monologue, just when the reader was learning how to enjoy and rely on them. The use of earlier parts of *Ulysses*, alongside the use of ancient classics, is a case of *reculer pour mieux sauter*: the radical innovator yet again dons the masks of tradition in order to attack his current problem with an unprecedented method. The book which has allowed all prior generic scaffoldings to be erected, used, and then fall away, now performs this act upon its own earlier episodes before attempting further newness. By cannibalising himself, Joyce ensures that no later writer can do to him as he has done to Homer or Shakespeare. In the same way that the self-accusations of Bloom in 'Circe' proof him against further allegations by others, so Joyce's own anticipatory strike against himself pre-empts future attacks.

226

While 'Circe' has its share of hysteria and chaos, Bloom himself is not inebriated, having prudently poured away his drink in the hospital. Even more interesting is the fact that in his mind he is no longer nervously jumping from point to point. Now he seems composed, better able to concentrate. As he approaches the brothel in Nighttown (the name Dublin journalists gave to their night shift), he stops to avoid collision with a street-cleaner: a few seconds of thought consume almost forty pages, for the unconscious process, as Freud observed, is timeless. He carries from his encounter with Gerty a phrase of hers about her monthly menstruation – 'that tired feeling' (567) – and as he feminises himself, his desire for a parenting experience grows maternal.

Although Bloom earlier feared that childbirth would kill him, now he fantasises about becoming a mother. 'Circe' is much concerned with Bloom's *anima*, his hidden female element, based on his accumulated experience of women, notably his mother, Ellen Bloom, scarcely mentioned until now. He is given a potato by his mother as a good-luck charm (his *moly* in Homer's word) to protect him against hunger and misfortune. He must humiliate himself before the madam, Bella Cohen, who asks whether he has forgotten their past meeting, only to receive a reply in which opposite possibilities are inter-woven: 'Yes. No' (642). As a female impersonator, Bloom twice tried on Molly's clothing in the past, but now before the massive whoremistress, he is transformed not into a proud mother but into an exposed, humiliated female. Here is enacted the revenge of his unconscious for what he did to Gerty, a perfect inversion of that scene, for now Bloom himself is 'on display' to a suddenly male Bello.

227

This is the moment when the prose passage in the style of John Henry Newman in the previous episode becomes crucial: 'There are sins or (let us call them as the world calls them) evil memories which are hidden away by man in the darkest places of the heart but they abide there and wait . . . Yet a chance word will call them forth suddenly and they will rise up to confront him in the most various circumstances' (552). That parody was not limited to its target but became the basis of this revolutionary episode – another example of how parody can generate wholly new forms.

Bloom's intense discomfort in this scene is also temporary – unlike that of the prostitutes who are forever in bondage to men. The whores, like those in Picasso's *Les Demoiselles d'Avignon,* are outwardly welcoming but inwardly filled with resentment and threat. They seem less like sirens than like judges at a trial, and many embody Bloom's fear of the feminine, a fear less intense in him but shared with Stephen and the other male characters. Bloom is troubled by the bondage of woman, and so his submission to a forced form of marriage reads like a terrified attempt to imagine what such a condition might be like. Joyce himself strongly rejected Nora's request that she at least be allowed to wear a ring in front of her relations. No wonder that Bloom wishes to purge sexuality of all possessiveness, or that he should want to transcend the sexual relation altogether ('Frailty, thy name is marriage' (656), not 'woman' as in *Hamlet*), replacing it with an idealised involvement with those asexual goddesses whose statues he saw earlier. The Bello phase of this episode is just a passing element of his aversion. Bloom has spent ten years of his marriage seeking a non-sexual goddess; but now, like Odysseus, he must forego all ideas of immortality and return to the very earthly Molly as his predecessor did to Penelope.

It is only *after* his recovery from this scene of embarrassment that Bloom is able to imagine the bedroom encounter of Boylan and Molly. The Boylan who features here is less like the man described earlier than an actor who conforms to a script written by Bloom: 'Show! Hide! Show!' (671). This is as close as Joyce gets to an account of the adultery, which may cause some readers to wonder whether it happened at all. The troubling thoughts, which he had so often briefly entertained and quickly dismissed, can now be confronted in a more sustained manner. He can now admit his own complicity in setting up and even stage-managing the affair, thereby using Boylan as a 'stud' who may help to restore the marriage.

Is 'Circe' itself being pressed into a somewhat similar service by Joyce? This does indeed seem to be the 'scapegoat' episode of *Ulysses*, whose monstrosity exists to make the rest of the book look more normal (much as Jean Baudrillard has said that Disneyland exists to make the rest of California seem real). 'Circe' is the book's unconscious rather than just Bloom's, yet we carry from it an astonished awareness of what Bloom may be experiencing as he moves into the later episodes. Although all characters speak here, our sense is that this is not really a dialogue of equals, but one that is so scripted by Bloom as to make many persons, even Boylan, sound quite like him.

Why did Bloom's watch stop when Boylan was with Molly in mid-afternoon? Perhaps, like other inanimate objects in his vicinity such as the bar of soap which sings here, it was endowed with enough consciousness to register the private feelings of its owner. His day, to all intents, ends at four o'clock, for once the adultery occurs he is freed of the burden which its anticipation carried. Anyway, after four o'clock *Ulysses* loses much of its own investment in time, beginning to skip over large tracts, because full reportage of the entire day would bring things to a standstill. This may be why 'Circe' is not really chronological, but set in the timeless zones of the Unconscious.

As he wrote *Ulysses*, Joyce sometimes wore four watches, each telling a different time. His characters live mostly in personal time, fortified in their privacy by the realisation that the city's many clocks keep public time anyway. That public time does not press too heavily on them, being forgotten in moments of happiness or reverie. Joyce was obsessed with notions of relativity and parallax, an obsession put into the mouth of Stephen, who begins to sense affinities with Bloom, and to realise that in meeting him he is confronted with a version of himself. Those who sally forth in the morning, as he joked in his Library talk, invariably run into themselves before evening:

> See? Moves to one great goal. I am twentytwo too. Sixteen years ago I twentytwo tumbled, twentytwo years ago he sixteen fell off his hobby-horse. (668)

Einstein had discovered in 1905 that time in one system at a certain velocity appears to slow down when viewed from a second system at rest in relation to it. Time was really 'a perspectival effect created by a relative motion between observer and the thing observed'. As with the parallax between Bloom and Stephen, so with the reader's own relation to time in *Ulysses* – it may slow down or speed up, depending on the reader's own state.

The modern world of public time tends to dominate and order lives – but the experience of attacks and retreats done to strict schedule through World War I had brought such time-bound efficiency into question, making people nostalgic for an Edwardian world in which people moved through time rather than feeling moved by it. *Ulysses* was a help in that regard, for it shows Bloom who can integrate his private past – even the memory of his dead mother – into a serene present and an open future. Stephen is quite different: he feels ravaged by guilt feelings about May Dedalus and smashes the chandelier in the brothel in an attempt to distract from these feelings. Bloom is better able to hold on to the present moment, because he can control his feelings about his personal past rather than being controlled by them. Stephen is still trapped in the nightmare, haunted by ghosts and dead breaths, so he shouts 'Nothung' (Needful) as the voice of Mrs Dedalus identifies with the suffering Jesus. But Bloom's 'second look' at a past experience shows how a man can be freed from it.

So he achieves his desired motherly role in saving Stephen from the whoremistress and from arrest by the police. As Bloom does this, the voice over of May Dedalus, though addressing Stephen ('who had pity on you when you were sad among the strangers?', 682) is guiding Bloom in his role. Hearing Stephen recite 'Who Goes with Fergus?', Bloom fails to recognise Yeats's poem and considers that the young man is muttering about a girl named Ferguson: 'best thing could happen to him' (702) is his verdict. Despite Mulligan's repeated suspicion of a sexual element to Bloom's interest, his anxiety is simply to protect his friend's son.

As if to symbolise their developing affinity, Bloom and Stephen have looked into a mirror, shortly after the Boylan scene, and seen reflected back at them the image of Shakespeare. Lynch at that moment quotes *Hamlet*: 'the mirror up to nature' (671). Why Shakespeare? He was the supremely androgynous artist whose lines have echoed through both men's minds all day. Bloom, the womanly man, represents a triumphant resolution of the problem Shakespeare could not solve: how to create a hero who is sensitive but also successful in the world? This mirror is the 'corrected' version of the servant's cracked looking-glass derided by Stephen in the opening episode. It epitomises how the older and younger man might come together, as spiritual father and son, Blephen and Stoom. Once again, of course, *Hamlet* has been somewhat rewritten, for Stephen is told to repent not by a father's spirit but by the ghost of his mother.

That face of Shakespeare in the mirror is paralysed by Joyce who may in his arrogance feel that he is about to transcend him. All father figures in *Ulysses* are revealed to be paralytic with drink, anger or rigor mortis itself. Bloom's father Rudolf killed himself rather than live for his son. Did Leopold so resent this that he could not fully come to terms with his mother, who was his rival for his father's love? The debate in the hospital about whether the life of a mother or a child should have priority acquires a further poignancy in this episode: but Bloom, unlike Stephen, works through his problems with the female. Stephen had had similar problems recalling his mother from childhood when he looked down at Sargent in the Dalkey school. Bloom's problem with his mother may also explain the thinness of *his* focus on his early years.

The child of an immigrant family is always engrossed in the act of assimilation to the host culture, and so it may be left to the next generation to recover the family's ethnic traditions. At the end of the episode, Bloom is rewarded for rekindling his lost parenthood with a vision of his dead son Rudy, attired in Jewish clothes and reading a Hebrew text from right to left. But the vision is ambiguous, even a little troubling. Although Bloom can see Rudy, the smiling boy lost in a book (like Hamlet *'lisant au livre de lui-même'*) doesn't even recognise his own father. This may be Joyce's way of insuring against a sentimental ending, but it seems more than that. The vision of Rudy carries a warning about the dangers of immersing oneself in a written text and losing the capacity for everyday living. Bloom has his finger on his lips in the style of 'a secret master' (702), but that mastery leaves him powerless before a boy who is stuck in a book. It was the problem of Hamlet; it is still Stephen's problem. Yet 'Circe' is also a kind of anti-*Hamlet*, with the son appearing as a ghost who comes to help his father rather than the ghost of a father seeking help from a living son. In some senses, the dead child may, even in his imperviousness, be parenting his own father, suggesting that he has another youth to look after now and so can let the sad memory of Rudy rest.

Bloom is ratified in the role of father at the end, taking control of the situation in the brothel and in the street outside. He is freed to be more virile, precisely because earlier in the episode he 'dared' to give expression to his own femininity. Moreover, his submission of the problems of everyday life to solution in dreams has become part of his new secret shamanic knowledge. He has accepted the fact that knowledge acquired by intuition is helpful to living the full life.

That is why Bloom had to pass through the animal state, with which he so empathised in earlier episodes – to suggest that the bond of life, from godlike to human to animal, is unbroken. Shape-changing had long been a feature of Gaelic literature and that tradition fed into Bloom's transformations. The goddess Circe ruled over swine, pigs who kept their noses to the ground in demonstration that evolution might go backwards as easily as forwards. Joyce shared Yeats's doubts about evolutionary improvement and would have understood his fellow artist's suspicion that monkeys might be degenerate men. But he also sensed that the goddess was weak enough to need docile animals to bolster her uncertain authority. In subjecting men, her authority was also a weakness, for their thraldom was only temporary, like that of Odysseus.

Nighttown was a strange place in which the over-organised city could be abandoned for an evening by those who were unable to escape for any longer a span of time. It attracted visitors on much the same basis as Philip Larkin's agreement to visit China – that he could 'return the same day'. Nighttown allowed straights to pose as swingers. It was never a true bohemia, simply a red-light district, and even as *Ulysses* was being published and the Irish Free State instituted, it was being closed down by the Gaelic League spies who worried the arriving Bloom and were now in political power.

Bloom calls the Walpurgisnacht a midsummer madness and he is set up as its Lord of Misrule, leader of a New Bloomusalem. The removal of Nighttown is like the journey into the woods in Shakespeare, a place in which identities split and fade and re-emerge, as youth has a final fling before adult life begins. Bloom's passing through the animal state recalls Bottom's brief spell as a donkey in *A Midsummer Night's Dream*, a play which lies behind much in 'Circe'. In Shakespeare's comedy, the old ritual world of fairies, folk festivals and fertility gods had been replaced by a more rational modern order: but in the woods, as in 'Circe', all that was confined to private 'analysis' could somehow be acted out, in a mode of reconciliation between 'a countryman's participation in holiday and a city man's consciousness of all those customs so recently lost'.

Ireland, in the half-century before 1904, had undergone a similar transformation, an attempted embourgeoisification of culture, leading to a denial of wakes, local saints' festivals, fire ceremonies and so on. Certain institutions like Nighttown functioned as safety valves, in which people could, like Shakespeare's lovers in the woods, play with alternative identities, and move between fact and fiction, a real and an imaginary world. The court fool – in this case Mulligan – was used for comic burlesque, on condition that he would finally be rejected, as Mulligan is by Stephen. Just as Bottom remains completely himself while being an ass, so does Bloom remain Bloom all the while he is a pig. The aim, in Joyce as in Shakespeare, is to extend the feeling of reality into a purely fictional construction; and by so doing to offer a social rather than private analysis of repression, 'accomplished

235

by dramatic action moving through release to clarification'.

Joyce was sceptical of analysts like Freud and Jung
mainly because he felt the need for resolution at a social
and not just a personal level. This he found in major
works of literature, from the Gaelic as well as the English
tradition. Brian Merriman's *Cúirt an Mheáin Oíche* (The
Midnight Court) was published in 1912 (but written in the
later eighteenth century) and dramatised a trial at which
Irishmen are arraigned by women for their failures of
virility and self-respect. Joyce, as far back as 1907, had
described an Irish-speaking peasant, speechless at the bar
of an English-speaking court, as a fair image of the
challenges faced by Ireland before the tribunal of world
opinion. Yet his own treatment of Bloom here is as much
a show trial as the one in Merriman's poem, for both
masquerade as adversarial dialogues between men and
women, while really being constructions of the presiding
male consciousness – of 'Merriman' in the poem and of
'Bloom' in 'Circe'. Yet, like Merriman's court, 'Circe' is
structured as a dream, and a dream which has many of
the phases of a modern psychoanalysis, from the posing
of the problem through the self-accusation of the guilty
male to a catharsis which appears to offer a solution.

16. Parenting

If *Ulysses* became intoxicated in 'Cyclops' and blind drunk in 'Circe', by 'Eumaeus' it is beginning to sober up, as Bloom embraces his 'parental' role. The late episodes, though frustrating some of the reader's expectations, do not seem so deranged. To offset the effects of alcohol, Bloom brings Stephen to the cabman's shelter in search of some coffee, but the fare served is bad. Joyce himself joked that Ireland would only become a liberated country when you could get a decent cup of coffee in every street.

Bloom chides the young man for fighting. Thinking of Pyrrhus and the futile battles of Roman history, Stephen agrees. He goes on to acknowledge his own ignorance in many practical matters, asking why chairs in cafés are stacked up on tables each night. As they left Nighttown Bloom said to Stephen 'lean on me' (769). He observed that if Stephen trusted him, he could 'go a step farther' (748) – that is, be a step-father. The warning given to Bloom by his own father Virag is now passed on to Stephen: Nighttown is a 'regular deathtrap for young fellows' (706). Earlier, he had wondered whether Stephen's upbringing might have been the cause of some of his problems; Stephen now admits that he left his father's house 'to seek misfortune' (713). Bloom warns him against Mulligan, the court jester who is picking his brains. Stephen has been deserted by all his friends but one, and that one – Lynch – was Judas.

Their exchanges are two-way, however, for Stephen is able to warn Bloom that the Italians around an ice cream car might sound operatic and romantic but are actually haggling over money. At many junctures in this episode, the men will exchange roles, as if freed by the company to explore their alternative side. The empirical Bloom becomes rather romantic, even as the poet turns matter-of-fact. Stephen's observation raises a major concern of the episode – the difference between things as they appear and things as they truly are. Bloom admits that his family name was changed; and he also observes that Haines, who presented himself as a Celtic scholar, is really just 'an English tourist' (713). As if to reinforce the sense of nothing being quite what it seems, the narrative voice hovers somewhere between that of Bloom and that of a returned old sea-salt, D. B. Murphy, neither of whom seems in total command of the language.

Bloom offers to stir Stephen's putrid coffee, and he also offers him a bun, while joking that it now looks more like a brick from a nearby building site. 'Couldn't' (733) is Stephen's strained reply. Here the idea of transubstantiation – that the body and blood of Jesus are presented at the consecration of the Mass under the appearance of bread and wine – is recreated, in the bread roll that looks like a brick and in the coffee which may well be something else. This is Joyce's heavily ironic climax to *Ulysses*. After all the fake consecrations, this is a true one, a real attempt at communion. Here Bloom becomes the distributing priest, as an act of common kindness tilts the moment towards the Eucharistic. The young Stephen had refused the Eucharist, saying he must wait for it to come to him – and now it has. In this moment both Eucharist and epiphany are rejoined – the sudden showing-forth of a hidden symbolic meaning of a seemingly banal exchange between two tired men. Earlier that day, Bloom had fed some Liffeyside birds, noting that they were not fooled by white paper made to look like bread. But now Bloom is distributing bread all over again.

If Stephen ate more solid food, Bloom counsels, he would feel a different man, a true transubstantiation indeed. Although he hasn't said a word about it, Stephen now remarks that he hasn't eaten all day, seeming to forget that small matter of an improvised breakfast in the tower. This hunger-striking is strange, for all day he had Deasy's payment in his pocket, some spent at the brothel and later a half-crown donated to the equally hungry Corley. Was Stephen doing some kind of penance, perhaps designed to relieve a sense of guilt about his dead mother?

The advice Bloom gives is the same as he offered himself after mid-day: 'Must eat . . . Feel better then' (214). It may be no more significant than that. But throughout *Ulysses*, Bloom has wished to animate everything, a redeemer wandering the world in search of bodies in which his spirit might become incarnate. If the appearance of things seems forever deceptive, that may be because godlike forces can fill them with new meaning. A person may be reborn as a tree or an animal. In such a cosmos, identity is strictly provisional, given and withheld by God or gods. So when the 'Eumaeus' episode speaks of eyes, it hedges its language about 'the person who owned them pro tem' (747). Bloom has refused all claims to being a prophet, much less a god, yet Stephen accepts his kindness in a phrase which will (it turns out) repeat Molly's words at their first tryst on Howth Hill. She said, 'As well him as another' (933); and here Stephen welcomes '*Christus* or Bloom his name is, or after all any other' (745).

The equation of Bloom with Jesus, up to now implied in mockery by incredulous anti-Semites, is made in full seriousness by the young man. Recalling the bitter encounter in Barney Kiernan's, Bloom takes particular pleasure in the fact that he told the men that their God was a Jew, 'because mostly they appeared to imagine he came from Carrick-on-Shannon or somewhere about in the county Sligo' (766). But why not, then, from Eccles Street? As always, Joyce guards against sentimentality: if so many appearances in this episode deceive, then maybe this consecration could too. But the unvarnished way in which it is told suggests that it may be more real for all that.

'The meeting of two personalities is like the contact between two chemical substances,' wrote C. G. Jung: 'if there is any reaction, both are transformed.' The choice by Joyce of 16 June 1904 was deeply meaningful, not just because he first walked out with Nora on that day, but also because that moment marked his return from the self-hatred and confusions of his youth, back to the sacrament of everyday life. Even the name 'Bloom' epitomises the idea of a flowering on a single day. What had caused much of Joyce's suffering was also what caused Stephen's: the inadequacies of an 'all too Irish' (718) father. John Joyce pressurised his eldest son by investing in him all the hopes of a shattered and declining family: 'The situation', said one of Joyce's classmates, 'was quite impossible.' Images of the Dedalus family's poverty flicker through Stephen's mind as he contemplates his own hunger in the episode. These images may have been rooted in Joyce's own feelings of guilt, for as one of his sisters recalled: 'Our father deprived the rest of the family to give to Jim. He saw in him a genius.'

In his panic-reaction to his hopeless father, Stephen tried to be self-sufficient – every man his own father. At moments in 'Eumaeus', he seems as dismissive of Bloom (his religious ideas, his taste in music) as he was earlier of the boys in the Dalkey school. Yet he needs to abandon that pose of self-sufficiency and to place himself in life's flow. Representing the middle generation, Bloom offers some hope that the conflicts between the old and young can be mediated and resolved. Without such a referee, the old and young run the risk of elaborating fantasies, less and less connected to reality. The myth of self-invention pursued by Stephen's generation was in part a response to the failure of their fathers to produce a safe, negotiable world. The transmission of wisdom from one generation to the other is a process that can never be fully described – it can only be evoked. Hamlet's growth in Shakespeare's play is never really explained: he simply disappears from some of its middle scenes to return a wiser man. Stephen, likewise, disappears from some of the central episodes of *Ulysses*, but returns as one of its two focal characters. His developing understanding with Bloom is narrated, but it remains finally mysterious.

Their rapprochement has elements of that between an older and younger man in the society of ancient Greece – Bloom, while walking, keeps to Stephen's right side, 'his tender Achilles' (769). Bloom plans a possible career for

Stephen as a singer with Molly, and he shows him her photograph, taken some years earlier, to whet his interest in the project. This may be his way of telling Stephen that he is not homosexual. It could also be Bloom's symbolic attempt to recreate a family ambiance in Eccles Street, with Boylan dismissed as the wife's manager and Bloom established in that role. Is Bloom also seeking the ratification of the better-educated younger man through the transitional object of his wife Molly in a way that is homosocial rather than homosexual?

Few of the men in the newspaper office had touched him, as they touched one another. Bloom seems, accordingly, to crave physical contact with other men; and as he links the right arm of the youth in his own left arm, Stephen 'feels a strange kind of flesh of a different man approach him, sinewless and wobbly and all that' (769). Back in the Ormond Bar, Bloom had been described as 'married' by the shared experience of music with Richie Goulding, who sat next to him (347); and at the close of 'Eumaeus', the two men leave, in the words of a popular song, 'on a low-backed car . . . to be married by father Maher' (775–6). Their alignment is, of course, strictly temporary.

Readers have sometimes wondered if both were stone-cold sober, how much would they have in common. Quite a lot is the surprising answer, for *Ulysses* has gone to great lengths to establish the unconscious harmony of their thoughts and activities throughout the day. For some readers, however, this is just not enough. They feel that both men are often at cross-purposes and that the long-promised meeting is an anti-climax. Their criticisms mostly focus on the banal language of the narration and on the broken, fragmented exchanges between Stephen and Bloom. But in a book which has repeatedly exposed the limits of language, why should the climax be verbal? Joyce was always haunted by the suggestive potential of the ellipsis at the trail-off of an unfinished sentence; something rather similar is happening here. Words are not all that important to Bloom, who has found conversations to be inconclusive all day – they cannot do your living for you. The real meeting of both men began in 'Circe', where they shared something as intimate as a dream life. How could any mere conversation measure up to that?

In 'Eumaeus' there are moments when Bloom and Stephen seem to know (without being told) each other's thoughts. So why should dialogue count for much now? Critics in search of a talking climax may be thinking in terms of a traditional novel and missing the deeper point of the new psychic layers uncovered by *Ulysses*. If Stephen had in his forecasting dream imagined an eastern gent's invitation, then perhaps the 'L. Boom', whose name is misprinted in the newspaper list of mourners at Paddy Dignam's funeral, may be the godlike noise in the street predicted during Stephen's conversation with Deasy.

Bloom knows anyway that the moment of the guru is but a brief flowering. He thinks of various grizzled old returnees, from Odysseus to Rip Van Winkle, coming back 'to show the understudy in the title role how to' (754), but 'coming back was the worst thing you ever did because it went without saying you would feel out of place as things always moved with the times' (757). This may be yet another of Joyce's dismissals of his own literary models, since by now he has become the main

243

man. But it is also an expression of Bloom's awareness that his role as honorary father of Stephen has its limits. It is the nature of sons to grow up fast and go away.

But not just yet. For Bloom's wisest lesson of all is his insistence that theory and practice, intellect and labour, must be reconciled. He suggests that Stephen solve his poverty by work. 'Count me out' (747) is the instant reply. Bloom hastens to clarify that he meant work in the widest possible sense: 'You have every bit as much right to live by your pen in pursuit of your philosophy as the peasant has. What? You both belong to Ireland, the brain and the brawn. Each is equally important' (747–8). Once again, Bloom is appalled by wastage – the wasted education of young men who promised brilliantly but under-achieved. Dublin is filled with the inhabitants of a fake Bohemia, undergoing a long-extended youth because they lack proper employment. (Guarding heaps of stones is no work at all for a man like Corley.) Their lives are built on promises never fulfilled and the sense that they will forever miss out. Their motto might be Lenehan's bitter catchphrase: expecting every moment to be their next.

Bloom understands that Nighttown is a fake Bohemia, a dead end for a man of Stephen's talent. However, Ireland is, in Stephen's opinion, a reluctant Bohemia as well ('We can't change the country. Let us change the subject', 748). Its young men are held to the age of thirty, trying out futile roles in a mode of endless experiment. So Stephen accepts the clear implication of Bloom's argument that the bourgeois and bohemian should be one and the same person. The days of life in the false Bohemia of pure theory unchastened by actual practice must be brought to a close. Stephen in this episode is no longer

244

posing for himself or for others, but engaging honestly with one other person for the first time. He shows the older man that he understands the hidden meaning of their encounter, describing variations on an old song, *Youth here has End.*

Joyce believed what he had Bloom say: that the bourgeois worker, whether in newspapers or advertising, was the conclusion of the book to which the bohemian was mere preface. The businessman, like the artists, was a broker in risk, who was willing to back an initial hunch with – if need be – years of hard work to explore the possibility. Joyce had opened the first cinema-house in Dublin and advertised Irish tweed in Trieste in this spirit of self-help. His *Ulysses* was not just an example of a high-risk business venture but also a sort of 'self-help' manual, in which an older Irishman teaches a younger one how to live and blossom. As an advertising man, Bloom thought and laboured at the very meeting point between the avant-garde artist and commerce, for the poster art of 1904 drew heavily on the aesthetic of *fin-de-siècle* painters. His devising of a logo of crossed keys for the form of Alexander J. Keyes is a modest effort in that tradition.

Joyce projected his own combination of values through Bloom. He wished to be at once the daredevil artist and the solid family man, avant-garde experimenter and respectable citizen. It was for this very reason that Sherwood Anderson lampooned him as 'Burjoice'. But Sylvia Beach found the combination touching: 'It didn't fit the artist of the *Portrait.* But it helped you to understand *Ulysses . . .* with Bloom taking over the whole show. I felt that Joyce fast lost interest in Stephen.' That last sentence is untrue. What Joyce was really seeking was a reconciliation between the two men. It is with the extended analysis of their meeting that the book comes into its own.

Bloom has his personal problems to solve, of course; and they centre on an attempt to invest bourgeois marriage with something of the freedom of the bohemian life. 'Can real love, supposing there happens to be another chap in the picture, exist between married folk?' (756). The story of Parnell and Captain O'Shea leads Bloom to fret about what happens with the husband not being up to the job. But he senses that the meeting with Stephen may help him to find a resolution. The stock examples of nineteenth-century adultery offered in this episode, with their scenes of volatile confrontation between husband and rival, all contrast with Bloom's gentler ethic of non-possessiveness. In a book designed to celebrate everyday verities, melodrama would be a dire distortion.

Stephen's passage from adolescence to maturity is intimately connected to the nature of Dublin. In a truly civic city such as Dublin was in 1904, all sorts of people pass through very different parts every day. Growth is possible, even for settled citizens like Bloom, through openness to the Other and a willingness to talk with those who might seem different. This free circulation in the inner city contrasts with life in suburbia, which is designated to answer the middle class's fear of a world which they cannot control. 'The essence of human development is that growth occurs when old routines break down,' writes Richard Sennett, 'but suburbs make it possible for us to hide from being adults.' Stephen cannot do that, for he is pulled by Bloom back into Dublin's centre. It is the sheer randomness of their meeting and discussion that Joyce wants most of all to celebrate, their

246

shared openness to all that is accidental. For him the wonder of a city is that it is a place in which behaviour can never be fully predicted or controlled. If today a twenty-two-year-old graduate would feel quite unsafe in taking up the invitation of an unfamiliar man to come home with him for cocoa and a chat, that may be our loss.

17. Teaching

As a student at Belvedere College, Joyce knew his catechism better than any boy in his class. The catechism was a manual of questions and answers, used to teach students the basic elements of Catholic doctrine. Its authors tried to anticipate the hardest questions which sceptics might raise and so forearm the faithful with clear, crisp answers. Its finicky precision of language and the methods used seemed almost scientific in the steady elimination of falsehood until you got to the truth.

But both the catechism and the science textbook had the same disadvantage: they asked a question not out of genuine uncertainty but only because the answer was already known. Yet there can never be a single answer to any question worth asking, for knowledge (as Emerson said) is the knowing that we cannot know. When Gertrude Stein was on her deathbed, she asked her concerned friends: 'What is the answer? What is the answer?'; and because they all failed to reply, she said dryly: 'Well then, would someone mind telling me what is the question?' The question-and-answer format is, of course, not peculiar to catechism or science; it also characterises all forms of *interrogation*. In a police state questions are asked only because the answers are already known and the 'right' answer must always be given, even

248

if that is not what the interrogated person believes. A novel about life under Nazi tyranny, *Hourglass* by Danilo Kîs, modelled much of its structure on Joyce's 'Ithaca' episode, showing how the ideological mufflers worn by interrogators prevented their hearing anything other than that which they wished to hear.

In 'Eumaeus' Joyce shows how the artists and citizen might be reconciled. Here another apparent polarity, that between religion and science, is addressed. The impersonal voice of the catechist is also able to ask questions about Bloom, Stephen and even Molly, which the characters could not ask themselves. Many things are revealed here which were up to now unclear – the extent of Bloom's wealth, for example. We learn that the Blooms have not enjoyed full sexual intercourse since Rudy's death eleven years ago – which may be why Molly has felt the need to take a lover.

Bloom has grown philosophical about Molly's lovers; he is even unsure as to exactly how many there have been. Coolly, he lists twenty-five possibilities (some quite ludicrous), but consoles himself with the thought that 'each one who enters imagines himself to be the first to enter whereas he is always the last term of a preceding series even if the first term of a succeeding one, each imagining himself to be first, last, only and alone . . .' (863). This could also be Joyce's reminder to himself that every version of the *Odyssey*, even Homer's 'first', is subject to such reservations and that none, not even his own, will be definitive. But it is also, within the logic of the narrative, an attack on notions of individuality. Boylan may think of himself as the cock-of-the-walk, but already he is being reduced to a single element of an open series.

A paradox lies coiled here. The more Molly is lusted after by other men, the more mysteriously desirable she becomes to her own husband.

The list of her lovers here, like other lists in *Ulysses*, has a levelling effect, reducing all to a common denominator. Bloom, a natural democrat, has no problem with this. Indeed, as he boils a kettle, the narrative voice informs us that what he prizes most of all in water is 'its democratic quality and constancy to its nature in seeking its own level' (783). In the years before and after 1904, a widespread distrust of the 'mob' in a mass society found a focus in a fear of sharing contaminated water. Bloom has already learned to share Molly's lovers and forgive her by comparing her passions to the rise and fall of sea water. The accord between Bloom and Molly is like that between Bloom and Stephen: they pursue parallel courses which never fully meet. But the wife remains fascinated by her husband, whom she loves: and the two men connect even though they never fully interact.

Using the Netaim prospectus to light an incense candle, Bloom expunges all trace of Boylan's presence. His action repeats the Mass of Holy Saturday, at which a cone of incense is lighted. Equally, when he and Stephen piss together under Molly's window (each man having urinated alone earlier in the day), this image of their solidarity repeats the moment in Homer when father and son shoot arrows at their enemies. But the arrows, like the lines traced by their voyaging, never truly meet. Stephen and Bloom share a sense of solitude – and that may be the deepest human solidarity of all. The surrealists of Paris believed that this was the most cultured type of community imaginable, one in which each person was free to pursue his or her own soliloquy, setting individuality in tension with that of others. This fits a modern world in which people often find it hard to attend to anything less interesting than their own thoughts.

Bloom grows even more androgynous in the presence of Stephen, who feels 'his firm full active passive masculine feminine hand' (832). To have so many contradictory attributes is almost like having none at all. Yet compared with the cosmic significance of such all-encompassing attributes, identity may seem a puny thing, well lost. The acrostic poem the young Bloom sent to Molly, where the first letter of each line read downwards spells the author's name POLDY, seems, by contrast, trivial and self-absorbed. By now, however, that charge might also be laid against the interior monologues themselves. All through 'Ithaca', Joyce continues to tease the reader with the discrepancy between the warmly human encounter of two very different men and the cold, clinical prose in which it is narrated. Although a reader might wish for a return of the monologues, the episode exposes their limits by disclosing much that they couldn't record.

What do we learn? That Bloom represents the scientific and Stephen the artistic temperament. But even that seems too neat, for at many moments Bloom has seemed like the poet whom Stephen can only play at being. We can now see that when Bloom *writes* poems, like the acrostic, they are dreadful; but when he keeps them in his head, his lines can be beautiful. We also learn that, although the duo epitomise Israel and Ireland, Bloom knows only a little Hebrew and Stephen a modicum of Irish. Neither is inarticulate, however, for Bloom can talk to animals and machines, while Stephen

251

can speak French and Italian. Bloom had a Victorian use for Shakespeare, consulting his plays as wisdom literature which might help him to resolve 'difficult problems in imaginary or real life' – and, like Stephen in the Library, he found the results 'imperfect' (790–1).

In a further act of communion, he offers his young friend 'Epps's massproduct, the creature cocoa' (791), which means God-food in Greek. In Homer's tale Odysseus was struck by a stool, and here Bloom bangs his right temporal lobe on the rearranged kitchen furniture. The loud crack emitted by the furniture may be the noise of a new code (eek), which will reduce the infinite to the quantifiable. For if Stephen has to proceed out from the known to the unknown, Bloom travels in the opposite direction, from the outside back to home, from the unknown back to the known.

Joyce imparts a sense of infinity to the episode, with the two men approximated to the stars at which they gaze. Their travels cease to be confined to Dublin, becoming interstellar; and the planetary voyaging of Bloom, begun with his ascension in 'Cyclops', is intensified here. The stars retain their aura, even as the humans lose some of theirs, but so also do humble objects, which a god on his travels might bring to consciousness. Joyce sees the great in the little because he sees the lie of considering them apart. So the sense of vast space often suggested in epic is countered by a notion of strict order among the homely objects kept by Bloom in his kitchen drawer. Confronted with the uncertainties of life, Bloom finds relief in the order of everyday settings.

This may account for the rather excessive play of detail in Bloom's monologues. He believes not just that there is a 'void' out there, but also that the human species will eradicate itself. The present episode called 'Ithaca', therefore, doesn't just describe a man reviewing the details of his day before sleep, but also a man reliving all the major events of his life. (This would explain Bloom's fascination with drowning.) The penultimate episode is like that moment in drama when, just before the denouement, the characters in flight from a collapsing world draw breath, as life comes to a brief standstill. Those fleeing the wreckage 'are sheltered in the presence of onlooking strangers, so that the familiar can be viewed in a totally new light'. 'Ithaca' similarly freezes the flow of life captured in the stream-of-consciousness episodes, so that readers can make their own cool assessments. These assessments would now have to register the further reasons behind Bloom's exhaustive inventories. He surrounds himself with objects, not just because he senses that the civic bourgeoisie is doomed, but also because he fears for the world itself. The listing of objects has to include almost everything, in case the world itself is about to be destroyed.

If Bloom epitomises the scientific temperament, it is applied science that interests him most. His schemes always have a practical value, none more so than one outlined here for making use of the chemical properties of human excrement. Throughout the day he had been troubled by waste, because of his fear that human life itself might lack any meaning. That is why Bloom tries desperately to make even random events fit into some sort of pattern.

This is the poignancy of science. Its desire for exactitude and certainty, far from being modern, is really

253

just the old familiar yearning of every man, woman, and child to feel secure in the world. So by using the catechism method Joyce implies that even as science has proclaimed itself the new religion, religion has been trying to become a new science. Joyce's Jesuit teachers had asked him to believe that there was a radical difference between the methods of religion and of science – but he couldn't agree. After the 1850s, with the emancipation of a Catholic bourgeoisie, the prelates of Irish Catholicism had tried to make its theology more rational, so they discouraged wakes, superstitions, and devotions to the healing power of local saints. Instead, a centralised church sought to rationalise its administration and equip all the faithful in an age of mass literacy with conclusive answers to the sort of objections made by agnostics, atheists and Protestants. Even as these changes began to take hold, around the turn of the century, science itself became more open to a principle of uncertainty and to a more mystical notion of physics. Joyce's tactic is clear. In a book of subjectivities, the claim of the catechism, like that of Victorian science, to an objective authority is made to appear quite ludicrous.

A catechism should be terse, graphic, quotable, but this one isn't. Instead, the narrative keeps tripping over itself, because of its honesty, its Bloom-like desire to spell out not just the rules but their justification. So, short questions produce long, often tedious, answers. Although the language appears to be clinical, it is not consistently so. Often, in fact, it's deeply emotional, as the word 'alone' is repeated to capture Bloom's isolation. The questions do not follow any logical pattern and repeatedly make the reader wonder: why is this being asked? They seem to follow a rambling, associative pattern, rather like Bloom's own monologues. The answers don't reveal all, and are sometimes even mistaken. At the start of 'Ithaca', the apparent exactitude of language promised relief from the chaos of interior monologue. By the close, the reader in all probability wants to go back to it. 'Ithaca' is a savage commentary on the overload of information in our modern world, information which oppresses more often than it illuminates.

Science proceeds on the same understanding as Bloom does. It holds that the unknown can be expressed in terms of the known, on the basis of sound present learning leading to new future knowledge. Stephen goes 'out there', as Bloom moves back to the familiar, but Bloom is never certain of anything for long. He questions his own strongest convictions: 'perhaps', 'maybe', 'probably', 'but' are key words for him. So also with *Ulysses*. It remains open to the idea of 'entelechy': that there are always new forms of knowledge destined to emerge, but which, despite that inevitability, will take us utterly by surprise. If ousted possibilities are never fully lost, but shot through with utopian potentials, then current systems of knowledge may soon be dismantled as new orders emerge in which opposites could be dissolved, whether art and science, bohemian and bourgeois, Greek and Jew.

Joyce's desire was not to destroy religion. He had far too much respect for the wisdom of the ages to want to do that. But he did wish to free the religious mind from its entrapment in discredited creeds and outworn social systems. He wished for a church which would cease trying to regulate human behaviour and would return instead to studying man's relationship to God and fate. However, in order to go forward in that way, Joyce first of all had to go back – to Homer, whose cosmos was a lottery based on accident and chance. In the *Odyssey* the gods are humanised and become playful, responsive to the needs of the passing moment; and so the reader feels that the journey of Odysseus was probably staged for their amusement. Likewise, Joyce insisted that *Ulysses* was a kind of cosmic joke.

But what sort of joke? Comedy tends to take the long, telescopic view. Seen from up close, the attempts by mankind to improve can often appear tragic; but, from a distance, they may seem very funny. *Ulysses* began to move towards such wisdom when in 'Wandering Rocks' it offered a god's-eye view of Dublin. By the time 'Ithaca' is reached, it is viewing the earth from outer space. Bloom, who so often took the anthropologist's view (of communicants, of burial rituals, of meals, of child-rearing) is now anthropologised himself. He is divested of personal identity in sentences which describe him as 'the man' (780) – actually bearing a light to Stephen. And Stephen in his premonitory dream had called his rescuer simply 'the man', who held out in promise some melons, which are now revealed to be Molly's rumps as the prophecy is fulfilled in the most absurd way imaginable.

Stripped not just of identity but also of self-respect in this scene, Bloom is the epitome of that kind of doomed, primitive order which is often studied by anthropologists just before it expires. But if *Ulysses* is elegiac, how can it also announce and celebrate the new? Nostalgia for a lost nineteenth-century world is not incompatible with the drive towards the twenty-first-century type of humanity. The account of the collapse of this civilisation might yet become the master-narrative of the next.

The modern world had known only a tragic split between the cold claims of abstract science and the hot passions of actual people. The two bore no relation, other than the likelihood that the latter might be studied by the former in the practice called Freudianism. One of Joyce's projects in *Ulysses* was to rejoin them, by employing scientific language at the moment of maximum feeling. He saw, too, that this was an answer to a wider modern problem: those who could feel did not always know how to express, and those who learned how to express often did so only when they had forgotten how to feel. No merely secular order could solve that problem, for the very notion of the secular was incomplete without the sacred that gave rise to it.

What Bloom, 'the man', epitomises for Stephen is the wisdom which accepts the limits of individual self-importance, even as it ratifies the importance of heroic self-acceptance. The only way to gain identity it to give a lot of it up – having first found *some*. Only then will you achieve enough negative capability to reach out and take on the identity of other things, be they persons, objects, animals, or even gods. The traditional nineteenth-century novel often had a question-and-answer session in its pen-ultimate chapter in which an older and younger person resolved their misunderstandings with the younger one abandoning false illusions. Here the catechism seems like Joyce's distortion-by-caricature of that time-honoured practice. But he does it to offer a contrast with the uncertain, wayward nature of the actual exchanges between Bloom and Stephen in 'Eumaeus'.

In their strangely opaque way these two episodes enact a radical new version of the *Bildungsroman*, the old novel of 'learning'. But where once the truths learned would be summarised in graphic, witty phrases of high-class dialogue – think of Elizabeth Bennett and Mr Darcy in Austen's *Pride and Prejudice* – that is no longer necessary. In *Ulysses* so much occurs in people's minds that the rapprochement between Bloom and Stephen needs little external depiction. 'Ithaca' offers a parody of the sureties of the nineteenth-century novel. Though seeming to be logical, it is itself as rambling as the earlier episodes of stream of consciousness, and even more weighed down by detail. All seems uncertain, caught between infinity and the local instance. Bloom's own ideal artwork and advertisement is in that context the very *opposite* of *Ulysses*: 'reduced to its simplest and most efficient terms not exceeding the span of casual vision and congruous with the velocity of modern life' (848).

Is Joyce therefore in bad faith, writing a book which celebrates the common man in such forbiddingly complex ways? Not really. The book was written to be enjoyed by ordinary men and women, but it is also an account of how the intellectual can return to the actual, an account of the complex path which such persons can take back to the ordinary. The method might be complex, but the thought was simple enough, said Joyce, who called himself 'the foolish author of a wise book'. A central element of that return to the ordinary is shown to be a willingness to accept chance. What unites Bloom and Stephen in the end, across differences of race, education and so much else, is a 'disbelief in many orthodox religions, national, social and ethical doctrines' (777). That is not a bad basis for a few hours of interesting conversation.

Yet Stephen prefers to go than to stay. Not that he has any fear of Bloom. He goes because it is his fate to leave the known for the unknown. As he leaves, he ponders a psalm on the deliverance of the Children of Israel from the house of bondage. In meeting Bloom, he embraced chance. Now, in order to be true to that moment, he must do so all over again.

So must Joyce. He had thought that 'Ithaca' would be the real ending of *Ulysses*, but once again the unexpected and the accidental intervened. The last episode, as Molly counter-signed her husband's passport to eternity, would prove the most astonishing of all.

18. Loving

'On the whole,' wrote George Simmel in 1919, 'we can describe the individual man better than the individual woman. Because of the social predominance of the man, the entire linguistic conceptualisation of our culture corresponds to the male coloration of the mental process.' He went on to suggest that 'the universe of language has not yet concerned itself with the individualised charac- teristics of woman'. By devoting so many of its pages to the thought processes of Stephen Dedalus and Leopold Bloom, *Ulysses* might seem to have borne Simmel out, but the closing episode throws his contentions into question – and it does so by an all-out assault on the conventions of language and of literature.

If the free circulation of people in city streets helps to open up unapproved routes, so also does language. Joyce's disruption of syntax all through *Ulysses* served to reroute many possibilities of English. Nowhere is this more evident than in Molly Bloom's closing soliloquy where eight sentences without punctuation fill up over fifty pages, while she muses on her strange life and even stranger day. As night trains sound in the distance, she masturbates to images of Bloom. His long-term strategy starts to pay off, as Molly turns against Boylan for taking all the pleasure for himself.

At first Joyce thought of having Molly write a set of letters about Bloom, but that would have been a rather old-fashioned ending in the style of early epistolary novels. Molly does recall having posted blank sheets of paper to herself in a literary equivalent of her masturbation – a fact which shows how lonely she has been in the years since leaving Gibraltar. Her fifty pages are commonly described as a soliloquy rather than a monologue, but here the soliloquist is female, as never in Shakespeare's plays. This soliloquy is not a mere spoken report describing a completed set of thoughts; rather it shows those thoughts in the very process of formation. You get the sense that neither Molly nor Joyce knows exactly where her musings might lead.

Many male authors have produced a female monologue of real power in their middle years: Yeats with the 'Crazy Jane' poems, Beckett with Winnie in *Happy Days*. It is as if their feminine element or *anima*, kept under strict control in their earlier years of literary struggle, can be suddenly released and brought into full consciousness as a major source of creativity. Having achieved so much already in *Ulysses*, Joyce is able to relax his self-censors. Of course, the inner female, so liberated, may turn out to be obscene, bitchy, even sluttish, after so many years of denial – and may be revealed to have an equally vulgar, equally repressed male dimension. The negative connotations of the word *animus* are proof enough of that.

Molly surely illustrates the point: she wishes she could have used four-letter words in bed with Boylan; she would like to possess a penis and even imagines what it would be like to be a man mounting her thighs. Such moments, the reader realises with a start, might have driven Bloom into seventh heaven. All day he has explored his own contrasexual side, imagining how women walk or give birth. He and his wife are true androgynes, embodiments of Freud's dictum that manly women are attracted and attractive to womanly men. The tragedy of their relationship is that their respective balances of masculine and feminine are no longer compatible. Molly still wants a rather conventional lover ('the right height over me', 886), whereas in Bloom the balance of forces is so poised that much of his desire seems to have ebbed away.

Yet, for all of Molly's conventionality, she is her own mistress. Her refusal to employ the usual niceties of grammar is a sign of just how little mastered she is by outside forces. In their monologues Stephen and Bloom used a staccato telegraphic language of logic, as if aware of the need to control otherwise threatening feelings which might take over. They internalised far more of the 'system' which she resists. Although Molly enjoys imagining how she might appear to an onlooking male, she refuses his invitation to sado-masochism: 'sure theres nothing for a woman in that' (890). Unlike Gerty, she refuses to turn herself into a fetish of male desire. Her insistence on affirming her actual sexual needs must have seemed radical in 1922, just as her self-acceptance must have been very moving.

As late as the 1980s, many older readers were still unready to meet the challenge, routinely denying that Molly could have been masturbating. When the Irish actress, Fionnula Flanagan, performed the soliloquy in this way, scholars in Minnesota walked out in protest, angrily handing back memberships of the James Joyce Foundation like war veterans handing back their bravery medals. The very idea of this lonely woman pleasuring herself was too much for them. These scholars had been educated in an upbeat American tradition which saw Molly as saying 'yes' to love and to life, in the spirit of Stephen's definition of literature as the affirmation of mankind. But Joyce, more sombrely, had been asking: does she? Her 'yes' might also be sad, since it is the strategy of a lonely monologist, who hopes that somebody might be there and listening. Like the self-posted letters, it is the device of a woman left with nobody to talk to but herself. By the end of her episode, the reader can see just how much the troubled couple have in common; but little of this is shared at the level of speech. Again, the tragedy of interior monologue is the poverty of its social occasions – how little gets said of what is un-knowingly shared. Early readers wished for an affirmative conclusion, as if to validate Oscar Wilde's joke: 'The good ended happily, the bad unhappily. That is what fiction means.' However, Irish interpreters could recognise a 'silent marriage' when they saw one.

Joyce's insistence on the painfulness of Molly's plight has not prevented some feminist readers from finding in the soliloquy too many stereotypes of a chronically self-contradicting womanhood. The same Molly who criticises a priest for disdaining to say 'bottom' goes on to denounce a priest for saying 'bumgut' (890); the same Molly who defends low-cut dresses early on attacks them by the end. She even says with delicious irony that she hates books with a Moll or Molly in them. This, of course, could be Joyce's warning that he is well aware of the dangers of stereotyping a female literary figure to fulfil the wishes of a male author, for that was precisely what Daniel Defoe had done in *Moll Flanders*. There the prostitute-heroine showed an easy, facile approach to emotional commit-ment, a mobility from place to place, and a financially acquisitive attitude – being in other words an 'honorary male' merchant, whose author had recreated his own mercantile lifestyle in the experience of an up-market whore.

Molly is contrasted with Gerty because she won't necessarily give men what they want. With Gerty, the reader feels the need to ask: from whom is this coming? Molly is utterly and solely present in her own words, like no previous character in *Ulysses*. She fully possesses her own voice, one reason why her episode is often called a soliloquy rather than a monologue. Her inventor may cause her to plead for release, like a Jungian *anima* seeking liberation – 'O Jamesy let me up out of this' (914) – but, though her body has been occupied, her thoughts are fully her own in a way that neither Gerty's, Stephen's, nor even Leopold's have ever managed to be.

How can this be so? In earlier episodes she was seldom present, but often described through the rumours and reports of disparaging men. 'A mirror never gives you the expression' (887), complains Molly, and she, even more than her husband, has been seen through the distorting mirror of other people's opinions. The cracked looking-glasses of servants can tell many lies. Never-theless, this final episode helps the reader to readjust her image, making a far more complete version possible. Molly grounds *Ulysses* in the end. If in the classic epics of Virgil or Milton a female muse is invoked at the start, here she is summoned only at the conclusion.

No other editorial voice intrudes on her thoughts. Bloom's stream of consciousness, though copious, was really just a series of separate snapshots of his thoughts, that were never continuous for long, because he was constantly subject to interruption or stimulation from without. Lying in total darkness, like the ancient Gaelic bards at their work of composing, Molly experiences no distractions other than the sound of church bells or passing trains. Though her grammar may be wayward, it becomes perfectly clear once the reader gets the hang of it. Her thoughts are fully connected – if you traced them on a graph, they would follow straight, clear, connected courses, whereas her husband's would zig and zag all over the place. What seems like reason in men – all those cropped sentences of Bloom and Stephen – may just as often be rationalisation, whereas women like Molly, being disadvantaged from the start, are compelled to take a more rigorously analytic view of every situation.

In the dark, just before sleep, the human censors are most fully relaxed. Hence Molly's obscene joke about the banana displays the sort of candour which she would hardly risk in a social encounter (with Boylan, she tried to curb her impulse to shout obscene words), but it can be safely tried on the reader to whom the soliloquist will not lie. The dramatisation of a woman's thoughts just before sleep allows Joyce to blend the hovering rhythms of 1890s poetry with the automatic writing so much in vogue during the 1920s. He does this in a way which may even connect his long, trailing sentences to the experiments of Marcel Proust, who wrote:

In 1919 my attention was completely absorbed by

those more or less fragmented sentences which, when one is completely alone, on the verge of falling asleep, appear in one's mind without its being possible to ascribe any previous deliberation to them.

Here again the role of chance is vital, but with it a sense that some external power may be directing things, as in the 'monitions' which guide the characters of Homer. Thus, when Robert McAlmon, typing Molly's soliloquy, altered the placement of some phrases, Joyce instructed him to let the accident stand.

The sheer plenitude of this soliloquy, and its speaker's magnificent self-possession, raise further doubts about Bloom. His mother, Ellen Higgins, was not Jewish, so he cannot make a final home in that tradition. If the *Odyssey* showed anything, it was the act of coming home, the state of having escaped a life of painful wandering. That was also a theme of the Old Testament. With each home-coming came the freedom to narrate a full account of things. But Bloom's very truncated version of his day, as given to Molly, seems sadly symptomatic of his life. For all of the hundreds of pages detailing his monologues, in the end he is denied access to his own story. The very 'lack' which some commentators have lamented in the traditionally gapped narratives of women seems to be present in the story of this man.

Why so? Molly's predicament in living with Bloom is like that of Odysseus when he attempts to live with a divine being. Bloom can be invoked and wooed but never fully won. Part of his initial attraction, indeed, was that he 'wasnt to be got for the asking' (879). He is like a blend of a coy, bashful maiden and an unknowable god. Because of their affinity within the silence of their marriage, each often intuits what the other is thinking, a truce that has allowed them to share a house, if not a life. Molly's relation to Bloom is therefore a bit like Stephen's: they meet, but there may not be enough traction in their exchanges to reopen full communication.

That is true of all the Dubliners in their dealings with Bloom. They know next to nothing about him, his Jewish background and his culture. Although he knows more of theirs, he is often quite baffled by what he finds. Because a detailed knowledge of cultural difference is lacking, the potential for relationship is lost as well. His desire to return to the womb, noted acerbically by Molly ('Theyre all mad to get in there where they came out of', 902), is really a wish to escape this stand-off. Yet it may well be Bloom's own maternal tendency that contributes to this paralysis for Stephen's mother had gone, having scarcely existed, and Ellen Higgins was all but erased from her son's consciousness. The fact that Bloom's unconscious poetry in his monologues will never be publicly recognised is what gives him something in common with the mother figure who can never express herself. The desire to return to the womb, to get back where he came out of, is both Homeric and biblical. Yet what seems like his desire for sexual conquest is astutely interpreted by Molly as also indicating a death wish.

It is strange that the main protagonist of this massive book can be both one of the greatest characters of world literature *and* a man who never gets to tell his own story. Instead, he must negotiate the unsatisfactory frameworks provided by others. Of course, Molly has to do that too, and her soliloquy is a triumphant indication of how the

trick can be done. The stunning *completedness* of *Ulysses*
only heightens the reader's awareness of the book's gaps.
If Bloom's lost Jewishness is part of the problem,
providing an insufficient basis for a more rooted
narrative, isn't the same thing true of the lost Irishness of
all the other characters, beginning with Molly? So little is
told of her past that we never really learn how she ended
up in Dublin. Irishness, like Jewishness, lacks essential
definition: it is whatever people say that it is. So, living
with Bloom is as frustrating for Molly as loving Hamlet
was for Ophelia. It's like co-habiting with an androgynous
angel, or maybe even a god.

Molly would like a way in to Bloom and wonders
whether a sexual act with another man could rekindle his
desire: 'I wish some man or other would take me some-
time when hes there and kiss me in his arms' (875). This
sounds promising, given Bloom's keenness to imagine
such scenes, suggesting once again that they may not just
be legal but ideal mates. But there seems no way in when
'the fellow you want isnt there' (925). So Bloom remains a
mystery to her, and in ways which simply add to her
desire. Freud asked the famous question: what does a
woman want? It carried the strong implication that the
woman herself did not know. Molly might reverse the
question: what on earth does a man want?

Is Bloom at fault? In rejecting full conjugal relations
after the death of Rudy, he may not have given much
consideration to his wife's feelings. His apparent indifference is all the more remarkable, given his sensitivity to the
difficult plight of other married women like Josie Breen,
and also given that Molly has invested so much of her
life's meaning in relationships with men. She says that she

found Lenehan's attention disturbing. Fighting a losing battle for Bloom's affection, she feels that she was forced into the role of adulteress. She remembers their love-making on Howth even more fondly than Bloom does. But, unlike Bloom, who in 'Ithaca' appears to despair of recapturing its intensity, she believes that perhaps they can. And this is what makes her so mesmerising.

Unlike the barmaids in 'Sirens', Molly knows how to sing – and sing she does. She is in fact the real Circe that the whoremistress only pretended to be. In the brothel, the game with Bloom was mere performance, but here in Eccles Street Molly lives the truth of the Homeric legend: 'Circe's power, which subjects men to her and makes them obedient, becomes her obedience to the men who through renunciation refused to submit to her.'

Can Bloom answer her renewed challenge? She laments that war has had the effect of 'killing any fine-looking men' (886). The doubts about Bloom's virility may have been Joyce's way of voicing a post-World War I anxiety also explored by T. S. Eliot and Ernest Hemingway: in the new sexual scheme of things, what can women do with their emergent masculine side and men with their feminine side? In order to meet that challenge, Bloom must be not no-man but Everyman. After World War I, many women had to impersonate absent men, including absent fathers. Even during the war, with women working increasingly in factories, some men began to impersonate absent mothers too.

Joyce declined to depict the central encounter between Molly and Boylan, rejecting all prurient interest on the reader's part. But he allows Molly to reveal enough to confirm that Boylan's love-making was as limited as we would have suspected – he failed to satisfy. That is why she feels the need to masturbate now, an act which links her strangely across the book to Bloom. Masturbation was one form of sexual activity that could not be controlled by state or church and, as such, had radical potential, especially for a couple who might wish to jump-start a relationship. As Bloom came to his lonely climax on Sandymount Strand, his thoughts returned to Molly. Likewise here, she quickly passes over Boylan to musings on Bloom.

In the *Odyssey* Penelope had one hundred and eight lovers but spurned them all, waiting patiently for her reunion with Odysseus; and even that was postponed for two days after his return, as the couple became 'co-conspirators in a plan requiring the utmost secrecy'. It may be that, in the Joycean version, this couple also can survive an act of adultery, achieving not the moment of perfected passion but something worth having nevertheless. The feeling is akin to that at the close of *Paradise Lost*, another epic of the mind, when phases of interstellar travel across the universe come to a final focus on a husband and wife facing an uncertain future together, after a period of being lost in a maze.

Ulysses in its later episodes suggests a transformation in Bloom, so that he may again become worthy of Molly's love. The secret accounts, shared unknowingly by the couple, of their first love-meeting on Howth complement other shared elements – Bloom's exploration of his contrasexual side in female clothing vis-à-vis Molly's taste for Turkish pyjamas and other male accoutrements. She wants at moments to be a man as much as he wishes to be a woman, and when these moments overlap, they know paradise. Even on their tryst at Howth, she had already sensed his need at times to play the woman in sexual activity: 'Mawkish pulp her mouth had mumbled sweet and sour with spittle. Joy: I ate it: joy' (224). In so doing she effectively implements her desire for a female priesthood, for the shared seedcake is truly a distribution of the viaticum, one which presages Stephen's own shared bun with Bloom. In this final episode, Molly sheds real blood into her chamber-pot, in contrast to the merely symbolic blood in the parody-chalice raised by the priest. That she menstruates is Joyce's way of showing that she has not been impregnated by Boylan, but also that, like her husband, she can offer a literal re-enactment of the sacrament of the Eucharist.

Through much of her childhood Molly had no mother, and her own maternal skills seem minimal. She talks as if her daughter Milly were more rival than child, more sister than daughter. Her dislike of the name Molly offers a focus for her own resentment about all this: 'my mother whoever she was might have given me a nicer name' (904). Growing up without a mother among the all-male regiment in Gibraltar may have freed her of certain inhibitions, even as it made her more aware of what men want. One of Bloom's fundamental desires is to mother people, and so she allows him to perform that unofficial role with her: 'where would they all of them be if they hadnt all a mother to look after them what I never had' (926). Thus, Bloom is the mother Molly never had, bringing her breakfast in bed and finding her special treats. She fears that at thirty-three years old she may be ageing and less attractive. In these moments of unhappiness, she turns to men, but what she seeks is not really sex so much as emotional security. Her childhood friendships were transitory, so her desire is for the desire of her man.

For his part Bloom is attracted by women, but mainly by women's bottoms – a rehearsal for the moment when he kisses his wife's luscious 'melons'. Molly doesn't understand this, of course, feeling outraged that he should focus on that part, where people haven't an ounce of expression, being all more or less alike. (She considers charging him for the pleasure in future.) She wants to be loved for herself, not for her sexual parts, even though she repeatedly fails to be discriminating about men herself. Mulvey on Gibraltar is transformed into Bloom on Howth, as Bloom's straw hat on Howth morphs into Boylan's on 16 June. Even her ecstatic acceptance of Bloom on Howth was somewhat qualified by her phrase of acceptance: 'As well him as another' (933). The limit to one's individuality at the most important moments of life is a central point to which Joyce always returns.

The contradictions in Molly's discourse that have long troubled readers might be resolved if, instead of being treated as a definite person, she were taken as *the voice of the book*, a voice that breaks out of gender confines and individual identity. At the limits of language, Joyce seeks to move beyond the bounds of consciousness. The Molly who says 'Im too honest' (910) is certainly speaking for him and for his attempt to see more than humans can decently see, to know men and women beyond gender, beyond even their limitation to a merely human role. If 'Ithaca' was at least in part devoted to moving Bloom into the zones of eternity, it might be wiser to see Molly in this way too, moving out of time and into the infinite.

The day on which Joyce first walked out with Nora is commemorated by this episode. All the male–male meetings are despatched back to this terminal, as if Bloom saw in them a rehearsal for the moment when he would be worthy of her again. If he had much to teach Stephen, *she* has a lot of wisdom to impart to Bloom – for instance, her refusal to lament excessively for Rudy over a decade after he has died: 'Im not going to think myself into the glooms about that' (927). If Bloom is still trying to purge sex of possessiveness, she has already done so with her indiscriminate mingling of Mulvey, Boylan, Bloom and God knows who else. But Bloom has his wisdom too. By respecting his wife's freedom, he ensures that she can never really be 'stolen' from him. People seek faithfulness in partners, yet they often wish to act free themselves. Joyce with Nora sought a freedom that would be completed rather than constricted by fidelity. The conduct of a couple in a good marriage may be a little like that required of a good translator of Homer's *Odyssey* – to be faithful without seeming so.

By this late stage of their marriage, Bloom has been purged of the desire to possess Molly or to revenge anything. She is fascinated and finds him still mysterious after so many years together, but she also accuses him of coldness in not responding more intimately: 'never embracing me except sometimes when hes asleep the wrong end of me not knowing I suppose who he has' (925). Compared to her, Bloom emerges as a more complete parent, but as a lover he has many buried or withheld feelings. Hers seem nearer to the surface, but to the point of naïveté, as she often equates a feeling with its expression. If she can express too glibly at moments even

273

those emotions which she doesn't fully feel, he can feel things which are not given full expression – a version of Stephen's problem. She was attracted by the challenge which he posed to a strong, feisty woman. Now she acts as if he needs to be wooed all over again, by recreating the ambience of Howth Hill in a house swarming with flowers.

Is some of this male wish-fulfilment on the part of Joyce? By any standard, *Ulysses* is an amazing anniversary present, but also a strange one, for its climax is a male–male meeting and its coda is a woman plotting to recapture the love of her husband. Nora, who repeatedly berated 'Jim' for not writing sensible books that ordinary people could understand, may well have had her own tactical reasons for affecting not to have read it. (On receipt of her presentation copy, she offered at once to sell it to Arthur Power.) When the psychologist C. G. Jung wrote to Joyce saluting the insights contained in 'Penelope', Nora laconically opined that 'Jim knows nothing at all about women'. Yet the marriage of the Joyces, solemnised in 1931, was described by Sylvia Beach as the happiest of any writer that she knew.

It was happy partly because it allowed Joyce to play the literary lover. In their earlier years together, he kept a collection of parchment poems, intending to present it to Nora on one of their anniversaries. The cover design was to be two interlocking rings, a symbol of infinity. This is indeed Molly's symbol, the figure 8 on its side (for her eight sentences and her date of birth). But there is an even deeper meaning. Giordano Bruno, whose work Joyce admired, used two interlocking circles as a sign of androgyny; and, as they sleep head-to-toe, the couple are (without knowing it) re-enacting the attempt at alchemical fusion by the saintly couples of early Christianity, St Francis and St Clare, St Theresa and St John of the Cross, all of whom sought the wisdom of an androgynous godhead. After baptism, there was to be neither male not female, but all were to be one in the figure of Jesus Christ at the centre of the interlocking rings. As Molly drifts off to sleep, Joyce tries to capture the subliminal forces at work in her conscious and semi-conscious mind.

'Penelope' lacks the narrative pretence of other episodes, but it does add complexity and depth to all that has gone before. It could hardly be called a conclusion: the end to a single day never brings much resolution. The characters will learn some new things, and forget many others. But it is the reader who can decide whether to change, the reader who has been made heroic by the act of working through the challenges posed by the book. Molly is, especially in the closing pages, the voice of the book as a whole. She is Joyce's Muse, his Nora, his inspiratrice, who impelled him to this act of radical creativity, and also the one for whom it was written.

At moments before sleep, couples can merge. Bloom has spoken his thoughts to his wife (well, some of them) as a prelude to dozing off, so his desires are very real to her in these moments. Although she will always reject his flagellation fetish, she does perform a surprising number of his fantasies for him. If the adultery with Boylan was a scenario partly drawn up by Bloom, she proves very willing to act it out. She views her body through the eyes of an implied male and will even let Bloom ejaculate on her bottom, the only way to make him want her. She is interested in what he wants as a man. Her feelings about Stephen are exactly those which Bloom would have wanted her to entertain. So fully does she implement many of Bloom's wishes that the whole episode could almost be read as another of Bloom's 'implied monologues', like Gerty's thoughts on the strand. What better climax to a male fantasy than to imagine a wife planning how to woo and win her husband all over again?

What can confidently be said is that in the final pages the identities of Leopold and Molly fuse, as in John Donne's poem that says 'we two, being one, are it'. Molly's famous 'yes' at the close is not just her word but her husband's too. It was he who asked her, all those years ago on Howth, to say yes. Even if language is largely controlled by men – a dubious proposition at this stage of *Ulysses* – the deeper power now established is that of the human body, and it lies with her: 'I gave him all the pleasure I could leading him on till he asked me to say yes' (932). Who owns the word at that point? 'I asked him with my eyes to ask again' (933). They both own the word and the book.

Ordinary People's Odysseys

'Odysseus is not a hero,' a Jesuit priest told James Joyce at Clongowes Wood College – but the young boy disagreed. All his life he would admire the canny wanderer who survived challenges by a combination of willpower and craftiness. He told Pádraic Colum that the Greek epics were 'outside European culture', a fact which left Homer free to experiment with new ideas of character and story. Much the same was true of Joyce himself – he wasn't yet 'James Joyce' when he wrote *Ulysses*, but a relatively unknown artist from a peripheral country, so he was at liberty to attempt strange, unprecedented things without provoking choruses of disapproval. Over one hundred generations of humankind separated him from Homer, yet somehow the *Odyssey*, because of its encounters with unfamiliar peoples, seemed the quintessentially modern story. Small wonder that modern publishers have sold far more copies of it than of the *Iliad*.

Through the centuries the *Odyssey* has had a magical appeal for authors who wished to retell it in poetry or in prose. But the chances of producing something worthy enough to stand beside the original were almost nil. Although as a child Joyce loved Charles Lamb's *Adventures of Ulysses*, he soon became rather scathing about second-rate versions by many other writers: 'There is little point in imitation on this scale,' says Richard Jenkyns, 'unless it is a means of saying something new.' Yet Joyce also realised that Homer had performed the repetition trick first, using the *Odyssey* to reduce its predecessor and rival the *Iliad* to the status of a footnote. Homer's own travel tale provided the first model of how a prior text could be trumped. Early on, he has Telemachus suggest that most people enjoy the latest version of a story far more than any of its predecessors.

If it would have been wrong to neglect Homer's masterpiece, the other great offence would have been to repeat it. Joyce felt himself filled with Homer's un-expected energies. 'The spirit of Homer was always beside me to sustain and encourage me,' he said of *Ulysses*: 'I believe that this was the first time that he did such a thing, since he could hardly have been concerned with all those feeble imitations that every second generation feels duty-bound to produce.' Homer's ghost may have been waiting for just such an adaptor, capable of taking a deeper X-ray of his narrative than any prior version could offer. For Homer knew that only the future would have critical methods subtle enough to bring out all the vital elements of the original work. The epic, being multi-plotted, always contains elements of many future narratives.

If Odysseus was destined to travel across space and time, so also was the *Odyssey*. It represents, in the words of Carol Dougherty, 'not so much the story of a journey as the journey of a story'. With its flashbacks, reveries, inscribed tales and multiple narrators, it has an oddly modern feel to it. Odysseus is a modern type of prot-agonist, whose authority to tell a story comes not just

278

from the Muses but from the pressure of experience – like Leopold Bloom, he has learned his lessons in 'the university of life' (798). When Calypso promises immortality if only he will stay with her, he says no, in what must be the first-ever tale in which a human refuses such an offer. His canny creator knew that there would be other, future Odysseys, even as Joyce sensed that there would be later versions of *Ulysses* (such as Derek Walcott's recent *Omeros*).

Odysseus was hardly a conventional military hero; he was more a kind of conscientious objector. He knew that the official reason for the war – the defence of the ancestral culture – was trumped up. Joyce believed, however anachronistically, that the more likely motive was a search for raw materials and new markets. Accordingly, Odysseus tried to dodge the recruiting sergeant, but to no avail. Much as he rejected military heroics, he also refused the role of sexual conqueror. Circe, the Sirens, Calypso – these women all take the sexual initiative in wooing their men, as Molly did with Bloom. Far from being a sexual predator, Odysseus seems rather like an absolute bourgeois, who knows how to be passive and vigilant, how to *wait* – a foreshadowing not just of the intellectual but of the secret charm of café society. He is supposed to be intent on his return to Ithaca, a journey which would have taken a couple of weeks, but it instead consumes many years. As he tarries, he anticipates the spectatorial pleasures of a Leopold Bloom who rates anticipation even more highly than fulfilment.

'Who will deliver us from the Greeks and Romans?' asked many a Romantic author, a question to which Joyce responded, 'I will.' The translator half hopes to displace the original text, or at least to release the energies that were latent in it but not yet fully expressed. It is as if one molecule, brought into contact with another, releases a new third energy after their collision. To remember any past work, one must agree to forget many of its elements; and so involuntary memory, often triggered by associative mechanisms, will have not just an element of surprise but also the force of a revelation. In Joyce's case, what is revealed is the modernity of Homer's tale. The world between 1914 and 1921, the years when *Ulysses* was taking shape, was a chaotic and frightening place. T. S. Eliot said that Joyce used Homer's story as a way of 'controlling, of ordering, of giving a shape and a significance to the immense panorama of futility and anarchy which is contemporary life'. But Homer was himself using his tale in the attempt to impose a semblance of order on a chaotic world which had in fact been shattered by his hero's travels and by what he had found on them. The *Odyssey* was 'trying to construct a reading of the worlds and peoples of its own mythic past in order to make sense of a tumultuous and volatile present'. So he decoded various alien cultures in order to recode them for his own, much as Joyce would turn Homer's 'then' into his own 'now'.

Theodor Adorno and Max Horkheimer described the project of the *Odyssey* as an attempt to destroy mythical thinking and replace it with the rational order of a trading world. In the tale, Odysseus is treated often as a travelling salesman or barterer, and he is even taunted for being a profiteering merchant rather than an aristocratic athlete. His refusal to be seduced by the song of the Sirens is a rejection of myth by a prudent rationalist, for the bourgeois wins by doing nothing, by simply waiting, by deferring gratification. Odysseus refuses to eat the lotus-plant or the sacred cows and opts instead to be both sacrifice and priest, in what can be seen as an astonishing anticipation of the role of Jesus – and of Bloom.

So the bourgeois ego owes its existence to the sacrifice of the present to the future, much as the *Odyssey* deferred some of its gratifications until *Ulysses*. In the old story, Odysseus saves his life at one point by losing his very name, just as Jesus will offer a 'new' code by which whoever loses his life will save it. Bloom too will be divested of his proper name to become simply 'the man' (780). In all of these narratives, a passive but caring person achieves a sort of semi-divine status, at once victim and god, by a sort of anonymous celebrity. The story of Odysseus was a parable of how you can use your ordinariness and anonymity to win a final victory, the technique of the 'everyday'. Among the lotus-eating sybarites, Odysseus triumphs just by working hard; when faced with the one-eyed monster, he learns the value of self-control, having been almost killed in a moment of imprudence. He bribes the monster with drink, in yet another anticipation of the words of Jesus consecrating the bread and wine: 'Take, Cyclops, and drink. Wine goes well with human flesh'. Bloom will offer his coffee and bun in a revised, gentler version. If sacrifice was once designed by humans to propitiate gods, now it is propounded by godlike humans as an offering made ultimately to themselves.

Joyce seized on this anti-mythological element in the *Odyssey* to free his own generation from their cult of war. In lacerating the earlier, now-sacred text, Joyce was guilty of nothing more than a rigorous application of Homer's underlying logic. The modern translator is never merely an aggressor, for he or she also helps to create the aura of the *original*. But by setting a new text to vibrate with an ancient one, the translator also serves to decanonise the original. In this process Homer becomes a botched, incompletely imagined, ur-version of Joyce, much as Simon Dedalus is presented as an unsatisfactory father to Stephen. Every major work of art contains and reinforces our sense of the strangeness of its original, even as it shows how elements of the modern may be found in the pre-historical. The converse is also true: aspects of the pre-historical may sometimes be found in the modern, which is forever in danger of lapsing back into mythological mentalities, as in the anti-Semitic attacks on Bloom. Autocratic nationalities have often despised and feared seafarers, who are notoriously hybrid and innovative in their sense of cultural identity.

Joyce sensed that in his world the surviving shreds of pre-modern thought might yet become the basis for a common culture. That, after all, was the understanding upon which Yeats and his collaborators were basing the Irish Literary Revival. The difference was that Joyce tried to imagine past heroes in our space, rather than us in theirs. If the story of Odysseus anticipates many features of the lives of the civic bourgeoisie, that may say more about the vulnerability of that modern class than it does about the permanence of the ancient world. For *Ulysses* is, among other things, a lament for bourgeois virtues that were fast disappearing.

A central theme throughout the *Odyssey* is its insistence that the solitary traveller really is alone, isolated by his own sophistication from the superstitious activities among primitive peoples, whose codes he views with the incredulity of a scandalised anthropologist. The song of the Sirens is, by definition, based on the pull of the past and, though haunting, it can only strike the busy Odysseus as an attempt to wish away the challenges of the present. Bloom repeatedly voices a similar reservation. Calypso, Circe, the Sirens themselves are all, according to Adorno and Horkheimer, 'nothing but a stylisation of what can no longer be celebrated'. Small wonder then that Joyce would key his own lament for a dying civic culture to such a story of lost worlds. Ithaca began to generate elegies to lost cultures at just that moment when it began to appropriate and abolish them, much as the modern discipline of sociology began to emerge only when society was no longer felt to fit like a glove. The logic of the *Odyssey* is that of many tales involving shipwreck – the answers to problems will be found only after the act of destruction. The catastrophe must precede clarification.

The gods of the Greeks were not remote. The Greeks felt no need of a messiah, for their gods were near at hand, social beings, possessed of a past and a present reality. They were made in man's image, not pictured as mythical monsters or fabulous birds but as people with human organs. This humanisation was itself a bold and modernising act, though it had some precedent in the Gilgamesh legend. If man could create gods in his image, then he might himself be godlike. The returned Odysseus at the close has the knowledge, even omniscience, of a god, although in his disguise he looks like a travelling beggar. By a similar logic, both Jesus and Bloom never seems more godlike than when they appear most bereft. To become a nomad is to have no place in which to lay your head. It is to give up all identity. Odysseus's great fear of dying at sea and of drowning without a clean burial is of becoming 'a nameless one'. The equivalent modern fear might be of massification, of being lost in the crowd, or at a more personal level of drowning in one's own unconscious. That may be why both Stephen and Bloom are haunted by thoughts of drowning throughout *Ulysses.*

One reason why Telemachus sets out in pursuit of his father is to establish a viable identity for himself. Years without that father have left a vacuum, and so his journey is a search for authority rather than a revolt against it. His mother hopes that it will at least make a man of him. Like father, like son. Telemachus never quite catches up with his target, finding in the pursuit a kind of happiness. His trajectory parallels his father's rather than intersecting with it, much as Stephen will trace parallel lines with Bloom through most of *Ulysses.* In the event, Telemachus learns little about his father, but he discovers something far more valuable: how to share in his journey. His journey to a self-formed identity is, like his father's, to an exemplary role.

Telemachus sets out to discover what men are saying about his father and, if necessary, to build an appropriate tomb. On his travels he enters that condition of non-identity, already well known to his father, because by definition a nomad can never be anything in particular: 'My mother certainly says I am Odysseus's son; but for myself I cannot tell. No man can be certain of his parentage.' The very separation of both protagonists epitomises the psychic problem. For Joyce this was the fear of many men that they were not the true fathers of their designated children. In Homer's work, as in *Hamlet*, that became a pressing problem for sons, no longer sure of their own fathers. Telemachus bravely and wisely concludes that he must take his given father on trust. All of these uncertainties help to explain the lure of Calypso or of the Sirens with their promise of immortality. Yet they are false muses whose poetry of the past would only empty men like Odysseus or Telemachus of their selfhood.

The true Muses are the gods, who guide the traveller to faraway places, often under cover of the darkness of the night, as if the *Odyssey* also functions as a sort of prospectus for settlers and tourists. This gives Homer's story its cinematic quality as a narrative filled with 'jump-cuts'. There are no gradual transitions from one scene to the next. At the start of each episode every setting is arbitrarily *there* as a given, with the weird but lucid discontinuity of a dream. Ulysses proceeds in a similar fashion with sudden shifts of scene from episode to episode. And neither Odysseus nor Bloom appears at the outset of either tale. Odysseus only comes into his story in book five, by which time he has evoked a crescendo of expectation, since all the earlier scenes emphasise the disastrous effect of his absence on his family, friends, and the body politic. Bloom, for his part, appears only in the fourth episode of *Ulysses*: and his emergence is quite sudden, arbitrary, unannounced, and unexpected, as the exponent of a kind of thought process very different from that of Stephen Dedalus.

Ulysses may have been the first artistic work to centralise the very process of *thinking*, but in doing so it was simply taking to a logical conclusion Homer's discovery that thought itself is godlike. For him it was not just a god but *the* god, not something to be bounded by human form. Athene is at once an external god and a projection of human thought processes – which is to say, the interior monologue. In the primitive world, people did not recognise thought as coming from their own minds, so emotions such as anger, nervousness, and desire were identified with organs of the body like the lungs, stomach or heart. Joyce's organ-for-every-episode scheme in Ulysses might even be interpreted as putting that world back together again, but in the form of a completed human body.

Like all storytellers and psychologists, Homer was intrigued by those vital moments in life when characters act impulsively, as if under the sway of forces beyond themselves. E. R. Dodds in *The Greeks and the Irrational* called these moments 'monitions' which 'allow us to ascribe all sorts of mental events to the intervention of some god'. Literature is filled with examples of people who act with decisive or tragic effect, as if their wills were not their own:

> Whenever someone has a particularly brilliant or a particularly foolish idea; when he suddenly recognises another person's identity or sees in a flash the meaning of an omen; when he remembers what he might well have forgotten or forgets what he should have remembered, he or someone else will see in it, if we are to take the words literally, a psychic intervention by one of these anonymous supernatural beings.

286

This sounds remarkably like some of the interior monologues in *Ulysses*. 'Often he is conscious of no observation or reasoning which has led up to them. But in that case, how can he call them "his"?', asks Dodds. This suggests that there may be severe limits to what modern people call 'individuality'. Some force has inserted such thoughts, outside the thinker's formal control, much as a lightning bolt seems to arise from a source outside the usual pattern of the weather.

What makes Homer so subtle is his recognition in the *Odyssey* that often the thinker alone can visualise the prompting god, who remains invisible to everyone else. This projection of inner states has led humans to create gods, by whom the creators then feel themselves possessed. It would explain some of the obsessive-compulsive behaviour of Stephen Dedalus and Leopold Bloom in 'Circe', as it also accounts for the way in which a proud person can offload responsibility for some types of behaviour:

> When he acts in a manner contrary to the system of conscious dispositions which he is said to 'know', his action is not properly his own, but has been dictated to him . . . Acts resulting from these impulses tend to be excluded from the self and ascribed to an alien origin . . . such as to cause acute shame to their author.

No deed done by persons is ever fully their own, for men and women never quite find the conditions in which they must act to be those which they would ideally have chosen. Joyce, by a weird kind of analogy with the monitions, installed Homer as one of his presiding spirits, so that *Ulysses* is not just his own work but also that of Homer.

For the epic poet (unless he is Walt Whitman) does not speak only of himself. Rather the Muse, goddess of inspiration, also speaks through him, her authority being invoked at the outset of works by Homer, Virgil and Milton. Homer used his own invocation in order to protest against rival versions of his stories, much as Joyce himself would prove jealously dismissive of the claims of other modern masters (calling D. H. Lawrence, for example, 'lush'). In *Ulysses* the inspiratrice speaks only at the end. But the entire book is a telling example of how the hidden gods intervene, by analogy with the Muse, through monitions and forces which are latent in the everyday self. At the close, it has developed a separate, independent consciousness which still sings through Joyce, but has moved well beyond him.

The wisdom to be gleaned from the *Odyssey* is clear enough: that there is nothing better in life than when a man and woman live in harmony and that such happiness, though felt intensely by the couple themselves, can never be fully described. It can merely be evoked, either by comparison or by contrast. Homer set out to heroicise the domestic, even as Joyce wishes to domesticate the heroic. Although these are not identical processes, the results have much in common. The major, characteristic device of Homer is the 'normalisation' technique of recalling a touching, homely image in the midst of a terrifying battle: 'as when the farmer ploughs his field . . .' The whole of *Ulysses* might be taken as just such an extended hymn to the dignity of everyday living, when cast against the backdrop of a world war.

It is as if Joyce has turned Homer inside-out and made the 'as if' similes the key to the entire narrative, rather

288

than simply passing moments of beautiful relaxation. In a more localised and concrete sense, the 'as if' similes of Homer might be taken to lie behind not just the interior monologues but also the daydreams and reveries of Bloom throughout *Ulysses*. It has been said that the epic similes of Homer are designed not only to escape battle, but 'to project the excruciating enormities of battle onto an integral world of peaceful and homely work'. This is like the effect which Joyce achieves, when responses to war break in upon the meditations of his characters (Molly thinks of war 'killing any finelooking young men', 886). Such references to combat are ancillary rather than primary, a final measure of the unsurpassable sweetness of the middle range of human experience. It is as if Joyce had anticipated Tom Stoppard's little joke: 'What did you do in the Great War, Mr Joyce?' – 'I wrote *Ulysses* – what did you do?'

All that might seem like a charter for a complacent banality, but at the time it was very much a minority viewpoint among intellectuals. Even the liberal Sigmund Freud was convinced that decades of peace had left the youth of Europe supine and spineless, so he welcomed the era of the mass grave. 'Life has become interesting again – it has recovered its full content,' he opined, bemoaning the fact that during the prolonged peace it had seemed 'as shallow as an American flirtation'. In the years before World War I, a cult of manly strength, cut loose from ethical moorings, had led to the jingoism finally unleashed in the conflict. As early as 1905, James Joyce had written to his brother Stanislaus:

Do you not think the search for heroics damn vulgar?

. . . I am sure, however, that the whole structure of heroism is, and always was, a damned lie and that there cannot be any substitute for individual passion as the motive power of everything.

In 'Nestor' Joyce derided the false use of classics in the classroom, designed to promote a style of imperial militarism. In *Ulysses* he offered a renewed version of how the classics might inform a more humane code.

Ulysses is brave enough to celebrate the feminine, while attacking the merely genteel: Joyce would probably have agreed with Henry Stanley that 'England is becoming effeminate and soft from long inactivity, long enfeeblement of purpose, brought about by indolence and ease, destruction of her own powers and shaken nerves'. Joyce, after all, was the man who boasted that he could find nobody in Ireland with a faith to match his own. At that time Georges Sorel was contending that epic still had a future, being 'an anticipation of the kind of work that ought to be carried on in a highly productive state of society'. Such a society would make for strong, self-reliant individuals, who could remain open to the 'strangeness' of Bloom.

Bloom's charm, like his heroism, is inadvertent. 'The healthy know not of their own health,' wrote Thomas Carlyle, 'but only the sick.' The real problem posed by the long peace was not the absence of a character-testing war but rather the fact that virtue, if it grows over-aware of itself, becomes sickly. It was in that context that William James could contrast 'the health, brightness and freshness' of 'the bloody old heathens of the *Odyssey*', and 'the essentially definite character of all their joys', with 'the over-cultivated and vaguely sick complainers of today'. Odysseus, like Mr Bloom, accepted the universe and the here-and-now. Hamlet, like Stephen Dedalus, wished that it might all dissolve.

The quotidian world of work to which people rise each morning is affirmed in the *Odyssey*. Penelope at her weaving and the farmer at his ploughing are among its defining images. Hamlet has no distraction from his worries other than the assumption (real or imagined) of madness, but for Odysseus this is a mere trick to outwit the recruiting officer. An epic character like Odysseus is no more subject to change than a Leopold Bloom. Theirs is not the world of the *Bildungsroman,* for at the end their experiences 'leave them more like themselves than ever'. *Ulysses* teases the reader by opening like a conventional coming-of-age novel: but from the fourth episode, it turns its focus on to Mr Bloom, at thirty-eight years of age a man too mature to develop as might the youthful protagonist of a nineteenth-century novel. Joyce sets up a meeting between his Telemachus and Odysseus near the end, but cannot really *show* how the younger man might turn into a convincing version of the older one.

Shakespeare had the same difficulty in demonstrating exactly how the naïve Hamlet of act one becomes the mature sage of act five, so he removed Hamlet, as Telemachus is removed by Homer, from some of the central episodes. Both young men had hoped (like Stephen at the close of *A Portrait of the Artist as a Young Man*) to excite the sympathies of ordinary people with their programme, only to fail utterly. The problem of writing such a *Bildungsroman* has been well captured by Eva Brann: 'we need an identity in order to learn but learning is supposed to confer an identity'. Growing into an adult state allows a person to absorb energies which, once selfhood is found, can be applied to an interpretation of the world. Lacking an identity, Stephen in *Ulysses* is not fully free to learn, yet he may at least study at close range just how an older man, possessed of selfhood, can take on the world. Bloom can no more explain this in words than Odysseus can for Telemachus. In each story both men 'arrive' at the same moment at a place that could be called 'home'.

Odysseus fears that Penelope's ardour will have weakened, Bloom that his wife is not faithful. The Greek wanderer speaks to his wife as if she were still young and to be courted over again; but in Joyce's version, it is Molly who sets herself the task of a renewed wooing. Bloom is less than wholly candid with Molly about the events of his day – in this, too, he recreates the mixture of shrewdness and tricksiness that was in Odysseus.

The famous digressive story of Eurycleia discovering the identity of Odysseus by seeing his old scar and recalling how he got that wound offers a long retrospective reverie in mid-action, told on the verge of the long-postponed finale. This is Homer's technical trick, by which he can deliver delayed gratification in yet another mode. It comes as a momentary pause in mid-narrative, a memory which consumes but a moment of consciousness-time, even though it takes far longer to hear or read it through. Joyce also opens many similar portals into the re-membered past at various moments of 16 June 1904. Both the *Odyssey* and *Ulysses* repeatedly cannibalise earlier sections of their texts; and each is written in a way which shows itself deeply alert to its own reception as a literary performance. Some of the internal audiences for sections within the works suggest parallels with the external audience, just as the listeners to Stephen in the National Library episode may be that part of Joyce's readership which he hopes to discomfit.

Interpreters of the *Odyssey* often try to recover its immediate effect on its first audience. So also do readers of *Ulysses* hope for the sort of 'innocent' analysis possible only to its initial audience in 1922. The problems posed for both sets of interpreters are in fact identical. Each work is now over-familiar to scholarly commentators, who may fail at given moments to open themselves to the exfoliations which might (but did not) ensue. Congealed readings need to be challenged, in order to allow to each moment in the unfolding text the openness it once had. There are missed meetings and missed accounts of vital meetings all through both stories. Each has plenty of time for the sort of nondescript individual who might well have been passed over in a more conventional tale. The drunken Elpenor was no great fighter, nor were his wits of the foremost, but in his death by falling from a roof he becomes the prototype for Paddy Dignam.

Many other ordinary people are given their moment of prominence by the aristocratic Homer: a nurse, a swineherd, a bard. When Odysseus returns to Ithaca at the end, he moves among his servants, a god disguised as a beggar, testing their fidelity, much as Jesus rejoins his disciples after the crucifixion or as Bloom returns with Stephen to his familiar ground at Eccles Street. Eumaeus grieves for the missing master who is in fact already present. He cries out for that which is lost, even as it has been already found. In its lament for a lost world, *Ulysses* may find even in the energy expended on elegy a basis for the recovery of that world's inner codes, as the dead white European male called Homer helped to make possible modernism's greatest masterpiece.

It's easy to isolate those elements in the story with which Joyce identified. Telemachus, tired of being the son of the fabled Odysseus, would far prefer to be the child of an ordinary man – a desire which must often have assailed James Joyce under the pressure of excessive expectation by his wayward but exacting father. Similarly, the role of Odysseus contained many parallels to his own, not least the fear that his stratagems would be famous across the world, while being all but forgotten among his own people. The depression brought on by exile could be transcended only by fully embracing the hero's own hidden feminine dimension: 'you must not refuse the goddess's favours, if you want her to free your men and look after you'. Like Odysseus, Joyce comes back from his amazing expedition in the guise of a beggar, seeking alms from Harriet Shaw Weaver and others who might bankroll the author. And he knew that his book, like the disguised Odysseus, would present the 'ordinary' as the canny disguise of the exceptional man. Being an artist aware of his own national traditions, he would also have been aware that the *Odyssey* was an example of an authentic *aisling*, that vision-poem in which an exiled prince returns over the water to free an occupied state and liberate his beloved from bondage.

Like Homer, Joyce belongs to everybody and to nobody – but to the lover of literature most of all, who might turn to his book, as the Greeks turned to the *Odyssey*, for their ideas of virtue and decency. The epics of other nations (and even those of the Greeks and the children of Israel) fed that mood of manic nationalism that drove Europeans over the edge of madness in 1914. But these past epics were subverted and reconfigured by Joyce. Nor was the surgery required all that radical. For both the *Odyssey* and the New Testament stood out from other epics in their willingness to treat ordinary life and ordinary people as subjects of innate dignity. These works had already questioned notions of militarism long before Joyce mocked those ideas even more scathingly.

Old Testaments and New

When asked why he chose Odysseus rather than Christ as a model for Bloom, Joyce was curt. Living with a woman was one of the most difficult things a man could do – and Jesus was a bachelor who never did it. Yet Joyce was haunted by the mystery he flouted. According to Francini Bruni, his friend in Trieste, 'He only completely admires the unchangeable: the mystery of Christ and the mute drama that surrounds it. I can well imagine that his head was full of this mystery when he wrote *Ulysses* and that therein lies the allegorical point of this story of new martyrdom'. Bruni noted how Joyce frequented the Catholic churches of Trieste all through Holy Week, 'so as not to miss a single syllable'. 'As a child he was very religious,' recalled one of his sisters: 'I think that all of Jim's loves were really created in the love of God.' His brother Stanislaus, who became a lifelong atheist, remarked sardonically of James's temperament that 'he who has loved God in youth can never love anything that is less than divine'.

Joyce was someone who snooped around old texts looking for a back door through which to effect an entry. The New Testament was one such text and a major element in the creation of *Ulysses.* What fascinated him was the audacity with which the gospel authors cannibalised and rewrote the Old Testament, much as he would reconfigure earlier classics, making *Ulysses* both their fulfilment and itself an open, prophetic book.

As well as the Bible writers, Joyce revered the English mystic William Blake as another bard 'who present, past and future sees', because all tenses blend in the no-time of God. Blake wrote a prophetic book on this understanding, as did Joyce. Even in the Old Testament, 'a saviour is born' because God-time is an eternal now and for Christian readers Jesus always existed. It was not God-the-Father who appeared on Sinai, but Jesus, the pre-existing Word. The words of the prophets were shot through with a utopian potential that was not completely realised until it was incarnated in the figure of the New Testament Jesus. Similarly, a previous work like the *Odyssey* achieved its destined form in *Ulysses*. But only when Jesus delivered certain lines or performed specific actions did his followers realise that he was the anointed one foretold. Only then did the sentences foretelling him become famous as prophecy, and, for Christians, more significant than the rest of the Old Testament. Joyce, likewise, selects key lines from the classics, even as he submits those texts to a 'retrospective arrangement' (113). The New Testament, in effect, establishes the utopian, forward thrust of the older texts – Joyce performs a similar service for it, and for them. In one sense, he liquidates all prior works; in another, he shows how much of them can be saved.

T. S. Eliot said that *Ulysses* manipulates a continuous parallel between contemporaneity and antiquity, and that this technique – he called it 'the mythical method' – had 'the importance of a scientific discovery'. But this method is at least as old as the New Testament. A number of crucial passages culled from the Old Testament helped the first Christians to give shape to the life of Jesus. The Exodus narrative of the people of Israel shows that, despite their occasional mutinies, God kept his promises and gave them hope of better things to come. The mutiny in the wilderness, the manna from heaven, the handing over of the Tables of the Law on Mount Sinai – each has later echoes in, respectively, the temptation in the desert, the miracle of the loaves and fishes, and the Sermon on the Mount. The twelve tribes of Israel find their equivalents in the twelve apostles. The edict of the Pharaoh that all male babies, including Moses, should die prefigures Herod's killing of children under two years old in his attempt to do away with Jesus.

So the Christian life was 'fitted' to the Exodus paradigm, with the forty days spent by Jesus in the desert as a reconstruction of the forty years of wandering in the wilderness by the people of Israel. This was the period of penitential wandering and waiting embarked on by Jesus, the 'agenbuyer' repeatedly mentioned in *Ulysses* (253, 511), to buy back a people, but also to redeem the old texts. This recapitulates the wanderings of Odysseus, and in a modern context it also anticipates the experience of the Irish diaspora awaiting Home Rule. The idea is that in their confused passage through the wilderness, those who were once the Pharaoh's slaves were transformed into God's free people; and that a period of forty years was felt necessary to allow time for the creation of a generation unaccustomed to bondage.

The mutiny in the desert enrages God but Moses mollifies him, coming down from the mountain carrying

298

what in *Ulysses* will be called 'the tables of the law . . . in the language of the outlaw' (181). That new dispensation on Sinai is not an action subject to any human control; it represents an irruption into the everyday human world of a divine force, which has been triggered by some sort of involuntary memory. This gives to the rediscovered past the excitement of surprise, the force of a revelation after a period of denial. It teaches people how to make a past moment contemporary, how to make the ancients live again in 'our' time. The event reverberates back into the past but also forward into an uncertain future.

After Sinai the people want laws, but not too many, because such a truth is less a statement in words than something to be felt from within. The radical innovation of the New Testament is its uncovering of an interiority even more subtle and deep than that known to Homer. Edward Said observed in one of his final essays, developing a point first made by Erich Auerbach, that in the *Odyssey* characters awaken every morning as if to the first day of their lives, and so for them the day becomes the unit to be seized. But in the Christian Bible, the lives of characters come heavy with implications, extending back and forward in space and time.

There a past event is only fully interpreted, and in that sense *completed*, by a present one, which may claim the status of the real, making the past seem mythical by comparison. If the epic bard is the person 'who present, past and future sees', then the Blake who noted that now-time also recognised that this extends Homer's insight that the gods are human creations – hence Blake's phrase celebrating the 'human form divine'. Certain protagonists, in moments of greatness, can seem both human and godlike, caught up in their historical period yet somehow enabled to float free of it too. For instance, Jesus can weep real tears at the sight of the dead Lazarus, while all the time knowing that he has the power to raise him. It is in a somewhat similar way that certain literary texts reverberate with predecessors and successors to such a degree that they transcend their time and partake, it seems, in the very creativity of the gods.

The covenant agreed on Sinai is less a legal formulation than a description of a developing relationship. The Egypt which the people of Israel fled – an Egypt repeatedly compared in *Ulysses* to the British Empire – is seen as a ruthless bureaucracy fixated on control and oppression. For the chosen people there can only be a life-relationship that is not rigid and requires them to confront in freedom the altered 'tasks of daily life'. In such a radical order, the new leader could never be charismatic. Hence Bloom's quiet, undemonstrative decency, and the fact that the new order is something which must be developed tentatively during a period of wandering. Galilee, the scene of the itinerant teaching ministry developed by Jesus, thus becomes a symbol of 'the periphery becoming the new', as the pilgrim arrives in a city like Jerusalem or Dublin and learns how to challenge its codes.

If the manifest content of the *Odyssey* is the scaffolding which eventually falls away to reveal the latent content of *Ulysses*, such a technique isn't necessarily taken from Marx or Freud. It can be found where they probably discovered it too – in the Torah as the source of Jewish tradition. 'People without understanding see only the narrations, the garment,' while 'those somewhat penetrating see also the body; but the truly wise . . . pierce all the way through to the soul.' The outer garments of earlier classics are removed from *Ulysses* like so many teasing veils, to disclose what lies beneath. The reader of a holy book in the Jewish tradition must accept the proposal that there is a divine wisdom in the text, before seeking to disrobe the bride in order to unite with her behind her many veils. The Jews, in fact, saw the cycle of literary history as a progression toward the revelation of such an unmapped interior. Homer was poetic but his work was secular. Virgil's writings in some elements anticipated the gospels, but only indirectly. Sacred scripture could, however, contain all the wise lore that was in predecessor works, retrospectively giving them '*salus*' (deliverance). Everything was in the holy book, including all that had been known to predecessors.

It was to this precise model that Joyce worked in *Ulysses*, '*ut implerentur scripturae*' (561), 'that the scriptures might be fulfilled'. The image of Rudy, Bloom's dead son, studying his Hebrew text 'from right to left' (702) at the end of 'Circe' is based on the idea that revealed teachings are a dead letter unless revitalised in the mouths of those who study them. Joyce understood that for the Jews the act of interpretation itself partakes of the holiness of scripture to which it adds. A criticism of the text in which God speaks might in itself also be an extension of the voice of God as universal author. Hence the strongly autocritical element all through *Ulysses* – those passages which help to supply that very apparatus by which the book might be interpreted.

Joyce's characteristic idea of a text as a work-in-progress is also central to the Jewish tradition. The fragments assembled drew strength not so much from a past totality as from the notion of a perfected work yet to be done. Hence the emphasis on *waiting*. An old Jewish joke concerns an unemployed labourer who is appointed, after many delays, to be the paid watchman on the look-out for the messiah. He soon grows disgruntled with the long hours and bad conditions. 'I can hardly feed my family on what you pay me,' he complains, only to be told: 'You should take comfort in the supreme importance of the work you do. Besides, unlike almost all others, yours is a permanent job.'

The first followers of Jesus used texts of the Old Testament to help make sense of the life, death and resurrection of Jesus. This was not done to convert anyone. After all, in those days, as Leopold Bloom rightly recalls, everyone was a Jew. Like Jesus, Bloom is cautious in his claims to any form of divinity. When he sees a handbill about a prophet, he humbly wonders whether it refers to himself, and when interrogated in 'Circe' he tactfully says, 'You have said it' (like the 'Thou sayest it' said by Jesus to Pontius Pilate). The humiliating death of a pretender mocked with a crown of thorns threw the claims of his followers into doubt. So a vast effort was undertaken to show the basis in ancient literature for the rejection and crucifixion of Jesus. Bloom seems utterly ludicrous when named the new messiah – a title first sarcastically conferred by the Citizen in 'Cyclops', before his mock-investiture in 'Circe'; Jesus himself was called messiah when he least looked like the foretold king of the Jews.

The death of Jesus was absolutely necessary. He had to become a sacrifice to textuality as much as to the Roman officials who condemned him. As Luke wrote, 'It is written that Christ should suffer and be raised from the dead on the third day' (Luke 24:46). His followers recycled fragments of the Old Testament before a new, coherent narrative was generated. So, the close interpretation of texts became for early Christians what it had long been for the Jews, a method of religious meditation. Each past fragment of text was only considered to be 'completed' or incarnate when it was understood for the first time within the new framework. Then it was free to disappear into the new narrative, much as Homer, the Bible, Dante and Shakespeare are intended by Joyce to vaporise into *Ulysses*. Just as *Ulysses* contains many fragments from earlier texts, so the New Testament has many textual passages of the Old written into its episodes.

The New Testament shows how the prophetic method works as a form of autocriticism. For example, Jesus foretells that Peter will deny him three times, and even as he is being taunted by his torturers to 'Prophesy', one of his most dramatic predictions is being fulfilled, 'as it has been written'. The Book of Psalms is often seen as giving shape and inner momentum to the story of Jesus, a story which moves through many moods from complaint to vindication, the same trajectory by which Bloom outfaces his detractors. Bloom exits Little Britain Street in a chariot, restrained in his seat by Jack Power, in a scene which is oddly true to the words of the New Testament which Mark the Evangelist attributed to Jesus at his own trial:

> You will see the Son of Man seated at the right hand of Power and coming with the clouds of heaven (Mark 14:62)

Apart from the blatant equation of Bloom and Jesus in the earlier scene ('I'll crucify him', 445), there are many more subtle echoes buried beneath the textual surface of *Ulysses*. In 'Aeolus' the newsboys mimic Bloom's walk, a scene which parallels Psalm 89:51, 'with which thy enemies taunt, O Lord, with which they mock the footsteps of thy anointed'. The chariot of brightness which bears Bloom to heaven comes out of Elijah as described in 2 Kings 2:11–12.

So many lines of the New Testament re-echo those from the Psalms that some Christians conclude (as Mark did) that the speaker of the Psalms must have been Jesus (and not David). Whether this could be true or not, all the evangelists asserted that again and again events in the life of Jesus recapitulated moments in the Psalms – the cry on the cross ('My God, my God, why hast thou forsaken me?') or the casting of lots for the dead man's garments. The premonitory dream which Stephen has of Bloom, holding out melons in the street of harlots ('Come . . . You will see who', 59) has its source in Matthew 26:64 and Mark 14:62 ('You will see'); and the Jesus who calls himself not God but Son of Man is repeated in Stephen's prophecy of 'that man' (59).

A literature which reveals a latent content in this fashion offers something more than a set of analogies, which any reader might notice. It also makes available, but only to privileged insiders or special decoders, a secret lore. The phrases deliberately echoed from the older text in the new one take on an extra charge and depth: they are shot through with prophetic potential, only fulfilled much later in the words and actions of a special man. Those words and actions in turn reverberate, as if they can no longer be merely factual records of a witnessed event, but may well have power to shape future, as yet unwritten, texts.

There is an immense danger in such writing. If this generation has witnessed the fulfilment of prophecies, that recognition can lead to an appalling smugness and complacency, as if 'we' are history's cutting edge. This is the terrible risk taken by the evangelists: of making Christianity seem like a victory over Judaism. But latent in the prophetic method was also a warning: if Jesus really was someone who surpassed Moses and Elijah, then some day the Christian gospels might themselves be superseded. If the Old Testament could be reconfigured by a reviser, so also in time might the New – as was done by followers of Joachim of Fiore in the thirteenth century. Ever the cunning scholar, Joyce knew that some day his book would be cannibalised, so he began that process himself.

The urge to create is also a destructive urge. The story of Jesus led to the superannuation of that very history it 'completed' as prelude to redemption. After Jesus, the Old Testament would be pre-history open to opportunist recasting by early Christians, just as after Joyce all prior forms of realism would be seen as two-dimensional. There was nothing meek or mild about the technical claims for a new narrative art latent in the work of the four evangelists. There were many other gospels that fell into oblivion, as there were many other modernist texts that never achieved the fame of *Ulysses*. These texts were lost for similar reasons: they did not offer such radical innovations of form – or such wisdom.

Before the New Testament, portrayals of lowly folk treated them in a somewhat condescending manner.

305

Even Homer does not use his more poetic style on the nurse or the swineherd. In comparison, the evangelists were democrats, because the teachings of Jesus warned that whoever exalted himself would be humbled and whoever humbled himself would be exalted. So the language used to describe the fishermen who followed Jesus is the same as was used for him. This is a truth recalled by George Russell in the Library episode of *Ulysses*: 'the movements which work revolutions in the world are born out of the dreams and visions in a peasant's hut in the hillside' (238). In its early days Christianity throve mainly among the common people – though some wealthy groups adopted it too – and its narrative art worked to similar effect. Ordinary lines, spoken seemingly at random by common persons (like a carpenter's son), were suddenly filled with world-historical implication.

What was remarkable in subsequent centuries was how few artists seemed to register the underlying point. Even Shakespeare tended to treat ordinary people as 'rude mechanicals', dropping from poetry to a prose register whenever they came centre stage, though he often gave his maids and clowns critical insight. Which simply shows that 'late Renaissance' society itself was still not answering the challenge posed by Jesus. In the eighteenth century Daniel Defoe, a writer whom Joyce admired, wrote his impure fictions in the voices of whores and tradesmen finding their way in a society of insecurity and chance, ruled by cruel punishments for those who strayed. Defoe was a figure on the edge of learned, polite society and, like Joyce, one who produced a radically new set of literary forms. It was only in the nineteenth century with the rise of the Romantic poets and with the move towards a universal franchise that a realist art in the hands of authors like Émile Zola and Thomas Hardy began to register the deeper aftershocks of the Christian transformation, but by this time many of the core elements of the Christian epic were already dying. One explanation of the fashion for modernising classical and Celtic stories at the start of the twentieth century may be that artists wanted to see how they would change if they were 'democratised'. Synge's use of common speech and everyday psychology in his dramatisation of the Deirdre legend may have given Joyce some pointers for *Ulysses.*

What is greatest in art is often achieved when a people is moving out of a period of primitivism but has not yet fully accepted the constraints of a new world. Their most intrepid souls retain some of the old energies even as they seek to contain them in newer forms. Often these new shapes, like subterranean popular movements, appear on the periphery of the great nations, which would help to explain why Ireland produced so many advanced modernists. But these resurgences often come after a period of trauma – what Gaelic poets called *longbhriseadh* (shipwreck), a terrible but challenging disaster which becomes the precondition of a change to a new future. In like manner, the new form evolved by the evangelists implies the abolition of the Old Testament, except as a source for the New.

The entire Jewish Bible was to be ransacked and broken up in order to confirm the historical truth of the Jesus story, yet its ultimate authority was necessary to prove the authenticity of Jesus to his followers. The earlier texts were to be, in effect, illuminated at that very moment when they were about to be displaced. After all, without these crucial lines given reverberative power by the life of Jesus, the earlier works might never have been felt to have major significance beyond their immediate place and time. However, in the act of being made flesh they were also superannuated. If there seems something humble about Joyce's arrogance and something arrogant about his humility, that is because he also presents his text as the one which lights up all previous elements of the cycle, according them a new dignity and meaning, even as he renders them subordinate to his own project. Within *Ulysses* itself he performs a similar feat: the closing soliloquy of Molly Bloom, though strictly speaking redundant in terms of the plot-line, gives an unprecedented degree of meaning and coherence to what has gone before.

Even this example is mere pre-text, however, since the whole thrust of *Ulysses* suggests that as we are the future of the past, with the right to remake the old for a new order, we also are the past of someone else's future, ourselves bound to be remade. In the Library, Stephen ponders how 'in the future, the sister of the past, I may see myself as I sit here now but by reflection from that which then I shall be' (249). The incursion of the future, as yet unknown, into a present narrative which shapes that future, even as its own self-accounting is shaped by it – that was Joyce's reason for setting his book a decade and more earlier than the time of its actual writing. This allowed him to show how shreds of the future, as well as of the past, are lodged in the present moment. As an advanced thinker, Joyce wasn't just ahead of his time.

Like the prophets of old, he could see so deeply into the present that the shape of the future became discernible. Nothing in the story of Jesus becomes fully interpretable until after the resurrection. In secular terms Joyce himself was seeking a vantage-point in the future from which the present would begin to make sense.

Nietzsche once said that people needed to be able to 'forget' in order to make a new thing possible, but that the present is always passing into a tradition which tries to maintain its claim on some future. Modernity needs history, even as past texts need present ones. They depend on one another even as they clash, and the modern text is always rapidly sacrificed to the tradition which absorbs it. This is the deeper meaning of that Eucharist around which not only the life of Jesus but also the meeting of Bloom and Stephen is organised. If the bread symbolises union, with its many grains fused by water, its breaking is the breaking open of the meaning of the words hidden in the texts. Such a 'feast day', proofed against destruction by ritual acts of remembrance repeated from year to year, recalls not just the first event but guarantees future acts of remembrance too. This may be yet another reason why there are no quotation marks in *Ulysses*. In a sense *everything* in the book is a quotation anyway.

Bloom is mockingly introduced in 'Cyclops' as a Jew in a gentile city, as a new apostle to the gentiles. One of the most innovative injunctions of Jesus concerned this very point – the need not just to embrace traditional enemies of Israel but to include and love them in an expanded definition of community. That community was redefined: 'whoever does the will of God is my brother and sister and mother'. Hence Bloom takes on maternal as well as

fraternal roles. The logic was latent in the Exodus
narrative: 'Thou shalt not oppress a stranger; for ye know
the heart of a stranger, seeing ye were strangers in the
land of Egypt.' The new covenant must be wholly free of
racial or territorial constraint; and on that basis a
narrowly nationalist messiah would constitute a defeat
for the politics of Exodus. Joyce's formula for Bloom as
the central presence in *Ulysses*, 'jewgreek is greekjew',
comes out of a letter of St Paul to the Galatians: 'There is
neither Jew nor Greek; there is neither slave nor freeman; there is no male and female. For you are all one in
Christ Jesus' (3:26–9).

St Paul has been described as the first Bolshevik, a
radical who wished in this way to universalise the Torah.
Yet this open-hearted approach led in time to that very
anti-Semitism which victimises Bloom, for it denied a
positive value to Jewish ethnic identity, presenting it
instead as a disgrace. By this means, Jews became the
Other of Christians, the sign of a terrible chasm in
Christianity. Paul, perhaps not noting the limits he was
setting to his own tolerance, presented the oneness in
Christ Jesus as the triumphant fulfilment of all previous
Jewish tradition. Joyce's Dublin Christians commit
similar errors. One asks Bloom, 'What is your Christian
name?' and another asks whether he thinks an acquaintance has a face 'like Our Saviour' (149). Yet Bloom
himself is valued by Joyce to the extent that he can
recognise the 'stranger' within himself. He is more
Christlike than any of his fellow citizens, being constantly
willing to put himself in the other fellow's position. Joyce
was following Paul of Tarsus in the attempt to imagine a
world without foreigners, a world made possible once

men and women accept the foreigner within the self and the necessarily fictive nature of all nationalisms.

The main emphasis in the New Testament is on the suffering humanity of Jesus. His identity as a foretold king is kept very secret, as if its announcement might precipitate even greater persecution. The problem faced by writers of the New Testament was how to present God in a man – the person *and* the thoughts in his mind, a God-man. Unlike Krishna, for example, Jesus is deeply human, someone whose willingness to answer for the sins of the world, despite his own goodness, was an even greater sacrifice than his death. But by becoming man, Jesus after his death made a higher evolution in mankind possible, so that all might find it possible to become 'the human form divine', to partake in God's presence and immortality. The identity of Jesus was really an open space into which people could read whatever they wanted; this space disrupted most of the official codes with which it came into contact. He even began to joke about this in moments of relaxation with the disciples. 'Who do men say that I am?' as a question leads to various suggestions: John the Baptist, Elijah, but ultimately 'the Christ'. Bloom also is an open identity, someone who often seems at any given moment to be whatever anyone says he is. But this is an experience well known to Irish people, whose image in the world has been generated by forces more powerful than they.

Nino Frank said that Joyce's privacy was that of 'someone entering a religious order'. It is an apt analogy. His book *could* be a divinely inspired text or a random gathering of words, for he worked on the borderline between religion and nihilism. He liked to joke that the

Catholic Church, like the See of Peter, was founded on a pun. When Gertrude Stein jibed that *Ulysses* was incomprehensible 'but anybody can understand' it, she was sarcastically alluding to its growing reputation in Paris as a sort of sacred text. Yet it is a book that called for years of study by scholars, while being at the same time open to all, as were the previous books of civilisations. 'You should approach Joyce', said William Faulkner, 'as a preacher approaches the Old Testament – with faith.'

Depression and After: Dante's Comedy

'I am 35,' wrote Joyce in 1918, shaving a year off his age to make things more symmetrical: 'It is the age at which Dante entered the night of his being.' Like Joyce, Dante was dignified, courteous, and thoughtful in his social manner; he also suffered from poor eyesight, and he wrote much of his *Inferno* while on the move, often 'hungry and threadbare', much as Joyce was when composing the early sections of *Ulysses*.

As the first parts of the *Divine Comedy* began to circulate, Dante was soon recognised as the greatest writer of his time, fame of the sort won also by Joyce as episodes of his book began to appear in avant-garde journals. In Genoa local women suggested that Dante's face and beard bore scorch marks sustained during his descent into Hell; in Zurich a woman in Joyce's apartment house referred to him as 'Herr Satan'. Joyce saw his youthful self as exemplifying a painful exile from his native city, like Dante eating salt bread in another man's house. He considered the Italian 'superior to Shakespeare', calling him 'the first poet of the Europeans'. Joyce treated Dublin as his predecessor treated Florence, not only as a birthplace but as 'the very context of his being'. If Dante celebrated a scholastic world that was already dissolving, Joyce himself tried to defend an idea of civil society which seemed in danger of collapse. If Dante had 'a feeling for the primacy of the civic over the factional, combined with a sense of the larger importance of the merchant class as against the nobility', so also did Joyce. But at a deeper level still, both men wrote in order to transform the psychological state of their readers by putting them in touch with their buried, innermost selves. In a letter to the Lord of Verona, Dante said that the *Divine Comedy* was intended not for speculation but with a practical object – 'to remove those living in this life from a state of misery, and to bring them to a state of happiness'. This aspiration was shared by Joyce, who set out to write the moral history of his people.

Both men excavated the very depths of the self and the world. The humble assumption by the son of God of a merely human form provided the inspiration for Dante's descent from Latin into the vernacular of his own Italian. In a somewhat similar way, Joyce transformed the possibilities of everyday language. Incarnation is a key to both the *Divine Comedy* and to *Ulysses*: if Dante gave to the human body a concreteness which Giotto achieved in painting, Joyce restored it to literature after a period of denial. The trapped, repetitive movements of bodies in the *Inferno* indicate a prior entrapment of the mind, its failure to free and control itself.

Both works begin in sadness, yet they end in happiness. The dominant feeling in the opening section of each is of a confused man who, fleeing a place of suffering, looks back over his shoulder at what he has just escaped. But the *Inferno* warns that no progress is ever possible to those who walk with heads twisted backward. Dante's work cannot therefore be exactly repeated. It

314

can be transcended, much as he sought to build on that of Virgil, Horace, Ovid, Lucan – a self-comparison which must have seemed outrageous when he first made it, but now appears quite just. His central interest is in the dynamics of creation, how newness comes into the world; like all radical innovators, he converts predecessors into versions of himself, boasting not that he follows the Gospel of John but that '*Giovanni é meco*', 'John sides with me'.

In an earlier work, the *Convivio*, Dante had spoken of the young man who 'would not be able to follow the right way in the wandering wood of his life, if his elders did not show it to him'. His *Inferno* begins, like *Ulysses*, with a soul mired in depression and helplessness, faced with formidable blocking agents, but with the means of escape also drawing near. '*Mi ritrovai*' – the famous words can mean, as Charles Williams has shown, either 'I found myself again in a place from which no mortal came alive' or 'I came to myself again' in the sense of recovery.

Stephen at the start of Joyce's book is himself lost, guilty of wanting to feel guilty. Like all of Dante's damned, he is punished not so much *for* his sins as *by* his sins, stuck fast and fixated on the almost unlimited forms of human pain. The worst thing about Hell, says Dante, is the number of sinners who seem to want to be there. He runs that risk himself until the voice of Virgil breaks in upon that gloom to rebuke all who wallow in negativity. The climactic scene of *Ulysses* is latent in the second-level meaning of *ritrovai* – that moment when the older man bends over the younger, as Stephen over Cyril Sargent, Bloom over Stephen, the wiser older one counselling his youthful self, recalling a time of deep misery which he could hardly bear to remember, except for the subsequent story of how it was transcended.

That story tells of how a man travels to 'refind' himself, after cruel mistreatment in his homeland leads him to sinful self-enclosure. The remedy will involve an 'exploration of the entire cultural world'. The underlying idea is that immersion in this world is central to a process of recovery, which can place a person's individual existence within a wider system of value. In that attempt the exile also recovers the sights, sounds, and textures of the lost but beloved city, which is somehow redeemed by its inclusion in this healing narrative.

Stephen's pain at the start of *Ulysses* is considerable – he seems helpless before the drifting aimless flickerings of his own mind. Like the poet at the start of *Inferno*, he 'does not know how to behave, how to act, what to say', and he is really a sort of 'social stumbler trying to figure things out'. Yet even as Dante depends on Virgil for fatherly guidance, he is also rescuing him from 'long silence'. So Joyce reanimates Homer as Dante reanimates Virgil. In both texts there will come a moment when the relationship moves from dependency to one of equality and thence to autonomy.

Who sent Virgil to Dante? Who summoned Homer to Joyce? Virgil did not actually carry Dante, nor did Homer guide Joyce's hand. If the journeys reported did not physically happen, in some psychological sense they did. the *Divine Comedy* is set in 1300, about nine years before Dante wrote the opening lines, as *Ulysses* is set in 1904, just ten years before Joyce embarked on it. Both works draw inspiration from a woman, Beatrice Portinari and Nora Barnacle. These were not only actual women but figures of the *anima*, the inspiratrice of art who brings matters into full consciousness. It was Beatrice who – prompted by the Blessed Virgin – sent Virgil to assist Dante. At the centre of such manoeuvres is a profound truth, known to all who seek to redeem their own unremembered history, to excavate a lost and painful past: 'no man can safely enter the dark gate of the shadow world without knowing that some deeply loved and trusted person has absolute faith in the rightness of his journey, and in his courage and ability to come through'. the *Divine Comedy* shows how to trust like a child in such a guide: 'Then as he bade, about his neck I curled / My arms and clasped him.'

Stephen lacks such trust to begin with and for an obvious reason: his father Simon (like John Joyce) tried to impose his own image on his son, with the pressure of a set of expectations that removed all his freedom, leaving the boy at once 'indulged and disesteemed' (20). Aware of the shadow that has descended on him, Stephen isn't making progress – despite his claim to be 'getting on nicely in the dark' (45). He is in despair, identifying with Lucifer and with all who sin against the light. But in the opening three episodes, which are really a modern *Inferno* – with examples of how *not* to live – most of Stephen's wounds are self-inflicted. The soul in such desolation needs to hit rock bottom before any recovery is possible. Only when he admits that he's lost can Stephen begin to re-find himself. Depressed, he needs someone who can show how to shine a light into the darkest depths and reconnect his buried self to his everyday personality. This will be done by the example of someone who knows how to make souls, animals, even objects articulate in the bright world above.

317

Virgil's strategy is clear. The only cure for the sin of despair is to show the many ways in which souls destroy themselves. Revenge itself is shown in the *Inferno* as an extreme form of despair, imaged in the figure of Ugolino gnawing eternally unsatisfied at the skull of Cardinal Ruggieri. Even at his lowest point, Stephen refuses the easy option of revenge. Urged by Mulligan to attack Haines, he refuses, saying, 'there's nothing wrong with him except at night' (7). On the beach he tells himself 'you will not be master of others or their slave' (56). For all his flaws, Stephen – unlike Dante's damned – is not over-attached to material things in a way that would prevent self-development. But he seeks perfection in the world without seeking also to perfect (or at least improve) himself. At first, therefore, he meets endless trouble. Only when he seeks his own individuation will he notice and engage with his rescuer, Bloom.

At the outset, however, he is as much an exile as ever he was in Paris, an alien to both numinous values and his inner self. For, as the Scholastics taught, every creature as a likeness of God must love itself, yet Stephen despises himself almost as much as he despises the world. In the *Inferno* help is at hand: from the dark, entangling wood the poet sees the light of the purgatorial mountain. The leaden, involuted sentences of Stephen are challenged, unexpectedly and unaccountably, by a voice from a completely different order of reality. After the anger of the youthful voice that whines comes the jaunty sentence which tells how someone called Mr Leopold Bloom ate 'with relish' (65) the organs of beasts and fowl – and so both narratives, after describing the Inferno, start all over again.

Virgil guides Dante, even though, not being a Christian, Virgil can hardly know the way – and so it is with Bloom. He too can guide without knowing, allowing the risen sun to show the way: 'Quick warm sunlight came running from Berkeley Road, swiftly, in slim sandals, along the brightening footpath. Runs, she runs to meet me, a girl with gold hair on the wind' (74). This is Joyce's vision of Nora, Bloom's of the young Molly, and it recalls Dante's of Beatrice: 'something like the glory of God is walking down the street to meet him'. A woman of such beauty makes Dublin or Florence a potentially Heavenly City, and girl and city become momentarily one. Stephen remains depressed, but Bloom lifts himself out of his torpor by resolving to restart 'those Sandow's exercises' (73).

If *Ulysses* is structured as an exodus-narrative of exile and conversion, so also is the *Divine Comedy*. In the Old Testament, the pilgrims crossed water, entering the subconscious zone before reaching the desert, a place of temptation, blockage and difficulty. Bloom, likewise, turns his thoughts towards the East ('a barren land, laid waste', 73), and he thinks of the Dead Sea and orange groves. Like other Jews in the Dublin of 1904, he might have reason to contemplate persecutions only just escaped, in the manner of Dante's poet. Also in 'Lotus-Eaters' he thinks of 'manna' as the bread of heaven that descended in the form of grace. If Stephen's attempt at getting a good start to the day failed, there can be no reason other than grace why Bloom's succeeds: his ability to face moments of discouragement and get beyond them. Stephen is haunted by the past but afraid of the dead, whereas Bloom feels that in order to progress one must first hit bottom. It is necessary to descend to Hades and confront the dead, the archive of all our rejected emotions, before we are ready to ascend. The Unconscious must be confronted, as surely as we must learn to imagine our own life after death. Unless there is a dying of old prejudices, the self will never blossom.

The gateway of Purgatory is Dante's metaphor for both the release of the people of Israel from bondage, and the freeing of the despairing soul from neurosis, from a world of monotonous repetition. The crossed keys logo which Bloom devises for the firm of Alexander J. Keyes does not just carry innuendoes of Home Rule and of the Vatican, but also symbolises the gates of Dante's Purgatory. In Dante, one key opens, the other doesn't. One offers affirmation, the other rejection – yet both are necessary for a full life. Bloom's affirmation, in short, will have to confront and contain Stephen's negations.

Dante's choice of Virgil as guide is as evocative as the choice of Homer by Joyce. To Virgil Dante accords a prophetic foreknowledge of the birth and life of Jesus in the *Eclogues*, which prefigure the New Testament and a period of peace ushered in by a holy child. Virgil could therefore glimpse a future world that he could not fully enter or understand. Yet, creative genius though he was, he could not fully transcend the world-view of his contemporaries, and so at the close of the *Purgatorio* he is not able to pass into paradise. Although his own inner longings are not fully satisfied – in this, too, he is like Bloom – he 'gives precedence to the needs of his pupil', being at once incomplete yet representing a consciousness as advanced as the pagan world can develop.

Virgil's record of the visit by Aeneas to the underworld prefigures Jesus's descent into Hell, Dante's into the

Inferno, and Bloom's to Glasnevin Cemetery. The blending of real historical passages with fictional characters, a blending also to be found in *Ulysses*, is the same technique which allowed Dante to see Moses as foretelling the life of Jesus.

The *figura* of the Bible carries a prophetic thrust, a sense of the 'not yet'. In like manner, Statius in the *Divine Comedy* tells Virgil that, because of his example in the fourth *Eclogue*, 'Through you I am a poet, through you a Christian.' This is one way of learning how to bear the tables of a new law in the language of the outlaw, to be, in the words of St Paul, 'a preacher to others but himself a castaway'. Before the close of the *Purgatorio*, Virgil leaves the narrative, knowing that the *Paradiso* will fulfil his own utopian longings. The greatest artists, it seems, will their own supersession by an even more audacious successor: 'I crown and mitre you over myself' From the beginning Beatrice had decreed that Virgil cannot enter Paradise, so in effect he tells Dante that the Florentine is free to go one better than he. This is wholly in keeping with Dante's conviction of the transformative, future-driven power of literature.

There are two Dantes in the *Divine Comedy*: the one who experienced dire confusion and the one who survived and much later reports it with clarity. Dante, like Joyce, becomes himself his own father and shows how art may help to integrate a past and present self. 'In the future, the sister of the past,' says Stephen Dedalus, 'I may see myself as I sit here now but by reflection from that which then I shall be' (249). Every judgement in the main parts of both texts is performed at the mercy of the moment of its enunciation. But the attempt in the last book of Dante, and in the last two episodes of *Ulysses*, is to find a present moment in which experience is no longer time-bound but is outside of the flow of time altogether. That moment when pilgrim and poet become one is hinted at in *Ulysses* when Bloom and Stephen together look up at the stars.

Left to his own devices, mortal man could not descend far enough to make 'atonement' for original sin, so God sent his son – as Haines says in 'Telemachus', 'the Son striving to be atoned with the Father' (22) – to assume the limits of a human body, but also to descend into Hell. The very pattern of Fall and Redemption, of Exile and Home-coming, is based on one of descent and ascent. The artist, like God, learning how to go down and embrace the submerged self, must return with a lucid report. The model, says Charles Singleton, 'was nothing less than God's way of writing'. Yet the movements of the wanderer, though often seeming purposeless, have a design. There was only stasis in the quicksands which im-mobilised Stephen in his Inferno, but there is a meaning to Bloom's travels, because they lead to a place of peace.

The simple truth is that Bloom purges his own sadness by reaching out to embrace that of others. His attention is given not to the broken person before him – a drunken poet and unhappy postgraduate – but to the full person whom he knows that man may become. If attention is a form of prayer, than Bloom is a lot more religious than he believes himself to be. His kindness to Stephen is like that of Virgil to Dante. It is not motivated by any self-interest, nor by any demand made by Stephen, nor even the desire to be released from his own suffering. It is wholly and magnificently arbitrary, offered to a youth he hardly knows, the son of a dead mother whose place Bloom instinctively assumes.

Bloom can perform this saving function because he has embraced and accepted his own melancholy and is thereby free 'to draw off the shadow of others'. The 'dark horse' (435) and 'coon' (134), assimilated to darkness in so many scenes, is the one who can set Stephen free. As Virgil had laid his hand on Dante, Bloom takes Stephen by the hand while they exit Nighttown, not as a clinical analyst, but as someone who feels an absolute sense of responsibility for his friend's errant son.

Dante had no first-hand knowledge of the *Odyssey*, since it was not yet translated into Latin in his time. But he knew of Ulysses from other authors and so could describe his journey beyond the known world of the Mediterranean into the Southern Hemisphere. His Ulysses, a largely imaginary creation, is cursed with the modern desire for total knowledge of an as-yet uncharted world, a geographical parallel to Joyce's exploration of the Unconscious. The achievement of both Dante and Joyce is to move well past their inherited intellectual systems, into a 'beyond' which becomes a new zone for the feelings and thoughts of humanity. They understood that a myth such as that of Ulysses, far from maintaining a static social system, may instead become the very means of changing it, 'so that one person's rediscovery of inner meaning can be a radical force for transformation'. The unknown world beyond our geographical limits is a physical embodiment of Hades, an archive for all our forgotten pasts and rejected thoughts, still redeemable through the power of language and art.

A profound element of that forgotten past, for both

Dante and Joyce, is the feminine consciousness. At the start of *Ulysses*, Stephen is an utter, if unconscious, misogynist. His excessive regard for the powers of reason leads to a devaluation of his own 'feeling' side, reduced to sarcastic references to the anatomical oddities of passing females. If Dante set out to show that the life of a person on earth is 'a brief moment of irrevocable decision', the opening episodes of *Ulysses* sketch 'the extreme peril of the situation, the depths of his distress'. Stephen's vision of the milkwoman in 'Telemachus', like Bloom's of the bent hag outside Cassidy's, is a sort of anti-*aisling* in which the old crone is most certainly *not* transformed into a young beauty by the wishing-power of the onlooking man.

But Joyce has learned the lesson of Dante's Sirens very well and applied it in a radical rereading of the Gaelic *aisling*. The Sirens in Dante are false fascinators, their monstrosity an image of what happens to the personality of a man when he loses the balance between reason and instinct. The converse happens when, as in the *aisling*, the hag is magically converted into a seductive vamp, for whose charms the male falls, a prey to every passing mood, yet 'quite incapable of seeing the actual woman except through a haze of projections'. This is the same temptation which assails the drinkers in the Ormond Bar in 'Sirens', as it assailed the sailors on Homer's ship. Bloom, like Odysseus, checks his tendency to bask in the Sirens' winsome smiles. Yet, even when able to summon such powers of resistance, no man is ever fully safe, because 'the more conscious a man becomes, the more dangerous are his lapses, small though they may appear' – as when Bloom falls for the image of Gerty in 'Nausikaa'.

Such a man is, however, able to expose the falseness of the Siren-song precisely because he keeps his mind on the truth of his feminine ideal, as Bloom keeps the image of Molly before him in the 'Sirens' and 'Nausikaa' episodes. The Sirens represent a false Beatrice, a false Molly, offering brief sensual pleasure but nothing more. Bloom invokes the image of water in his moment of forgiveness of Molly, having recognised that nobody can finally own such a thing. Dante himself had given a famous lecture on water at Verona, arguing that it nowhere rose higher than the earth's surface, and praising what Bloom celebrated in *Ulysses*, its democratic qualities which lead it always to find its own level. The *Purgatorio* comes to an end at the waters of Lethe, where forgiveness is freely offered and life restored. As at the close of *Finnegans Wake*, the human being is likened to a drop which gratefully rejoins the ocean. The spirit of the Lord first moved on water, in the primary act of creation, and this generative consciousness is the point towards which both Dante and Joyce return.

Dante's poem had its source, as did *Ulysses*, not in a theory but in a human event – the sighting of a woman on a city street. Wisdom literature often arises from the pressure of such a felt experience. For all the symmetries between the *figurae* of Old and New Testaments, many of the central statements in the life of Jesus – the parables, the events at the wedding feast at Cana – have no parallels in ancient prophetic texts. Indeed, their randomness adds to their persuasiveness. These moments of lived experience were often lost in the centuries after Jesus, because of the necessity of reducing his story to 'polemics of missionary statements' designed to appeal to 'the mentality of various peoples to which the doctrine was carried'. In a similar way, because of an obsession with the Homeric grid among early commentators, *Ulysses* itself got simplified for transmission. 'In the end,' says Erich Auerbach of Dante, 'little remained of the doctrine but a sequence of dogmatic abstractions' as the ancient images lost their concreteness and lapsed into cold allegory.

These were the centuries, also, of that early Christianity which sought to replace the goddess of pagan lore with a more controlling and rational masculine consciousness. But such a condition could not last indefinitely. The preaching of St Dominic and St Francis in the century before Dante held that any learning which did not spring from love was contemptible, a matter of worthless theory divorced from good works. Linked to all this was a re-emergence of a feeling for concrete, sensual reality in the cults of the Virgin Mary and in the related images of the beloved in the poetry of the Trecento. 'Where does new beatitude lie?' became the pressing question, and Dante's answer was: 'In words that praise my lady.'

Joyce could be critical of that image with which, as Stephen complains, Italian thinkers dazzled the plain people of Europe, but he was critical only because he was so deeply attracted to it. He was, after all, born towards the end of a Victorian era in which a muscular, masculine form of Christianity held sway, with a corresponding cult of Mariolatry sponsored by the Papacy in Rome; and he felt the need to make his own Danteesque counter-assertion. *His* Madonna, embodied at the book's close, is no false Siren, but a true Star of the Sea, who will guide travellers home, rather than see them shipwrecked.

The fireworks display recorded in 'Nausikaa' was only a display, a performance. In the *Paradiso*, Beatrice says that if she flames now in a fire of love beyond all earth, onlookers should not be astonished. As Bloom and Stephen look up to Molly's window and beyond it to the stars, whose burning intensity offers a 'corrected' version of the display on Sandymount Strand, theirs is a vision of a redeemed world. At the prompting of Beatrice, Dante sees the living star of the Virgin Mary and then – in a remarkable anticipation of the famous NASA photograph of the earth taken from the moon in 1969 – the insignificance of that earth beneath all the planets. 'From this point', says Beatrice, 'hang the heavens and all nature' – that 'heaventree of stars' (819) celebrated for its beauty in 'Ithaca', echoing the final line of the *Inferno*: 'And thence we issued forth to see the stars.'

These moments of sweetness were hard won. The young Joyce had written most sarcastically of his country in a Trestine newspaper of 1907: 'If she is truly capable of reviving, let her awake, or let her cover up her head and lie down decently in her grave forever.' Dante had written to the city of Florence: 'you are like a sick woman who cannot find any rest on her soft bed, but turns continually to ease her pain'. By the close of both works, the love affair has been redeemed, as the woman and city, utterly renewed, come to reflect one another in a zone of eternity outside of time and process: 'The star itself was changed and laughed.'

For Christians it was the bodily incarnation of Jesus in the womb of Mary that gave meaning to human history. This is why Dante uses the phrase beloved of Joyce and repeated by Stephen: that Mary is '*figlia del tuo figlio*', 'daughter of your own son', a phrase which shows how the godhead might fulfil its decreed mission by assuming a human form. In the *Odyssey* the gods who briefly touched down on earth travelled incognito, so 'their divinity remained intact, unaffected by the world of men'. They remained gods at all times, unlike Jesus, who was both god and man. This is the truth at the heart of both Dante's and Joyce's humanisation of epic: they do not treat Beatrice as a symbol of grace, or Molly as a version of the earth mother; they refuse all petrified allegory and see each woman as caught up in a concrete, personal history. Both Dante and Joyce can render every surface and depth of the known world, yet somehow also position themselves above and beyond human life. They rewrote their flawed, personal pasts in order to extract the hidden significance and immense value of everyday experience. The more chancy and capricious every action seems in these texts, the more predestined it may turn out to be.

By moving his book towards a sense of eternity, Joyce also underlines its status as a comedy. In such an order, it would be a dire form of sentimentality to invest earthly things with even more significance than God would accord them. Only a philosophy which looked not just *at* but *through* death could give the wisdom which life, alone and unaided, cannot provide. Yet the central paradox of both works is that this world, however flawed, is the only medium through which such deeper meanings can be intuited.

Dante and Joyce insist on describing as real events the assumption of their characters into the heavens. They both treat these supernatural moments as existing within the same order of reality as random meetings in a city street.

The lament for the shattered world of the Scholastics or for the coming fragmentation of the civic bourgeoisie is subsumed into a larger, less melancholy narrative, which looks forward, beyond the end of days, to a place of supreme peace, a heavenly city. There are, as Robert Hollander joked, but two classes of reader offended by such claims: 'believers and non-believers'. The pilgrim and the wanderer share a nostalgia for origins, the return to God which is the true atonement of father and son. If 'love loves to love love' (433), that love which Dante says absolves no loved one from loving will draw Leopold, as Dante's pilgrim, back into a world 'swimming in roses' (931), '*de la rosa sempiterna*'. But Molly chooses the red rose, while Beatrice opts for the white.

The Catholicism in which Joyce was raised was a rule-bound affair of external proprieties meticulously observed, and any infraction filled the sinner with scruples. But Joyce went deeper, seeing the life of the individual as a series of choices, which involved the death of the old man and the birth of the new. Jesus, begotten not made, finds his inversion in Stephen, made not begotten, not yet fully born or parented, as yet a Stephen rather than a Dedalus. In *A Portrait of the Artist as a Young Man* he had felt false when he performed his religious duties, a hopeful enough frustration since it suggested the existence of some deeper self that he was being false to. In 'Lotus-Eaters' the experience of taking communion is itself routinised, as Bloom observes the halter-clad women approach the altar rail. If ritual has been all but stripped away, even Bloom, though lacking Stephen's instruction in Catholic lore, feels a pang at its passing. In fact it is Bloom who draws Stephen, all unconsciously, into a Eucharistic fellowship, offering Stephen his own cup, that supreme image of the known world.

Dante made the first major appeal to a national readership in its own language, and in doing so laid the basis for the literature of the modern world. Joyce developed that programme, pioneering a form of vernacular modernism. Both men produced narratives which repeatedly address the reader in the very act of inventing a new sort of reading: but they do so in the conviction that a work, reaching very far into both past and future, can base itself on the conviction that 'the highest knowledge must be set before every man'.

Shakespeare, Hamlet and Company

On a walk home from Belvedere College one afternoon, Joyce was asked by his classmate Albrecht Connolly to admit that Shakespeare was the greatest poet. He refused. Connolly, a far more robust boy, began to twist Joyce's arm and to frogmarch him along the footpath, in hopes of extracting the concession. Joyce was in tears but he did not submit. In *A Portrait of the Artist as a Young Man* that scene was recast as Stephen's refusal to 'admit that Byron was no good', but the real-life version shows Joyce in a more immodest light. He really did see Shakespeare as his antagonist, someone whose greatest work might nonetheless be trumped.

In his mind a play like *Hamlet* had untapped potentials which he might fulfil. After all, that very sense of the gap between an idea's possibilities and its working-out was one of the play's innermost themes:

> Sure, he that made us with such large
> discourse,
> Looking before and after, gave us not
> That capability and God-like reason
> To fust in us unused.

The problem for Shakespeare as much as for Hamlet was that the multiple possibilities opened up by his story become almost an end in themselves rather than the basis for a clear action. This is why T. S. Eliot could find the flaw of the play in its summoning up of emotion in excess of the facts as they appear. For Joyce, *Hamlet* the play as well as Hamlet the character was a dire warning that interior monologue might displace action rather than enable it. His soliloquies immobilise Hamlet: instead of doing, he theorises about doing, in ways that just deepen his depression. There may be no resolution in the world of *nacheinander*, just one thing after another. A man can, as Hazlitt said, lose the power of action in the sheer energy of the resolve, for the relation between an idea and an act is always uneasy. Goethe put it best when he said: 'Few people have the understanding and simultaneously the ability to act. Understanding extends, but also immobilises; action mobilises, but it also restricts.'

Like Stephen, Hamlet appears in mourning clothes at the start. Stephen's dark clothes are ridiculed by Mulligan and others because they make him look like a priest. Both men insist on the depth of that inner wound which justifies their clothing. Hamlet says 'But I have that within which passeth show / These but the trappings and the suits of woe.' Like Stephen, however, he knows that in a world which judges by appearances, it's important to dress in character. He has his Wittenberg style while Stephen has his 'Latin Quarter hat'. Yet both men are troubled by how little their clothes manage to say: their sadness remains unexpressed in 'inky cloaks', and certainly unresolved.

Polonius illustrates the underlying problem, with his glib assurance to his son that 'the apparel oft proclaims the man', a too-easy equation between outer avowal and

332

inner feeling. Polonius is one of those shallow, courtly souls who judge only by appearances. The cloud shown him by Hamlet is variously described by him as like a camel, a weasel or a whale, depending on what his prince in a passing moment deems it to be. The little cloud seen by Stephen and Bloom at the start of the day, though it appears in different locations, is clearly the same entity, not to be reduced to simile or metaphor. Yet that Dublin skyscape also recalls the pillar of cloud in the desert which drew on the people of Israel.

Like Hamlet, Stephen at the outset lacks advancement and suffers from bad dreams. When he sleeps in Sandycove Tower, which Haines likens to Elsinore, he is unquiet, haunted by the spirit of his dead mother. His response is less ambiguous than Hamlet's to his dead father: 'Ghoul! Chewer of corpses! . . . Let me live' (11). He does, however, share Hamlet's doubts about the revenger's role, rejecting Mulligan's invitation to attack the Englishman Haines. In fact he refuses to identify himself with *any* role, for that would be a dreadful self-simplification. To entrap the self in a role would be to know again the humiliation reported in *A Portrait of the Artist as a Young Man* of holding down an unworthy, unconvincing part.

In the past Stephen had some involvement with the actors of Yeats's emerging national theatre ('But I would not accounted be,' scoffed Joyce, 'One of the mumming company'). However, he knows that Hamlet was too shrewd ever to play a part himself, contenting himself merely with writing or directing them. Hamlet is in fact an early warning system for Stephen that the intellectual may be one who can play every part except his own. His sense of the theatrical quality of everyday life means that he can feign madness, puncture the facile acts of Rosencrantz, Guildenstern and Osric, coach the players in their roles, and teach the queen how to assume virtues which she lacks. Obsessed with role-playing in a court of dissemblers, he is the modern discoverer of the interior monologue that goes well beyond the stage soliloquy of earlier Renaissance drama. As Harold Bloom says, he overhears or catches himself saying things and thinking things.

What he overhears is precisely that part of him which 'passeth show', which cannot be expressed in mere action and which no mere actor can represent. Those inner promptings recalls the monitions ('that within') which revealed themselves to Homer's protagonists and to the Cúchulainn of the Irish saga, to such a degree that Standish O'Grady argued that epic should never be played by mortal actors but should simply be left to the imagination. But tragic drama likes to break this inter-diction. Invariably, it describes a protagonist whose self never quite fits his or her appointed role, and whose awareness can never become fully incarnate in the action. The ghosts which appear from the past epitomise that problem: they return like Hamlet's dead father precisely because of unfinished business, because they did not fully express themselves when alive. Yet they are crippled by their status as pure spirits. Unable to do anything for themselves, they ask others to act on their behalf. For them the ignominy of such powerlessness is akin to that of a Homer, a Dante or a Shakespeare who has left some of his work undone. 'You had to come back. To show the understudy in the title role how to,' says the narrator of 'Eumaeus', but 'coming back was the worst thing you ever did because it went without saying you would feel out of place as things always moved with the times' (757).

In that sense, fathers are always like ghosts. That is why Stephen identifies Shakespeare not with his greatest creation, Prince Hamlet, but rather with the ghost of the dead king whose impossible part he played. By the time he wrote *Hamlet*, Shakespeare knew that according to *The Book of Common Prayer* it was no longer proper or even legal to talk *to* the dead – they 'had gone beyond the reach of human contact'. What is suppressed in life often re-appears in art: and *Hamlet* certainly suggests that people, however sceptical, will continue to talk to the dead. As the Irish farmer said of the fairies whose local mound he had dug up: 'I don't believe in them – but they're there anyway.' The dead themselves will talk back in hopes of achieving through their children what they failed to do in life – to have a second chance.

Hamlet is never sure whether the ghost is honest: or even whether he is his father's son, for if Gertrude's love is fickle in the present, it may have been so in the past as well. Joyce also was troubled by this fear, which assails fathers as well as sons. Hamlet's inky cloak may in fact be designed to cover over his *lack* of feeling for his dead father, as well as masking his consequent hesitation over the need to avenge him.

Whether he really sees a ghost or merely conjures one up from his fevered mind is irrelevant, for he talks to his dead father as surely as Stephen addresses his dead mother. A great deal of *Ulysses*, as of *Hamlet*, concerns our commerce with the dead, but also with the act of dying

335

and even more with the state of being dead. Despite their powerlessness in the present – perhaps *because* of this very powerlessness – the spirits of the dead seem endlessly demanding, even peremptory. To a remarkable degree, the plot of *Hamlet* is dictated by the ghost. He sets it up, directs his son on how to proceed, intervenes when the son's resolve appears to weaken, prevents rough handling of his former wife, and sees to it that there is a bloody catastrophe. Compared to all that, the son might seem pallid, a mere cipher; however, the ghost – and Shakespeare knew this – is really Hamlet's own interior monologue. So the play's hidden logic – that the re-imagination of past lives comes to dominate all that is achieved in the present – becomes in Joyce's transmutation the principle underlying the whole of *Ulysses.*

Nor should that be surprising, for Joyce had always been obsessed with the flow of the past through the present. Like Hamlet and Shakespeare, he was seeking to depict something that had never been quite so fully represented before. To do this, he had to enter unknown territory ('the undiscovered country from whose bourn / no traveller returns') and to write out of unprecedented depths. Coming out of such depths, the act of writing, no less than that of revenge, cannot be one man's only. Marx observed that whenever people are about to do something radical, they nervously summon onstage the spirits of the dead, and they seek to portray themselves as secret sharers of past heroes. Thus, the French revolutionaries of 1789 pretended to be risen Roman democrats. Marx saw the need for the frightened revolutionary to connect the dead voices of the past to the as-yet unutterable, unrepresentable forces of the present, to 'that within which passeth show'. So the ghost speaks to Prince Hamlet, as Homer speaks to Joyce. So the play-within-the-play is used by Hamlet, and by Stephen in 'Circe', to show how much is still left unsaid. The problem is clear: how to complete an action which fully expresses, rather than falsifying, the inner self.

Hamlet at first rejects the old plot of the prior play, because he is beyond such crude simplifications; what he wants is not revenge but wholeness and self-acceptance. The past text exists only as a scaffolding which must fall away, like the costumes in a theatrical wardrobe which must make way for the actors' own clothes. About the age of thirty, after a protracted education as a courtier, scholar and soldier, Hamlet was about to come into his own – but he met a ghost. Henceforth, he could never fully become himself. Although the role of revenger was one to which he was ill-suited and ill-disposed, once the ghost had seized centre stage, Hamlet was destined to fill it.

For Joyce as for Marx, he became an example of what *not* to do, of how *not* to capitulate to the past. He became a prisoner of the costume drama that he himself had mocked. To know his deed he has to postpone and finally cancel the moment when he might know himself. To murder the king, he must first murder his scarcely born self. But, even as he dies, that self hasn't gone away, and the nearer it comes to the truth, the harder it is to express in words:

> Had I but time – as this fell serjeant, death
> Is strict in his arrest – O, I could tell you –
> But let it be. Horatio, I am dead.

This is a hint by Shakespeare at the emotion in excess of

337

the facts which could not be uttered, at least not by him or by his players. Perhaps it never could be, but the speech has remained a challenge for all subsequent writers. Hamlet, on the edge of death, found the experience almost unutterable. Odysseus, Jesus and Hamlet all descended into Hell, only to find some of their insights unnegotiable in any human language. But *writing* is that undiscovered country from whose bourn some intrepid travellers do return every few centuries with the ability to articulate just a little more of what it's like to be in and out of the world. And that may be why the young Joyce, who always knew his destiny, could not say what Albrecht Connolly asked him to.

Joyce recognised in Hamlet the problem of the neurotic modern intellectual in whom the balance between inner and outer worlds has been lost. Stephen's intellectual activity, likewise, is so great as to immobilise him. If Hamlet wondered whether the dead king had really been his father, that doubt may help to explain why he appointed the court jester Yorick to that role, for it was Yorick who had borne him on his back a thousand times, while regaling the solitary child with jokes. In similar fashion, Stephen will appoint Leopold Bloom as his surrogate father, from whom he may learn how to act in a world which is uncertain in its meaning. So Joyce presents us with Bloom, the normalised Hamlet, the intellectual as Everyman.

This move is possible in Shakespeare's play because of the ambiguity of Hamlet's age. He is a matured man, between the ages of Stephen and Bloom. Romantic interpreters think of Hamlet as an unresolved youth, but by the standards of 1600 he was well on his way, more a

Leopold than a Stephen. The skill with which Joyce eases Bloom into the role suggests the value of the second analogy. The large-scale irony here is that Stephen in 'Scylla and Charybdis' uses the play to represent his family's problems, yet his version of Shakespeare's life better reflects Bloom's. Like Hamlet, Bloom has 'lately foregone all custom of exercises', but resolves to put that right – with Sandow's body-building scheme. He has a tendency to melancholy, but never fully gives in to it, preferring to immerse himself in the world. Like Hamlet he stands in a graveyard and imagines what it must be like to be dead, quoting, 'Alas poor Yorick.'

Joyce invented Bloom in the attempt to solve a problem which eluded Shakespeare: how to present a womanly man who is nonetheless admirable and successful in the world. In the comedies Shakespeare dealt with androgynous women, in the tragedies with androgynous men; but the former were triumphant while the latter failed utterly. In the comedies, Viola can duel with a sword almost as bravely as any male; Portia can show a sharper analytic wit than any lawyer in court; and Rosalind can outdo any man in intelligence. When these women adopt male disguise, they simply enhance their underlying womanhood. They are enabled by this disguise to mingle with the men they love, seeing them as they truly are, rather than as gallants posing to impress a lady – and the men, for their part, are able to respond to such lovers, seeing them as persons rather than as women. Which means that the concluding marriages exemplify true bonding. Not so in the tragedies, where Shakespeare shifts the focus of his investigation from the manly woman to the womanly man. Now the effects of androgyny are disastrous. Richard II's sensitivity and effeminacy leave him open to usurpation by the wily Bolingbroke; Hamlet describes himself as 'passion's slave', but he fails to bring out a corresponding male element in Ophelia; and Lear gives up power, only to be destroyed by vengeful women. Three hundred years after Shakespeare, Joyce seeks to create an androgynous male who is more comic than tragic.

If Bloom is a womanly man whose marriage has stalled, then Hamlet as passion's slave seems at least as effeminate. On the night of 15 June 1904, Mrs Bandman Palmer played the part, prompting Bloom to think that Hamlet's womanly qualities might have driven Ophelia to suicide. Bloom is well aware of his wife's sexual frustration, whereas Hamlet's own problems with women derived from his shattered faith in his mother after her over-hasty marriage to Claudius. Addicted to the theatrical, he feels nonetheless free to denounce it in pouting performances of femininity by such soft souls as Ophelia:

> I have heard of your paintings too, well enough; God has given you one face, and you make yourselves another; you jig, you amble, and you lisp, and nick-name God's creatures, and make your wantonness your ignorance. Go to, I'll no more on 't; it hath made me mad.

His obscene innuendoes to Ophelia are designed to bring out a more 'manly' side in her to complement the woman's part in him. But in this he fails, doomed by his very sensitivity. Having idealised woman, he is revolted by her humanity. Having worshipped abstract ideals, he is disappointed to love merely mortal flesh. The fact that his dead father seems more concerned about Queen Gertrude than about him increases Hamlet's sense of loneliness and of the betrayal of women. The thought that he may not really be the dead king's son is one more reason to delay or abandon the act of revenge. In telling Ophelia to go to a 'nunnery', Hamlet knows that the word can mean brothel as well as convent.

Joyce too was obsessed by the dichotomy between the virgin and the whore in western images of womanhood. He once told his brother that Irishmen were interested in women only as street-walkers and as house-keepers – and having sampled the former, he fled the latter. He was never a believer in a spotless womanhood, seeing all too clearly how Ophelia's double bind to play both virgin and trollop leads to her suicide. The obscene folk songs which Ophelia sings in the fourth act were the predictable result of such repression. Joyce knew by heart Queen Gertrude's later speech describing how the crazed girl strewed her flowers and then herself into the river. Yet he transferred on to Gertrude all his guilt about his dead, unprayed-for mother. The fear of the father figure is equally strong in both Joyce and Shakespeare. *Hamlet*, like *Ulysses*, is not so much a celebration of a son's fidelity to his father as a lament for the lost integrity of the father–son relation, which will never again achieve the unproblematic tenderness that it had in the *Odyssey*. This may be one reason why the references to *Hamlet* are manifest in *Ulysses*, while those to the *Odyssey* remain implicit. Unknown to its sponsor, Stephen's theory of Shakespeare highlights many analogies with Bloom's own life – from the incident in which he was overborne in a field by a feisty woman to the moment when a lordling woos for him by proxy. But central to Stephen's conception is his rather self-flattering proposal that in questions of paternity, the son holds the initiative.

Much as Joyce was free to convert *Hamlet* into a botched ur-text for *Ulysses*, so Stephen contends that the son always has the power to reverse human chronology, dictating to the father. Shakespeare's loss, says Stephen, is also his gain, because he is a son when he writes, but he is also aware as Joyce was that he too may be trumped, that futurity will father him. Paternity is a legal fiction, because no man can know for sure that his legal child derived from him; it's also a fiction in a narrative sense, because the corpse of John Shakespeare rests, 'disarmed of fatherhood, having devised that mystical estate upon his son' (266). Joyce wished to speed up the process of his own reception by a futurity willing to father him, that new democratic reader with a fresh way of interpreting old texts.

Bloom in the bath had contemplated his penis, 'the limp father of thousands' (107). Stephen implies as much of Shakespeare, who had become a father by the time he wrote the play, and who lost his son Hamnet as Bloom lost Rudy: 'He was not the father of his own son merely but, being no more a son, he was and felt himself the father of all his race, the father of his own grandfather, the father of his unborn grandson' (267). Stephen believes that Shakespeare wrote *Hamlet* after his father's death, at that moment when men realise that they're not going to live forever and when a son may seem like a rival rather than an offspring. Having unconsciously read Bloom's life as Shakespeare's, Stephen converts Shakespeare's attitude to sonship into little more than an anticipatory illumination of his own sonship of Simon.

In such a scenario, the son is a new male, 'his growth is his father's decline, his youth his father's envy, his friend his father's enemy' (267). There can be no love between fathers and sons in such a scheme, where any son with a poor father is compelled to reinvent him by the simple act of fathering himself. Not that this was anything new. It was a story at least as old as the New Testament: 'He Who Himself begot, middler the Holy Ghost, and Himself sent himself, Agenbuyer, between Himself and others' (253), to redeem the past and to make the words of the Old Testament into incarnate actuality.

Stephen uses Shakespeare in the attempt to solve a real problem in his own life, that of the feckless, improvident father. But he can have no idea just how prophetic of Bloom his portrait is. There is in his critical discourse a thrust into the future, a psychological 'surplus' coming from his Unconscious, which prepares him for the meeting with Bloom. Already he has dreamed of the eastern-looking gent who will care for him. Crazy and monomaniacal though his theory of Shakespeare is, it does contain the shape of his own future. Even as he ousts one despised father, he begins to embrace a more positive substitute – along lines well described by the Player King in Shakespeare's play-within-a-play:

> But, orderly to end where I begun,
> Our wills and faces do so contrary run
> That our devices still are overthrown;
> Our thoughts are ours, their ends none
> of our own.

343

People, like texts, often subvert their own intended out-
comes, as the Unconscious undoes the will and brings
those people to a place where they never expected to be.
No ghost from the grave will impel either Stephen or
Bloom; only what they themselves embrace in the present
will have reality for them. But neither man can see that
shaping future just yet – in both cases the Unconscious
still has work to do.

One way of explaining this would be to return to the
New Testament, and the saying of Jesus, that every hair
on a human head is numbered. That text is much in
Hamlet's mind after he returns from a death intended but
somehow overcome. His statement that there's a special
providence in the fall of a sparrow is a self-comparison to
Jesus. There is a higher, if inscrutable, divine will which
may be at work behind the seeming folly of human
actions. Another way of accounting for this would be to
see it as the Unconscious, the uncharted inner depths
slowly and unpredictably being excavated and mapped
onto the everyday mind. On either reading, the over-
wrought intellectual, Hamlet or Stephen, must learn not
to take on as a burden all the woes of the world. Both men
have sought to give their personal problems a
transcendent importance by mapping them onto world
events. Hamlet plays at God by deciding himself whether
the new king should live or die, while Stephen eventually
learns that it is inside his own head that he must kill the
priest or the king.

The script of a life is never entirely self-assigned. It is
sometimes better to act on instinct ('praised be rashness')
and ask questions later. Near the end of his life, Hamlet
grows reckless in the knowledge that democratic death

levels everything anyway: 'A man may fish with a worm that hath eat of a king, and eat of the fish that hath fed of that worm,' with the consequence that 'a king may go a progress through the guts of a beggar'. By a similar logic, you might, if you stood in a graveyard, find the dust of Alexander the Great 'stopping a bung-hole'. This was something Stephen knew in 'Proteus' – that matter exists only to be transformed into something more or less exalted than that with which it began: 'God becomes man becomes fish becomes barnacle goose becomes feather-bed mountain' (63). The Neo-Platonic lore studied by Joyce in Marsh's Library stated no less – that in Hamlet's words man was: 'In action how like an angel! In apprehension how like a god!' But an elegiac note is also present, for the same Renaissance man is also 'this quintessence of dust'. Even in 1600 the finest text produced in the era is a lament for a potential greatness lost.

Ulysses does, however, keep faith with *Hamlet*'s deeper thesis. Bloom, cuckolded like King Hamlet, seeks a son. Dressed in mourning, he enters the hospital wearing a black suit as if lamenting his sundered marriage. The meeting between him and Stephen is beyond any human control – but of course nothing is random when an epic Fate is at work behind the scenes. Stephen has the ability to think, Bloom the inclination to act. Stephen needs to learn how to converse, and Bloom, who yearns for conversation, may be the one he seeks. The danger is that Stephen's consciousness is so luxurious as to become an end in itself, unless it can become engaged with realities by a Bloom who offers a way of reconciling thought and deed.

Conclusion: The Long Day Fades

Joyce was upset to hear that his favourite aunt, Josephine Murray, who had helped him in so many ways in his life and in his art, disapproved of *Ulysses*. She put it away in a press and, later, had it removed from her house. 'If *Ulysses* isn't fit to read,' its author responded, 'life isn't fit to live.' In saying as much, he was thinking of it not just as an honest imitation of life but as a celebration of the minutiae of any given day. Yet by offering different schemas to men like Carlo Linati and Stuart Gilbert, he may unwittingly have impoverished future interpretations of his book. It became 'a text to be deciphered, not read'. Henceforth, scholars would work, scoffed Leo Bersani, with 'a kind of affectless busyness' within those rigid grids which the author had laid down. They would elucidate textual references rather than face the more challenging question of what Joyce was actually saying. But the very works with which Joyce asked for his to be compared all dealt with the same question: How to live? He knew that, in order to be original in his answers, he would have to go right back to the origins of world culture.

In the *Odyssey* Homer presented the hero's voyage as the journey of a soul in the process of discovering itself. In the New Testament Jesus said that such a person-in-formation would have to leave father, mother and family

347

in the act of individuation, knowing the sadness of exile before the joy of a renewed community. In the *Divine Comedy* Dante demonstrated the path back from depression to serenity. In *Hamlet* Shakespeare showed how a special providence shaped human ends, despite the accidents which frustrate us. These are all works of wisdom literature, and Joyce placed his own work in this series of texts which taught people how to live. In Elizabethan times, joked Stephen, Shakespeares were as common as Murphies. It is the ordinariness of life, the everyday quality of its lived wisdom, which attracted Joyce to such classic works and made him want to add one of his own. Some previous writers like Dickens had escaped the ordinary by resorting to melodrama. Others like Flaubert had heaped scorn on the dullness of everyday life, treating ordinary people as similar to the buffoons of old-fashioned comedy. Joyce, on the contrary, wished only to capture the poetry of everyday life.

He was also aware that the ancient classics contained much of the old-world lore now lost to most modern people, but which he hoped to restore. That lore was buried in the human psyche, as fragments of those thoughts which had been rejected in the dogmatic forms taken by most religions, but it could still be reactivated as wisdom. At their first meeting, Joyce said to Yeats that he 'owed nothing to anything but his own mind which was much nearer to God than folklore'. That over-stated his independence of Gaelic lore and of the classics just mentioned, but it was not wholly wrong.

At the start of *Ulysses*, Stephen suffers from a self-inflicted wound. He is lonely, depressed and melancholy, mainly because, like so many intellectuals formed in the

1890s, he has chosen art over life. He has done this in the conviction that in an industrial mass society, what 'life' there is survives only in the most elite types of art. His inwardness is brave, even audacious, but it leaves him disconnected from the everyday. Over-developed in intellect, he is under-developed in the life of the emotions. His learning, which has intimidated too many readers of *Ulysses*, is probably his greatest liability, for it constantly comes between him and the life he might live. At various moments of the day, but especially in 'Circe', he will have to confront many unclaimed experiences and unlived truths, which he has repressed for far too long. He must grasp life through the flow of actual experience rather than through academic concepts. It is not the reader of *Ulysses* who needs to be more educated to understand all of Stephen's references, but Stephen who needs to be *less* learned. Culture sometimes consists not in acquiring opinions but in getting rid of them.

The way out of Hell, as Dante observed, lies at its dead centre. Stephen wishes to escape his pain, as any sensible person would, but first he must fully live through his own desolation in all its raw immediacy. He gets drunk in search of an elation which might allow him to forget, if not escape, his depression. But he needs to go right through the depressed state, if he is to remove all its poisons. Only when he sees that his problems are linked to those of all humanity will his pain begin to lose some of its sting. The dreams and nightmares which trouble his unquiet sleep are those repressed parts of himself, especially his relationship with his mother. They erupt again in the night world of 'Circe', asking to be lived out and redeemed. Like Joyce, Stephen is intrepid and brave enough to dive down into the hell of his Unconscious, to bring into awareness all that has been lost or denied. Genius, as Yeats said, is a crisis which joins our buried self to our everyday mind. That is why Stephen is so obsessed with the Catholic ritual of Holy Saturday: the Paschal Candle lit in the darkened church is an image of lost consciousness finally coming back into everyday recognition. The resurrection of Jesus from the tomb on Easter Sunday is scarcely more miraculous than the fact that every morning the sleeper who has abandoned himself to darkness awakens to a new world.

Stephen's interest in the early fathers of the Christian church and in the occult lore of Neo-Platonic tradition resonates with his sense that a new self can be born for him, if he has the courage to accept psychic change. Much will be left behind, so that that new person can be born. The need is not to fixate on either the unhappy past or uncertain future, but simply to let things happen. His problems are, nonetheless, acute: life has been reduced to a sense of *nacheinander*, one thing after another, without order or design. Meaningful experience has been displaced by random sensation. The interior monologue is the perfect medium for registering this impasse, for it is really a study of the passive nervous system, the sensitive soul in pain registering constant shocks. Its focus is even more on personal response than on the actions and events which are responded to.

Joyce shows Stephen's 'overload' in the third episode, before proceeding to depict in Bloom an older man who copes rather better with the problem of an unhappy consciousness. But even Bloom feels besieged, and so *Ulysses*, in due course, moves from a study of the frustrations of

Stephen and Bloom to a consideration of those social forces which block their full self-expression. That will also involve probing the languages of professional discourse, the subconscious, and the information overloads of modern life.

Joyce's project was indeed to rejoin the sacred to the everyday. Whenever he heard intellectuals using pretentious phrases, he said: 'Don't you wish they'd talk about turnips?' The official churches had made the same terrible error as the writers of modern literature: they had removed their special activities from the practice of everyday life. Only mystics and Gnostics still believed in such a reconciliation at the level of religious practice. Along with the surrealists, Joyce was one of the few major figures committed to it in art. The wisdom at the origin of human culture in such figures as Homer, rather than fixating upon mankind, saw the person as part of the continuum of life, between gods and spirits on one side, and animals and plants on the other. Rejecting the idea of a text, the devotees of mystical knowledge preferred voices, which 'encouraged subjects to see themselves outside their historical moment' – for instance, to make Odysseus walk again in contemporary Dublin streets. They sought to fill the gaps in knowledge left by the creedal dogmas of the major religious traditions.

In his abjection Stephen has to pass through a fallen world of sin and error. What Joyce found in the art and life of Oscar Wilde was the same truth recorded by William Blake: people are educated by their sins, and they must learn first how to go wrong in order later to go right. Only in that way could the actual everyday be re-enchanted. The mistake made by the generation of 1914 was the same

351

one made by the follower of *fin-de-siècle* art: their pursuit of extreme situations was too knowing. Not only did it devalue the middle range of experience, but it was too programmatic. Better to be overtaken by experience, to learn how to watch and to wait.

Stephen tries to live as if life itself could be a work of art, but Bloom offers a humbler sort of art that captures the wisdom of life. Stephen's over-intense programme leads to a terrified recoil from the body, so different from Bloom's acceptance of the flawed human form. Many readers recoiled similarly from the frankness of *Ulysses*, which Joyce jokingly linked to the Bible as two books which no proper Catholic could ever be allowed to read.

As Walter Benjamin noted, a conviction emerged after World War I that experience was no longer communicable in stories of good counsel. People now had mere sensations, and as one vibration replaced another, none was worked through to a conclusion. The art of High Modernism, with its search for extreme moments of joy or abasement, proved no more meaningful a resolution than the trench warfare of 1914–18. But *Ulysses* offered an answer by reconnecting elite art and everyday living. It arose from the pressure of felt experience. Modern living had been devalued by gloomy intellectuals who failed to appreciate just how intelligent, cheerful and resourceful people were in their daily lives. Yet Bloom shows himself skilled in both the conceptual and the selling techniques of advertising, devising the logo of crossed keys, and outlining its underlying psychology. A practical stroller, he also illustrates how people can use the city's newspapers, hoardings, and handbills as a way of negotiating the urban maze. The blend of theory and practice which he calls upon to instruct Stephen is based on a firm conviction that experience and intellect are not opposites; that everybody thinks about the meaning of what happens to them some of the time and that nobody can afford to think about it all of the time.

Bloom constantly compares life to a stream, a flow of things. That stream can never be fully grasped, just experienced, for to analyse it fully it would be necessary first of all to stop the flow. Happiness can be felt but never really described, though it can sometimes be prolonged by a deferral of gratification. In sexual love, only the couple themselves – Odysseus and Penelope, Leopold and Molly – can *feel* such contentment, while the only paradise people can actually know in an analytic way is the one they have already lost. Nevertheless, Joyce insists that the life of the individual is far more important than major political events in the world. Even revolutions are generated by new thoughts dreamed up by peasants on some remote hillside. So also the radical new forms of art are created on the edge of things. It is the insights of marginal people that bring grace.

The sharing of a bad cup of coffee and a stale bread roll may be a real moment of blessedness. For Bloom, food is sacramental. Unlike other events, eating can be controlled without immodest strain. While the other Dubliners rush their meals, guzzle their meat, or talk with their mouths full, he takes care over every culinary detail. At his lunch, he cuts his cheese sandwich into slender strips, and he follows that action with a whole page of personal thoughts before eating it. *Ulysses* proceeds by the same almost tantric sense of delayed gratification.

The lost knowledge of the Gnostics was to be gleaned

353

from those signatures of all things which Stephen wished to read on the landscape of Sandymount Strand. That knowledge which he rather portentously sought in rocks, sand and sea is discovered by Bloom to be secreted in objects – in waste, soap, paper, even piss or shit. Some of the magic of the ancient world expelled from the human mind can now be found in things. Life's meaning is in the flow of making such discoveries, and in the ability of persons to remember past lives, past flows, by connecting with a wisdom that was always buried deep in the self. Hence Joyce's use of Homer, the Bible, Dante and Shakespeare; but also Bloom's ideas on metempsychosis, by which people may remember past lives lived not just as a person but maybe as a bird or a tree.

Bloom exemplifies rather than teaches most of these ideas. He embodies far more than he explains. For all his literary pretensions, his written work is brief and dire. Like Stephen with his brilliant theory of Shakespeare, he cannot set his wisdom down in the constrained forms of writing. 'Neither Christ nor Socrates nor Buddha wrote a book,' said Yeats, 'for to do that is to exchange life for a logical process.' The flow of life is captured in oral energies – old saws, proverbs, witty quotations – which stand in marked contrast to the rather stilted forms of the catechism. 'Ithaca' is Joyce's parody of a world in which storytelling has been replaced by information. Other episodes mock the ways in which abstract systems have too often become more real for modern people that the selves on which they are imposed.

Joyce shared the common fear that the pace of social change had become so fast that it left the generations no common ground on which to meet. Instead, horizontal bonding within each generation was the new reality. As Scott Fitzgerald said, an artist writes for the youth of today, the critics of tomorrow, and the schoolmasters of ever afterward. 'Who will attempt to deal with young people', asked Walter Benjamin, 'by giving them the benefit of their experience?' Bloom's overture to Stephen breaches all the new protocols, by drawing the young man into the process of transmission. When he was young, Joyce had tried the reverse trick on a thirty-eight-year-old W. B. Yeats, only to conclude that the poet was too old to be helped. But at least he made the attempt to reach across generations.

In the oral transmission of wisdom, errors are an intrinsic and even useful part of the process. Needing correction and rebuttal, they help to draw others into the debate about where truth may be found. Amidst the comings and goings of men in the National Library, Stephen's own attempt at playing the guru misfires: but the one-to-one exchange set up by Bloom in 'Eumaeus' works far better. Bloom as an adept seeks not to impress a crowd but to locate just one special person to whom to pass his ideas. The fact that Stephen feels that he must leave is also within this spiritual tradition. Zarathustra said that the individual can experience himself only at the end of his wanderings, as Bloom is now, but Stephen must first of all go away and get to know the world and find his own identity before he can return.

Having rescued Stephen from his depression, Bloom also manages to transform his domestic situation. He lets the affair between his wife and her concert manager go ahead, because he feels guilty about his own marital shortcomings for which he needs her forgiveness. Yet

Molly's soliloquy shows that Bloom's mention of Stephen as a possible new vocal partner has worked in exactly the way he hoped. Compared to Stephen's cultured sensitivity, Boylan is an ignoramus 'that doesnt know poetry from cabbage' (924). Molly herself decides to get Turkish clothes, the very sort that animated Bloom's fantasies of a manly wife – and these facts are interpreted astrologically in 'Ithaca' as portending a change in the dynamic of their relationship. Their shared memory of their Howth tryst gives grounds for hope of a revival in their marriage. From Socrates to Shakespeare, great teachers have had trouble with their wives and sought out the company of young men, whom they might more easily impress with their wisdom. But this one, at least, returns happily enough to home and to hearth.

Bloom's responsiveness to the needs of a confused young man is one way through which he can express his attachment to his city and to his community. The labyrinth through which they move might be the maze through which so many have struggled to find wisdom at the centre. The free movement of bodies through city streets reflects the circulation of blood through the human body: and that steady circulation is what keeps a body healthy. Joyce wished to show that people had nothing to fear from the masses who passed through streets every day. Each member of the crowd, far from being a barbarian, was like Bloom a person in search of stimulation – but not too much. Bloom is akin to the man in the mackintosh at Paddy Dignam's funeral, for either could be the thirteenth mourner; but when he is asked to name the stranger, Bloom cannot do so. Part of his great charm is that he cannot recognise himself, even when he meets himself in others, whether in Odysseus or in the mackintosh man. But meet others he does, and all day long. It is in part because he has a troubled sense of himself that he is prompted to reach out and address the pain of his fellow citizens. But it is also because he enjoys and relishes accidental, unscheduled encounters, as the very basis of civic life.

The aim of art is not to depict a set of incidents, for that would be no more than information. It is rather to relate each event to the life of a storyteller, so that it can be conveyed as lived experience. *Ulysses* is the work of a storyteller, not a novelist. It is a narrative which uses the streets as a guide to the received wisdom of an entire community. A life so lived finally reveals an order hidden from those caught up in the day-to-day accidents of its unfolding. What seemed like random incidents are revealed in the end to be part of some fore-ordained plan. There is a providence in the fall of a sparrow, the hairs on our heads are numbered, and the man of genius makes no mistakes. His errors are the portals of discovery.

Notes

How *Ulysses* Didn't Change Our Lives

3 *a reader of 'Ulysses':* W. R. Rodgers, *Irish Literary Portraits*,
London, 1972, 46

– *at the box office:* Willard Potts (ed.), *James Joyce: Portraits of
an Artist in Exile*, Dublin, 1979, 272

– *never met a bore:* Sylvia Beach, *Shakespeare and Company*,
London, 1959, 40

5 *a penny a line:* cited ibid., 264

– *tight from hunger:* Eugene Sheehy, *The Joyce We Knew*, ed.
Ulick O'Connor, Cork, 1967, 17

6 *the Hitler Mystique:* Henri Lefebvre, *Critique of Everyday Life*,
vol. 1, introduced and translated by John Moore, with preface
by Michael Trebitsch, London, 1991, 131

8 *in many of his exams :* Richard Ellmann, *James Joyce*, Oxford,
1982 (2nd edn), 756 contains a chart of Joyce's marks

– *a very long way:* C. P. Curran, *James Joyce Remembered*,
Oxford, 1968, 54ff.

– *a socialist artist:* James Joyce, *Collected Letters*, vol. 2, ed.
Richard Ellmann, New York, 1966, 68 (letter to Joyce's brother
Stanislaus on 31 October 1904)

– *both rich and poor:* cited by Christopher Lasch, *The Revolt of
the Elites*, New York, 1995, 41

9 *than my contemporaries:* ibid., 89

– *a self-taught Dublin working man:* Virginia Woolf, *Collected
Letters*, vol. 4, ed. Quentin Bell, London, 1972, 63

– *'Les Demoiselles d'Avignon':* see Robert Hughes, *The Shock of
the New*, London, 1980, 21–4

9 *solid and inspiring:* Richard Hoggart, *The Uses of Literacy*,
    Harmondsworth, 1958, 319
− *this is Illyria:* Anew McMaster, 'The Fit-Ups Recalled',
    Newsbeat programme, RTE television, 22 October 1966
10 *across the drawing-room floor:* cited in C. P. Curran, *James
    Joyce Remembered*, 22
11 *of being unperceived:* Maurice Blanchot, *The Infinite Conver-
    sation*, translated by Susan Hanson, Minneapolis, 1993, 242
− *things of every day:* Samuel Taylor Coleridge, *Biographia
    Literaria*, ed. George Watson, London, 1975, 169
12 *call the results a newspaper:* Friedrich Nietzsche, *Thus Spoke
    Zarathustra*, translated by R. J. Hollingdale, Harmondsworth,
    1961, 77
13 *was fabulous:* Mary and Pádraic Colum, *Our Friend James
    Joyce*, New York, 1958, 55
− *backers from overseas:* see Ellmann, *James Joyce*, 300–11
14 *what are called Bohemian qualities:* Mary and Pádraic Colum,
    Our Friend James Joyce, 206
− *a great family man:* W. R. Rodgers, *Irish Literary Portraits*, 65
15 *naïve, even innocent, interpretations:* F. R. Leavis was one
    critic willing to celebrate writers whose work conveyed the
    pressure of felt experience and a sense of the full ethical life:
    but his views on literary form and language were so narrow
    that he dismissed *Ulysses* as a dead end

How It Might Still Do So

17 *has taken to teaching:* Oscar Wilde, *The Artist as Critic*, ed.
    Richard Ellmann, London, 1970, 291
− *ignorance about the world:* Christopher Lasch, *The Revolt of
    the Elites*, 181
− *the exacting silence of a text:* cited by Susan A. Handelman,
    *Fragments of Redemption: Jewish Thought and Literary
    Theory in Benjamin, Scholem and Levinas*, Bloomington,
    Indiana, 1991, 63
19 *heroic deeds and language:* J. F. Byrne, *Silent Years*, New York,
    1953, 87ff.

20 *as we meet them in the real world:* James Joyce, *Critical
Writings*, ed. Ellsworth Mason and Richard Ellmann, New
York, 1959, 45

– *usylessly unreadable blue book of eccles:* James Joyce,
Finnegans Wake, ed. Seamus Deane, London, 1992, 361

23 *consumerist middle class:* on this social shift, see Richard
Sennett, *Respect: The Formation of Character in an Age of
Inequality*, London, 2003, passim; and his *The Corrosion of
Character: The Personal Consequences of Work in the New
Capitalism*, New York, 1998, passim; also relevant is
Christopher Lasch, *The True and Only Heaven*, New York,
1991, passim

25 *idea of a neighbourhood:* see Jane Jacobs, *The Death and Life
of the Great American Cities*, London, 1962, passim

– *nobody in my books has any money:* cited by Pádraic Colum,
The Joyce We Knew, 101

– *other things as well:* cited by Ellmann, *James Joyce*, 576

26 *swingers by night:* Daniel Bell, *The Cultural Contradictions of
Capitalism*, London, 1979, xxv

27 *students of Trinity College:* cited by C. P. Curran, *James Joyce
Remembered*, 60

– *their own clothes:* Karl Marx, 'The Eighteenth Brumaire of
Louis Bonaparte', *Surveys from Exile*, ed. David Fernbach,
Harmondsworth, 1973, passim

– *not an adventurer:* cited in César Graña, *Bohemian versus
Bourgeois: French Society and the French Man of Letters*, New
York, 1964, 165ff.

28 *of the modern artist:* cited by Graña, ibid., 20

– *think like a demigod:* cited ibid., 195

29 *about a third party:* cited by Richard Lehan, *The City in
Literature*, Berkeley, 1998, 109

– *'foredreamed' his own epic:* Noel Riley Fitch, *Sylvia Beach and
the Lost Generation*, London, 1985, 229

– *in emergencies:* Carl Van Doren (ed.), *The Portable Walt Whitman*, New York, 1952: the quotations are from pages 42 and 382

30 *discernible:* in Willard Potts (ed.), *James Joyce: Portraits of an
Artist in Exile*, 114

30 *need of an editor:* Roddy Doyle, New York, 10 February 2004

Paralysis, Self-Help and Renewal

31 *in the midst of life:* Ellmann, *James Joyce,* passim

33 *on the roads of the world:* cited in Willard Potts (ed.), *James Joyce: Portraits of an Artist in Exile,* Dublin, 1979, 216

– *mere Englishness:* this point and the preceding quotations are to be found in Andrew Gibson, *Joyce's Revenge,* Oxford, 2002, 7

– *might have produced:* Pádraic Colum in *The Joyce We Knew,* 107

34 *took centuries to emerge:* The American classic *Moby-Dick* (1851) was another encyclopedic narrative of an intergeneric kind, sometimes filed as non-fiction in libraries because its densely factual discourse on whaling is interspersed through its fictional narrative. It also projected the values of a nation still in the process of making itself. The analogies with *Ulysses* would repay yet further study

– *novelist of a new kind:* W. B. Yeats, letter to Secretary of Royal Literary Fund, 1915: cited by Ellmann, *James Joyce,* 391

35 *a decline in cultural standards:* R. A. Breatnach, 'The End of a Tradition', *Studia Hibernica,* no. 1, 1960, 142

36 *go no further:* on this blockage, see Cathal Ó Háinle, 'An tÚrscéal Nár Tháinig', *Promhadh Pinn,* Átha Cliath, 1978, 74–98

– *which means 'ourselves':* on these themes the definitive study is P. J. Mathews, *Revival,* Cork, 2003

37 *just like individuals:* James Joyce, *Critical Writings,* 154

– *a fuair siad:* Feardorcha Ó Mealláin, 'Mairgne ar an nDíbirt go Connacht', in Caoimhghin Ó Góilidhe (ed.), *Dánta Árdteastais,* Átha Cliath, 1967, 42–3

38 *cherishing all the children of the nation equally:* Proclamation of the Irish Republic, Easter 1916

39 *seemed long decayed:* Karl Marx, 'The Eighteenth Brumaire', *Surveys from Exile,* 94

1. Waking

42 *father to yourself:* Friedrich Nietzsche, *On The Advantage and Disadvantage of History for Life*, translated by Peter Preuss, Indianapolis, 1980

– *bitter mystery:* W. B. Yeats, *Collected Poems*, London, 1950, 49

45 *his face in a mirror:* Oscar Wilde, Preface to *The Picture of Dorian Gray*, London, 1891

– *false to several others:* see Lionel Trilling, *Sincerity and Authenticity*, Oxford, 1972, 118–22

46 *the most belated race in Europe:* James Joyce, *Critical Writings*, 70

47 *English-bred lie:* Patrick Kavanagh, *Collected Pruse*, London, 1973, 13

49 *seeks to overturn:* Richard Sennett, *The Fall of Public Man: On the Social Psychology of Capitalism*, New York, 1978, 184

– *ld ddr saol:* on this proverbial wisdom in the autobiographies of the Blasket islands, see Pádraig Ó hÉalaithe, 'Na hOiléanaigh agus a dTréithe', *Irisleabhar Mhuighe Nuadhat*, 1966, ┰ 18

– *selves in transformation:* see Michael Sheringham, *Everyday Life: Theories and Practices from Surrealism to the Present*, Oxford, 2006, 367ff.

50 *of a morning reprieve:* cited and discussed by John McCole, *Walter Benjamin and the Antinomies Tradition*, Ithaca, New York, 1993, 284

52 *their true faces:* Carlos Fuentes in *Terra Nostra* bases his novel on the thesis that a revolution is the struggle by a people to have faces rather than masks

2. Learning

53 *'made a man' of him:* Ellmann, *James Joyce*, 159ff.; also 378–9

54 *opening stories of 'Dubliners':* Marian Eide, *Ethical Joyce*, Cambridge, 2002, 30–9

56 *all taken to teaching:* Oscar Wilde, *The Artist as Critic*, 291

57 *or blossom shew'th:* John Milton, *Poetical Works*, ed. Douglas Bush, Oxford, 1966, 105

57 *not your father:* on this phenomenon, see Angela Carter, *The Sadeian Woman: An Exercise in Cultural History*, London, 1979, 15ff.

59 *greatest scrapper that ever lived:* cited by Ann Douglas, *The Feminization of American Culture*, New York, 1978, 326

60 *to the noise of the street:* cited by Robert Hughes, *The Shock of the New*, 71

62 *young man:* on the Jewish migrations to Ireland after 1860 see Cormac Ó Gráda, *Jewish Ireland in the Age of Joyce*, Princeton, New Jersey, 2006, 9–42

3. Thinking

67 *seeing of an object:* cited and discussed by Stephen Kern, *The Culture of Time and Space*, Harvard, Cambridge Mass., 2003, 22

– *stone to stone:* quoted by Robert Hughes, *The Shock of the New*, 281

68 *child of his own writings:* this is the general thesis underlying Michael Holroyd's multi-volume biography of Shaw, but it is initially and more specifically articulated in his 'GBS and Ireland', *Sewanee Review*, Winter 1976, LXXXIV, no. 1, 39–54

– *to conceive of himself:* for a full analysis of the literary workings of this process, see Harold Bloom, *The Anxiety of Influence: A Theory of Poetry*, London, 1975, passim

69 *after a picnic:* this satirical image, though widely attributed, seems to have originated with George Moore

– *Platonic conception of himself:* F. Scott Fitzgerald, *The Great Gatsby*, London, 1994, 105

– *derive only from myself:* Jean-Paul Sartre, *Words*, translated by Irene Clephane, Harmondsworth, 1967, 71

– *liberation of a rhythm:* cited by Pádraic Colum, *The Joyce We Knew*, 66

70 *perfect work will do both:* Walter Benjamin, *The Origin of German Tragic Drama*, translated by John Osborne, London, 1977, 44

– *hour of the day:* quoted by Stephen Kern, *The Culture of Time and Space*, 21

71 *a bung-hole:* William Shakespeare, *Hamlet*, Act 4, Scene 3 and
Act 5, Scene 1, ed. O. J. Campbell, A. Rothschild and S.
Vaughan, New York, 1961, 124 and 154

– *very like a whale:* ibid., 106

73 *that walked the waves:* John Milton, *Poetical Works*, 147

76 *and so cold:* William Carlos Williams, *Collected Poems*, ed.
A. Walton Litz and Christopher MacGowan, New York, 1986,
372

4. Walking

77 *goes to war:* Frank Budgen, *James Joyce and the Making of
Ulysses*, Oxford, 1972, 75

85 *men without imagination:* J. E. Rivers, *Proust and the Art of
Love: The Aesthetics of Sexuality in the Life, Times and Art of
Marcel Proust*, New York, 1980, 35

87 *achieve sexual gratification:* Sigmund Freud, *On Sexuality*,
trans. James Strachey, ed. Angela Richards, Harmondsworth,
1977, 209–15, 299–302

88 *picture of the human soul:* Anthony Kenny, *Wittgenstein*,
Harmondsworth, 1973, 65ff.

– *Adaline Glasheen:* 'Calypso', *James Joyce's Ulysses: Critical
Essays*, ed. Clive Hart and David Hayman, London, 1974, 51–70

5. Praying

93 *tenacity in conviction:* Ellmann, *James Joyce*, 368

94 *by a sexual explanation:* see Jolande Jacobi, *The Way of
Individuation*, translated by R. F. C. Hall, New York, 1967,
especially 106–31

97 *than most citizens:* Cormac Ó Gráda, *Jewish Ireland in the Age
of Joyce*, 34–5 and 167–9

6. Mourning

101 *embalms himself alive:* Theodor Adorno, *Minima Moralia:
Reflections from a Damaged Life*, translated by E. F. N.
Jephcott, London, 1974, 38–9 and 120

106 *beautiful form of life:* Ellmann, *James Joyce,* 96 and 252

– *a power of dissolution:* Maurice Blanchot, *The Infinite Conversation,* 244

– *'last till doomsday':* the preceding three quotations are from *Hamlet,* op. cit., V.ii.159 and V.i.153, 148

110 *six-foot plot:* in Leo Tolstoy's 'The Death of Ivan Ilyich'

111 *to talk about it:* Samuel Beckett, *Waiting for Godot,* New York, 1954, 40–1

7. Reporting

113 *'something happens':* Maurice Blanchot, *The Infinite Conversation,* 243–4

114 *'filled with thought'* : quoted by Robert Hughes, *The Shock of the New,* 125

– *it was beautiful:* cited ibid., 63

117 *not unjust description:* James Joyce, *Collected Letters,* , vol. 1, ed. Stuart Gilbert, New York, 1966, 297

– *previous twenty-four hours:* Peter Fritzsche, *Reading Berlin 1900,* Harvard, Cambridge Mass., 1996, 178ff.

120 *the design of the horse-carriage:* Susan Buck-Morss, *The Dialectics of Seeing: Walter Benjamin and the Arcades Project,* Harvard, Cambridge Mass., 1990, 101ff.

– *colonisers and merchants:* cited in Willard Potts (ed.), *James Joyce: Portraits of an Artist in Exile,* 68.

8. Eating

124 *better nutrition:* Ó Gráda, *Jewish Ireland in the Age of Joyce,* 171–6

129 *sit in the shade:* Jane Austen, *Emma,* ed. Ronald Blythe, Harmondsworth, 1966, 354

– *in their direction:* Carol Shields, *Jane Austen,* London, 2001, 136

– *'sublime' or beautiful?:* Thomas Bartlett (ed.), *Life of T. W. Tone,* Dublin, 1998, 151.

136 *being limited by it:* Michael Sheringham, *Everyday Life,* 373

9. Reading

137 *to their quarters:* Mary and Pádraic Colum, *Our Friend James Joyce*, 29

– *not nailed to it:* C. P. Curran, *James Joyce Remembered*, 36

138 *on the inner sanctuary:* ibid., 35

140 *professors at Trinity College:* see Lady Gregory, *Cuchulain of Muirthemne*, Gerrards Cross, 1970, 5; and on the row with the professors, see Tomás Ó Fiaich, 'The Great Controversy', in *The Gaelic League Idea*, ed. S. Ó Tuama, Cork, 1972, 67–8

141 *rest of their lives:* see Ó Fiaich, 'The Great Controversy', 68

– *spit into the Liffey:* quoted by Gerald Griffin, *The Wild Geese*, London, 1938, 24

142 *by advertising:* cited by Richard Wolin, *Walter Benjamin: An Aesthetic of Redemption*, New York, 1982, 119

143 *treasure-house of myth:* Eva Brann, *Homeric Moments: Clues to Delight in Reading The Odyssey and the Iliad*, Philadelphia, 2002, 203

10. Wandering

153 *map of it:* Ellmann, *James Joyce*, 28

155 *on their souls:* This contrast between behaviour of missionaries and imperial officials is noted in E. M. Forster's novel *A Passage to India* (1924)

156 *by the Easter Rising:* on the decline of deference, see David Fitzpatrick, *Politics and Irish Life: 1913–1921*, Dublin, 1977, 234ff.

157 *pieces of silver:* Joyce, *Critical Writings*, 196

162 *deindividualising small town:* George Simmel, *On Individuality and Social Forms*, 333

163 *had no consciousness:* Ellmann, *James Joyce*, 372

166 *the pawns:* I owe this point to José Venegas of Duke University, who made it the basis of a fine essay in 2004

11. Singing

168 *condition of music:* Walter Pater, *The Renaissance*, Oxford, 1967, 106

169 *scorn of syntax:* J. M. Synge, *Collected Works: Prose*, ed. Alan Price, Oxford, 1966, 143

170 *stringed instrument:* on this, see Declan Kiberd, 'Synge, Yeats and Bardic Poetry', *The Irish Writer and the World*, Cambridge, 2005, 70–90

176 *'sweets to the sweet':* William Shakespeare, *Hamlet*, Act 5, Scene 1, line 156

177 *a savage breast:* William Congreve, *The Mourning Bride*, Act 1, Scene 1

12. Drinking

183 *vocabulary be revealed:* C. P. Curran, *James Joyce Remembered*, 70

186 *national parallelism:* Séan de Fréine, *The Great Silence*, Dublin, 1965, 108

192 *admirer of Bloom:* Frank Budgen, *James Joyce and the Making of Ulysses*, 169

– *conscience of his race:* James Joyce, *A Portrait of the Artist as a Young Man*, ed. Seamus Deane, London, 1992, 276

13. Ogling

193 *drawersy style:* Frank Budgen, *James Joyce and the Making of Ulysses*, 210–11

194 *'Idylls of the King':* J. M. Synge Manuscripts, Trinity College Dublin, MS 4393, f.6

195 *to use their skills:* see J. J. Lee, 'Women and the Church Since the Famine', in *Women in Irish Society: The Historical Dimension*, ed. Margaret McCurtain and Donnchadh Ó Corráin, Dublin, 1978, 41ff.

197 *saturated in sexuality:* Donald Davie, *These the Companions*, Cambridge, 1982, 50

200 *its own flawed formation:* Edward Mendelson, 'Encyclopedic Narratives', *Modern Language Notes 91*, 1976, 1267–75

201 *'Heavenly God!':* James Joyce, *A Portrait of the Artist as a Young Man*, 186

– *vocation as a writer:* Stanislaus Joyce, *My Brother's Keeper*, 157–8

202 *mentioned by Bloom:* Katherine Mullin, *James Joyce, Sexuality and Social Purity*, Cambridge, 2004, 128

203 *thick lips:* see L. Perry Curtis Jnr., *Anglo-Saxon and Celts: A Study in Anti-Irish Prejudice in Victorian England*, Bridgeport, 1968, passim; L. Perry Curtis Jnr., *Apes and Angels: The Irishman in Victorian Caricature*, London, 1971, passim; and Richard Ned Lebow, *White Britain and Black Ireland: The Influence of Stereotype on Colonial Policy*, Philadelphia, 1976
   – *for land-lubbers:* Angela Carter, *The Sadeian Woman*, 15
   – *have made of them:* Stanislaus Joyce, *My Brother's Keeper*, 164

14. Birthing

209 *act of coition:* Frank Budgen, *James Joyce and the Making of Ulysses*, 220

210 *how sad!:* quoted by Ellmann, *James Joyce*, 204
   – *in our bodies:* cited in Willard Potts (ed.), *James Joyce: Portraits of an Artist in Exile*, 159

212 *William Peacock:* for a fine analysis of this, see Andrew Gibson, *Joyce's Revenge*, 172–6

214 *no religion:* Ellmann, *James Joyce*, 514

217 *the subject of his book:* Stuart Gilbert, *James Joyce's Ulysses*, London, 1963, 76
   – *goahead plot:* James Joyce, *Collected Letters*, vol. 3, ed. R. Ellmann, 146

220 *of a miracle:* Walter Benjamin, *The Origin of German Tragic Drama*, 178
   – *anatomical dissection:* ibid., 218
   – *with a miracle:* ibid., 234

15. Dreaming

222 *Sigmund Freud:* 'The Theory of Dreams', in *The Modern Tradition*, ed. R. Ellmann and C. Feidelson, New York, 1965, 572
   – *medical 'symptom':* Jacques Lacan, Le Séminaire, Livre XXIII, *Le Sinthome*, établi par Jacques-Alain Miller, Paris, 2005, passim

223 *more deeply afterwards:* Sigmund Freud, *The Interpretation of Dreams*, passim
  - *the dreamer:* August Strindberg, Preface to *A Dream Play*, translated by Michael Meyer, London, 1971
224 *'a purely . . . Cuchulanoid' world:* quoted by Ann Saddlemyer, 'Synge to MacKenna: The Mature Years', *Irish Renaissance*, ed. R. Skelton and D. Clark, Dublin, 1965, 67
  - *in the real world:* James Joyce, *Critical Writings*, 45
  - *stranger in the house:* the phrase gained currency not just as a description of colonial occupation in Yeats's and Gregory's *Cathleen Ni Houlihan* (1902) but also as an account of the marital situation treated in Synge's *The Shadow of the Glen* (1904)
225 *most realistic episode of 'Ulysses':* cited by Mullin, *James Joyce, Sexuality and Social Purity*, 73
  - *good things will come:* quoted by Ellmann, *James Joyce*, 360
229 *seem real:* this joke is usually attributed to Jean Baudrillard
230 *the thing observed:* Stephen Kern, *The Culture of Time and Space*, 18
234 *degenerate men:* Allan Wade (ed.), *Letters of W. B. Yeats*, London, 1954, 108
  - *the same day:* Andrew Motion, *Philip Larkin: A Writer's Life*, London, 1993, 26.
235 *so recently lost:* C. L. Barber, *Shakespeare's Festive Comedy: A Study of Dramatic Form and Its Relation to Social Custom*, Princeton, New Jersey, 1972, 17
236 *to clarification:* ibid., 139
  - *self-respect:* the best modern edition is Liam P. Ó Murchú (ed.), *Cúirt an Mheon-Oíche*, Átha Cliath, 1982
  - *of world opinion:* James Joyce, *Critical Writings*, 198

16. Parenting

237 *in every street:* James Joyce, *Exiles*, Harmondsworth, 1973, 51
240 *both are transformed:* William McGuire and R. F. C. Hall, *C. G. Jung Speaking*, Princeton, New Jersey, 1977, 286
241 *'was quite impossible':* C. P. Curran, *James Joyce Remembered*, 68

– *in him a genius:* cited in W. R. Rodgers (ed.), *Irish Literary Portraits*, 35

245 *'Burjoice':* Sylvia Beach, *Shakespeare and Company*, 42

– *lost interest in Stephen:* ibid., 43

246 *to hide from being adults:* Richard Sennett, *The Uses of Disorder*, New York, 1970, 98 and 139

17. Teaching

248 *any boy in his class:* testimony of Willie Fallon, *The Joyce We Knew*, 56

– *we cannot know:* on this type of 'negative capability', see Richard Poirier, 'Superfluous Emerson', *Poetry and Pragmatism*, Harvard, Cambridge Mass., 1992, 37–78

253 *a totally new light:* Walter Benjamin, *The Origin of German Tragic Drama*, 66

258 *author of a wise book:* quoted by Ellmann, *James Joyce*, 471

18. Loving

260 *characteristics of woman:* George Simmel, *On Women, Sexuality and Love*, translated by Guy Oakes, New Haven, 1981, 125

262 *womanly men:* see June Singer, *Androgyny: Towards a New Theory of Sexuality*, London, 1979, passim

263 *fiction means:* Oscar Wilde, *The Importance of Being Earnest*, in *Four Plays*, Harmondsworth, 1954, 275

264 *up-market whore:* on this, see Ian Watt, *The Rise of the Novel*, California, 1956, 108–15

265 *all over the place:* Urs Bucher, 'Stream of Consciousness in the Work of James Joyce and Dorothy Richardson', University College Dublin, PhD, 1982

266 *deliberation to them:* quoted by Dan Frank, *The Bohemians: The Birth of Modern Art: Paris 1900–1930*, London, 2004, 340

269 *refused to submit to her:* Theodor Adorno and Max Horkheimer, *Dialectic of Enlightenment*, translated by John Cumming, London, 1979, 73

270 *the utmost secrecy:* Eva Brann, *Homeric Moments*, 275

274 *sell it to Arthur Power:* Ellmann, *James Joyce*, 525
   – *nothing at all about women:* ibid., 629
   – *any writer that she knew:* Sylvia Beach, *Shakespeare and Company*, 42
   – *interlocking rings:* Ellémire Zolla, *The Androgyne: Fusion of the Sexes*, London, 1981, 68–9
276 *are it:* John Donne, 'The Canonisation'

Ordinary People's Odysseys

277 *not a hero:* quoted in *The Joyce We Knew*, 104
   – *'outside European culture':* ibid., 79
278 *something new:* Richard Jenkyns, *Classic Epic: Homer and Virgil*, London, 1992, 53
   – *to produce:* quoted in Potts (ed.), *James Joyce: Portraits of an Artist in Exile*, 158
   – *journey of a story:* Carol Dougherty, *The Raft of Odysseus: The Ethnographic Imagination of Homer's Odyssey*, Oxford, 2001, 75
279 *new markets:* quoted in Potts (ed.), *James Joyce: Portraits of an Artist in Exile*, 70ff.
280 *force of a revelation:* on this mechanism as outlined by Walter Benjamin, see Richard Wolin, *Walter Benjamin: Aesthetics of Redemption*, passim; and Susan A. Handelman, *Fragments of Redemption: Jewish Thought and Literary Theory in Benjamin, Scholem and Levinas*, passim
   – *contemporary life:* T. S. Eliot, '*Ulysses*, Order and Myth', *The Dial*, LXXV, 1923; reproduced in Ellmann and Feidelson (eds), *The Modern Tradition*, 681
   – *volatile present:* Carol Dougherty, *The Raft of Odysseus*, 9
   – *trading world:* Theodor Adorno and Max Horkheimer, *Dialectic of Enlightenment*, translated by John Cumming, London, 1979, 1–80
281 *with human flesh:* ibid., 67
282 *cultural identity:* ibid., 44
283 *no longer be celebrated:* ibid., 43
284 *a man of him:* Professor John Dillon of Trinity College Dublin

made this point at a lecture in University College Dublin on 10
April 2006
- *of his parentage:* on this, see Eva Brann, *Homeric Moments*,
148
286 *supernatural beings:* E. R. Dodds, *The Greeks and the
Irrational,* Berkeley, 1951, 11
287 *'call them "his" ':* ibid., 11
- *to their author:* ibid., 17
288 *'lush':* Ellmann, *James Joyce,* 615
289 *homely work:* Eva Brann, *Homeric Moments,* 139
- *What did you do:* Tom Stoppard, *Travesties,* London, 1975, 44
- *an American flirtation:* on this, see Sigmund Freud, *Character
and Culture,* New York, 1963, 124–5
290 *motive power of everything:* James Joyce, *Collected Letters,* vol.
2, 81
- *shaken nerves:* quoted by Christopher Lasch, *The True and
Only Heaven: Progress and Its Critics,* New York, 1991, 299
- *faith to match his own:* James Joyce, *Collected Letters,* vol. 1,
ed. Stuart Gilbert, New York, 1966, 53
- *state of society:* cited by Christopher Lasch, *The True and Only
Heaven,* 314
- *only the sick:* ibid., 236
291 *complainers of today:* ibid., 287
- *more like themselves than ever:* Franco Moretti, *The Way of the
World: The Bildungsroman in European Culture,* translated by
Albert Sbragid, London, 2000, 114
292 *to confer an identity:* Eva Brann, *Homeric Moments,* 51
294 *look after you:* Homer, *The Odyssey,* translated by E. V. Rieu,
London, 1991, 149

Old Testaments and New

296 *who never did it:* Frank Budgen, *James Joyce and the Making
of Ulysses,* 191
- *of new martyrdom:* quoted in Potts (ed.), *James Joyce: Portraits
of an Artist in Exile,* 35
- *a single syllable:* ibid., 35

296 *in the love of God:* Mrs Shaurek, cited in W. R. Rodgers (ed.),
     Irish Literary Portraits, 29
   – *less than divine:* Stanislaus Joyce, *My Brother's Keeper,* 159
297 *and future sees:* William Blake, *Selected Poems,* introduction
     by Basil de Selincourt, London, 1927, 53
   – *the importance of a scientific discovery:* T. S. Eliot, '*Ulysses,*
     Order and Myth', *The Modern Tradition,* 681
299 *involuntary memory:* Robert Alter, *Necessary Angels: Tradition
     and Modernity in Kafka, Benjamin and Scholem,* Cambridge
     Mass., 1991, 75 and 104
   – *unit to be seized:* Edward W. Said, *Humanism and Democratic
     Criticism,* New York, 2004, 100–1. Said acknowledges the
     influence of Erich Auerbach on this analysis
   – *human form divine:* William Blake, *Selected Poems,* 47
300 '*tasks of daily life':* Michael Fishbane, *The Garments of Torah:
     Essays in Biblical Hermeneutics,* Bloomington, Indiana, 1992,
     96; see also Michael Walzer, *Exodus and Revolution,* New
     York, 1985, 53ff.
   – *becoming the new:* Séan Freyne, *Galilee, Jesus and the Gospels:
     Literary Approaches and Historical Investigations,*
     Philadelphia, 1988, 271–2
301 *through to the soul:* cited by Michael Fishbane, *The Garments
     of Torah,* 34
   – *unmapped interior:* ibid., 34–40
303 *on the third day:* for analysis of this utterance, see Donald
     Juel, *Messianic Exegesis: Christological Interpretation of the
     Old Testament in Early Christianity,* Philadelphia, 1988, 14
306 *would be exalted:* the most brilliant analysis of the
     unprecedented realism of the New Testament gospels is
     conducted by Erich Auerbach, *Mimesis: The Representation of
     Reality in Western Literature,* translated by Willard Trask,
     Princeton, New Jersey, 1953, 72–3
   – *rude mechanicals:* William Shakespeare, *A Midsummer
     Night's Dream,* Act 5
309 *claim on some future:* Susan A. Handelman, *Fragments of
     Redemption,* 154ff.
   – *hidden in the texts:* Garry Wills, *The Rosary,* London, 2006, 103

- *and sister and mother:* on this, see Willard M. Swartley,
  *Israel's Scripture Traditions and the Synoptic Gospels: Story
  Creating Story*, Peabody, Massachusetts, 2003, 52–3 and 93
310 *the land of Egypt:* Michael Walzer, *Exodus and Revolution*,
  140
- *the Other of Christians:* on this, see Willard M. Swartley,
  Israel's Scripture Traditions, 252; also Julia Kristeva, *Strangers
  to Ourselves*, translated by Leon S. Roudiez, Hastings, 1991
311 *a God-man:* Anthony Tyrrell Hanson, *The Prophetic Gospel: A
  Study of John and the Old Testament*, Edinburgh, 1991, 281
- *a religious order:* cited in Willard Potts (ed.), *James Joyce:
  Portraits of an Artist in Exile*, 76
312 *anybody can understand it:* quoted in Ellmann, *James Joyce*,
  529
- *with faith:* Frederick J. Hoffman and Olga W. Vicery (eds),
  William Faulkner: Three Decades of Criticism, interview with
  Jean Stein, New York, 1960, 77

Depression and After: Dante's Comedy

313 *of his being:* James Joyce, *Collected Letters*, vol. 2, 433
- *'hungry and threadbare':* R. W. B. Lewis, *Dante*, London, 2001,
  121–2
- *'Herr Satan':* on Dante's scorched beard, see William
  Anderson, *Dante the Maker*, London, 1983, 384; for Herr Satan,
  see Frank Budgen, *James Joyce and the Making of Ulysses*, 36,
  who attributes the comment to women who worked in the
  Stadttheater
- *of the Europeans:* Ellmann, *James Joyce*, 61; and Mary T.
  Reynolds, *Joyce and Dante: The Shaping Imagination*,
  Princeton, New Jersey, 1981, 11
- *of his being:* R. W. B. Lewis, *Dante*, 2
314 *against the nobility:* ibid., 6
- *state of happiness:* William Anderson, *Dante the Maker*, 6
- *twisted backward:* Charles Williams, *The Figure of Beatrice: A
  Study in Dante*, New York, 1961, 136
315 *show it to him:* ibid., 109

315 *recovery:* ibid., 108

316 *entire cultural world:* R. W. B. Lewis, *Dante*, 12

 – *to figure things out:* Edward Hirsch, 'Summoning Shades', *The Poets' Dante*, ed. Peter Hawkins and Rachel Jacoff, New York, 2001, 398

317 *to come through:* Helen M. Luke, *Dark Wood to White Rose: Journey and Transformation in Dante's Divine Comedy*, New York, 1993, 11

 – *clasped him:* Canto XXXIV, 70–1

319 *to meet him:* Charles Williams, *The Figure of Beatrice*, 20

320 *will never blossom:* see Helen M. Luke, *Dark Wood to White Rose*, passim

 – *needs of his pupil:* William Anderson, *Dante the Maker*, 342

321 *through you a Christian:* Canto XXII, 73

 – *himself a castaway:* Charles Williams, *The Figure of Beatrice*, 169

 – *over myself:* ibid., 174

322 *God's way of writing:* Charles Singleton, 'In Exitu Israel de Aegypto', *Dante: A Collection of Critical Essays*, ed. John Freccero, Englewood Cliffs, New Jersey, 1965, 112

323 *the shadow of others:* Helen M. Luke, *Dark Wood to White Rose*, 64

 – *force for transformation:* William Anderson, *Dante the Maker*, 382

324 *irrevocable decision:* Erich Auerbach, *Dante: Poet of the Secular World*, translated by Ralph Mannheim, New York, 2007, 177

 – *of his distress:* ibid., 171

 – *haze of projections:* Helen M. Luke, *Dark Wood to White Rose*, 83

 – *small though they may appear:* ibid., 83

326 *lapsed into cold allegory:* Erich Auerbach, *Dante: Poet of the Secular World*, 15

 – *praise my lady:* R. W. B. Lewis, *Dante*, 47

327 *and all nature:* Helen M. Luke, *Dark Wood to White Rose*, 184

 – *in her grave forever:* James Joyce, *Critical Writings*, 174

 – *ease her pain:* Charles Williams, *The Figure of Beatrice*, 154

– *and laughed:* on this, see Charles Williams, ibid., 198
329 *'believers and non-believers':* Robert Hollander, *Dante: A Life in Works*, New Haven, 2001, 36
– *'rosa sempiterna': Paradiso* XXX, 124–6
330 *set before every man:* Erich Auerbach, *Dante: Poet of the Secular World*, 98

Hamlet, Shakespeare and Company

331 *the greatest poet:* Willie Fallon, *The Joyce We Knew*, 46–7
– *no good:* James Joyce, *A Portrait of the Artist as a Young Man*, 86
– *fust in us unused:* William Shakespeare, *Hamlet*, Act 4, Scene 4, 128
332 *excess of the facts as they appear:* T. S. Eliot, *The Sacred Wood: Essays on Poetry and Criticism*, London, 1920, 101
– *also restricts:* quoted by Alexander Welsh, *Hamlet in His Modern Guises*, Princeton: New Jersey, 2001, 75
– *suits of woe:* William Shakespeare, *Hamlet*, Act 1, Scene 2, 33
– *oft proclaims the man:* ibid., Act 1, Scene 3, 42. On the split between avowal and inner feeling, I am deeply indebted to Harold Rosenberg, *Act and the Actor: Making the Self*, Chicago, 1983, 74–103
333 *the mumming company:* James Joyce, *Critical Writings*, 150
334 *and thinking things:* Harold Bloom, *Hamlet: Poem Unlimited*, New York, 2003, 118–19; see also Alexander Welsh, *Hamlet in His Modern Guises*, 64
335 *'of human contact':* Eamon Duffy, *The Stripping of the Altars*, New Haven, 1992, 475
– *need to avenge him:* see Harold Bloom, *Hamlet: Poem Unlimited*, 8; and William Kerrigan, *Hamlet's Perfection*, Baltimore, 1994, 90
336 *state of being dead:* C. S. Lewis, 'The Prince or the Poem', in *Hamlet*, ed. Campbell, Rothschild and Vaughan, 248
– *no traveller returns:* William Shakespeare, *Hamlet*, Act 3, Scene 1, 87
337 *passeth show:* ibid., Act 1, Scene 2, 33

337 *Horatio, I am dead:* ibid., Act 5, Scene 2, 172
339 *custom of exercises:* ibid., Act 2, Scene 2, 73
– *true bonding:* see Juliet Dusinberre, *Shakespeare and the Nature of Women*, London, 1975, 257–8
340 *'passion's slave':* William Shakespeare, *Hamlet*, Act 3, Scene 2, 94
– *made me mad:* ibid., Act 3, Scene 1, 89
341 *brothel as well as convent:* O. J. Campbell, Introduction, in *Hamlet*, ed. O. J. Campbell, A. Rothschild and S. Vaughan, 6
– *as house-keepers:* Stanislaus Joyce, *My Brother's Keeper*, 164
343 *none of our own:* William Shakespeare, *Hamlet*, Act 3, Scene 2, 99
344 *'praised be rashness':* ibid., Act 5, Scene 2, 159
345 *guts of a beggar:* ibid., Act 4, Scene 3, 124
– *a bung-hole:* ibid., Act 5, Scene 1, 154
– *like a god:* ibid., Act 2, Scene 2, 73
– *quintessence of dust:* ibid., Act 2, Scene 2, 73

Conclusion: The Long Day Fades

347 *isn't fit to live:* Ellmann, *James Joyce*, 537
– *deciphered, not read:* Leo Bersani, 'Against *Ulysses*', *The Culture of Redemption*, Cambridge, Mass., 1990, 175
– *affectless busyness:* ibid., 174
348 *to God than folklore:* Ellmann, *James Joyce*, 107
349 *getting rid of them:* Frank Tuohy, *Yeats*, Dublin, 1976, 175
350 *everyday mind:* W. B. Yeats, *Autobiographies*, London, 1955, 272
351 *about turnips:* Ellmann, *James Joyce*, 702
– *outside their historical moment:* Gauri Viswanathan, lecture at University College Dublin, 11 April 2007
352 *ever be allowed to read:* Ellmann, *James Joyce*, 540
– *good counsel:* Walter Benjamin, 'The Storyteller', *Illuminations*, translated by Harry Zohn, London, 1974, 142
354 *logical process:* W. B. Yeats, *Autobiographies*, 461
355 *ever afterward:* in Matthew Bruccoli, *As Ever, Scott-Fitz*, London, 1973, 184

– *of their experience:* Walter Benjamin, *Selected Writings,* vol. 2, 730
– *end of his wanderings:* Friedrich Nietzsche, *Thus Spoke Zarathustra,* 227
356 *body healthy:* Richard Sennett, *Flesh and Stone: The Body and the City in Western Civilisation,* London, 2002, 255-65

Index

Abbey Theatre, 13, 19, 36, 45, 141, 224

Adorno, Theodor, 101, 280, 283

advertisements: ascendancy over writing, 142; Bloom places ad in paper, 115–16; Bloom uses language of, 93–4; as link between commerce and art, 245; as prompters of Bloom's inner thoughts, 91, 125–6, 222; and stream of consciousness, 128

aislings, 294, 324

Allen, Woody, 98

Anderson, Sherwood, 245

androgyny: Bloom's, 85–6, 90, 92, 146–7, 157, 251; Jesus's, 190; male distrust of, 188–9; Molly's, 147–8, 261–2; Shakespeare's androgynous characters, 91–2, 339–40, 340–1; symbols of, 274–5

Anna Karenina (Tolstoy), 110

anonymity, 181–2, 204, 256, 281, 284

anthologies, 212–13

anti-heroes, 35

Aristotle, 148–9, 152

Arius, 52

Arnold, Matthew, 144

art: and advertising, 245; change in artist's role in twentieth century, 26; Dedalus's and Bloom's different models, 352; Dedalus on artist's role, 103; Joyce's attitude, 19–20, 25, 122; as procreation, 208, 211, 210; relationship between poet and citizen, 13, 244–7; Yeats on writing, 354; *see also* culture

Artifoni, Almidano, 165

At Swim-Two-Birds (O'Brien), 34

Atkinson, Robert, 140–1

Auerbach, Erich, 299, 326

Austen, Jane, 128–9, 258

authority figures *see* father figures

bards, 32, 170

Barnacle, Nora: attitude to Joyce's books, 274; as Joyce's inspiration, 316; and Joyce's writing habits, 33;

381

385